Helen Thornham is Research Fellow at the Institute of Communications Studies, University of Leeds. She is the author of *Ethnographies of the Videogame: Narrative, Gender and Praxis* (2011) and co-editor, with Simon Popple, of *Content Cultures* (I.B.Tauris, 2014). Her research focuses on gender and mediations, narrative, discourse and power and she is currently researching transformations of broadcasting.

Elke Weissmann is Senior Lecturer in Film and Television at Edge Hill University. She has published widely on television, in particular in the area of television drama and global television, as well as representations of violence. Her books include *The Forensic Sciences of CSI: How to Know about Crime* (2011). She is Vice-Chair of the Television Studies Section of the European Communication Research and Education Association (ECREA).

Edited by
Helen Thornham and
Elke Weissmann

Renewing
*f*eminisms

Radical Narratives, Fantasies
and Futures in Media Studies

I.B. TAURIS
LONDON · NEW YORK

Published in 2013 by I.B.Tauris & Co Ltd
6 Salem Road, London W2 4BU
175 Fifth Avenue, New York NY 10010
www.ibtauris.com

Distributed in the United States and Canada
Exclusively by Palgrave Macmillan
175 Fifth Avenue, New York NY 10010

ISBN: 978 1 84885 825 1 (HB)
         978 1 84885 826 8 (PB)

A full CIP record for this book is available from the British Library
A full CIP record is available from the Library of Congress

Library of Congress Catalog Card Number: available

Printed and bound in Great Britain by T.J. International, Padstow, Cornwall

MIX
Paper from
responsible sources
FSC® C013056

Contents

List of Illustrations   vii

List of Abbreviations   ix

Acknowledgements   xi

Contributors   xiii

Introduction: Renewing–Retooling Feminisms   1
Helen Thornham and Elke Weissmann

1   The BFI Women and Film Study Group 1976– ?
    Christine Geraghty   11

Section 1: Relaying Feminism   29

2   Rebranding Feminism: Post-Feminism, Popular Culture
    and the Academy
    Sue Thornham   32

3   Third-Wave Feminism and the University: On Pedagogy
    and Feminist Resurgence
    Kristin Aune   47

Section 2: Lived Feminist Identities   63

4   Classy Subjects
    Maureen McNeil   67

5   Imagining Her(story): Engendering Archives
    Roshini Kempadoo   84

6   Weaving the Life of Guatemala: Reflections of the Self
    and Others through Visual Representations
    Sonia De La Cruz   104

Section 3: From Soap Opera to . . .   121

7   'They're "Doped" by That Dale Diary': Women's Serial
    Drama, the BBC and British Post-War Change
    Kristin Skoog   124

8 Scheduling as Feminist Issue: UK's Channel 4 and US
   Female-Centred Sitcoms
   Elke Weissmann   140

9 Separating the Women from the Girls: Reconfigurations
   of the Feminine in Contemporary British Drama
   Vicky Ball   155

Section 4: Futuristic Feminisms   173

10 New Media, New Feminism: Evolving Feminist Analysis
    and Activism in Print, on the Web and Beyond
    Andi Zeisler   178

11 Articulating Technology and Imagining the User:
    Generating Gendered Divides across Media
    Helen Thornham and Angela McFarlane   185

12 Feminism, Expertise and the Computational Turn
    Caroline Bassett   199

13 Renewing Feminisms in the 2000s: Conclusions and Outlook
    Anita Biressi and Heather Nunn   215

Bibliography   229
Index   251

Illustrations

1 Roshini Kempadoo (2007): *Amendments* (screen still)   89

2 Erika Tan (2005): *Persistent Visions* (screen stills)
   (reproduced with the kind permission of the artist)   92

3 Stacey Tyrell (2001): *Position As Desired*
   (reproduced with the kind permission of the artist)   95

4 Nicole Awai (2006): *Bikini Beach: Maracas*
   (reproduced with the kind permission of the artist)   98

5 Backstrap loom weaving   106

6 Amparo (left), Oralia (middle), with a student from USA   108

7 The working girl in *Secret Diary of a Call Girl*   156

8 Role reversal with the working woman in *Prime Suspect*   163

Abbreviations

ABC	American Broadcasting Company
ASTMS	Association of Scientific, Technical and Managerial Staffs
BARB	Broadcasters' Audience Research Board
BBC WAC	British Broadcasting Corporation's Written Archives Centre
BFI	British Film Institute
BSA	British Sociology Association
C4	Channel 4
CBS	Columbia Broadcasting System
CCCS	Centre for Contemporary Cultural Studies
ECREA	European Communication Research and Education Association
FHM	*For Him* Magazine
HBO	Home Box Office
ITV	Independent Television
LWT	London Weekend Television
MeCCSA	Media, Communication and Cultural Studies Association
NBC	National Broadcasting Company
NOW	National Organization of Women
NUS	National University of Singapore
PCL	Polytechnic of Central London
SEFT	Society for Education in Film and Television
TVS	Television South
UPN	United Paramount Network
VDU	visual display unit
VJ	video jockey
WFSG	Women and Film Studies Group
WMSN	Women's Media Studies Network

Acknowledgements

This book initially emerged from a lively and passionate debate about feminism during a conference we both attended. We had just heard an increasingly familiar construction of feminism as apolitical, individualistic and focused on consumption, and we were sitting, talking to so-called 'second-wavers' and highlighting how the same issues were continuing to structure our struggles. It seemed time for an intervention. The idea of a symposium that would bring different generations of feminists together to debate continuities, lived and shared experiences and the political, social and cultural tensions that emerged through these experiences, was born. With support from Anita Biressi and Heather Nunn of MeCCSA's Women's Media Studies Network and Heather Sutherland de Moreno, we organized what turned out to be the first of many feminist events at different institutions that, together, formed the basis of this book.

Thus, as always, this book has a complex history and wouldn't exist if it wasn't for the support of different people and institutions. This starts with MeCCSA's Women's Media Studies Network, Anita Biressi, Heather Nunn and Heather Sutherland de Moreno, without all of whom the symposium would not have happened. Máire Messenger Davies, who supported the funding applications and the book project throughout. Sue Thornham, Maureen McNeil and Christine Geraghty, for being the inspirations that they continue to be. The University of Reading, in particular Jonathan Bignell, which allowed us to use their premises for the symposium. All the wonderful presenters at the symposium and the people who came to listen; it was a fantastic day and gave us the courage to go forward with this book. The excellent scholars who shared their feminist thinking with us, wanted to engage with old and new debates and contributed to this book. The reviewer whose feedback helped us to strengthen our own narratives in the introduction. Philippa Brewster, who showed interest in this project from the word go and has been a helpful and supportive editor. Our families, for hosting meals and providing wine so we could spend all evening talking about the book. And each other, for such an excellent working relationship.

Contributors

Kristin Aune is Senior Lecturer in Sociology at the University of Derby. Her research and teaching interests lie in the areas of gender, feminism, religion and youth. Recent publications include articles in *Feminist Review* and *Men and Masculinities* and the book *Reclaiming the F Word: The New Feminist Movement* (co-written with Catherine Redfern; Zed Books, 2010). She is editing a special issue of *Social Movement Studies* about new feminist movements in contemporary Europe.

Vicky Ball is Lecturer in Film, Media and Cultural Studies, University of Sunderland. She is currently writing a book on the British female ensemble drama (1969–2011) for Manchester University Press and co-editing (with Melanie Bell) a special edition of the *Journal of British Cinema and Television* on the topic of women's work in the British film and television industries. She has published on gender and television, and she is a member of the Executive Committee of the Women's Film and Television Histories Network: UK/Ireland.

Caroline Bassett is Reader in Digital Media at the University of Sussex and co-leads the digital media stream of ECREA, the European Communication and Research Association. She is widely published on gender, mobile computing, narrative and cultural form and is currently completing research exploring hostility to computing across a series of professional and community arenas using historical archives in the UK and USA.

Anita Biressi is Reader in Media Cultures at Roehampton University. Her research interests include popular journalism and tabloid culture, media spectacle, reality programming, documentary and factual film and television. She is currently writing a book with Heather Nunn about class in contemporary British culture.

Sonia De La Cruz is a PhD candidate at the University of Oregon, where she also teaches. Her research explores the relationship of cultural work and traumatic experiences in Latin American cultures. Her research is partly practice-based and has so far produced a 52-minute documentary. She is part of the Centre for Latino/a and Latin American Studies.

Christine Geraghty is an Honorary Research Fellow at the University of Glasgow and at Goldsmiths, University of London. She has written extensively on television and fiction, her first work being an early study of narrative in the British soap opera *Coronation Street* (BFI, 1981). She is the author of *Women and Soap Opera* (Polity, 1991) and co-edited (with David Lusted) *The Television Studies Book* (Arnold, 1998). Both of these books are seminal texts for this publication. She has contributed to debates on television and quality through articles in *International Journal of Cultural Studies* and *Critical Studies in Television* and is an editor of the *Journal of British Cinema and Television* and a member of *Screen*'s Editorial Advisory Board.

Roshini Kempadoo is a photographer, media artist and lecturer. Her research, multimedia and photographic projects combine factual and fictional reimaginings of contemporary experiences with history and memory. Having worked as a social documentary photographer for the Format Women's Picture Agency, her recent work as a digital image artist includes photographs and screen-based interactive art installations that fictionalize Caribbean archive material, objects and spaces. They combine sound, animations and interactive use of objects to introduce characters that once may have existed, evoking hidden and untold narratives.

Angela McFarlane is Director of Public Engagement and Learning at Kew Gardens and Visiting Professor at Kings College London. Until 2008, she was Professor of Education at Bristol University. She is responsible for the public programme at Kew, including the visitor experience of the gardens, visitor services, marketing, PR, publishing, digital media and education.

Maureen McNeil is Professor of Women's Studies and Cultural Studies at the University of Lancaster. Her research intersects cultural studies, feminist studies and science/technology studies and she has published widely in these areas. Her work is instrumental to this book, and in particular her seminal book *Gender and Expertise* (1987) is a landmark for this publication. She is currently researching collective projects on the imaginary and on publics.

Heather Nunn is Professor in Culture and Politics at the University of Roehampton. She is vice chair of the Media, Culture and Communications Studies Association (MeCCSA) and co-chair of the MeCCSA Women's Media Studies Network with Anita Biressi. She has published widely in areas relating to gender, feminism, television, celebrity culture and identity.

Kristin Skoog is Lecturer in Media at the Media School, Bournemouth University, UK. Kristin completed her doctoral thesis, *The 'Responsible' Woman: The BBC and Women's Radio 1945–1955*, at the Communications and Media Research Institute, University of Westminster, in 2010. Kristin has a broad interest in the social and cultural impact of broadcasting; her research is currently focused on radio in post-war Britain and a historical perspective on women's radio in Europe.

Helen Thornham is Research Fellow at the Institute of Communications Studies, University of Leeds. She is the author of *Ethnographies of the Videogame: Narrative, Gender and Praxis* (2011) and co-editor, with Simon Popple, of *Content Cultures* (I.B.Tauris, 2013). Her research focuses on gender and mediations, narrative, discourse and power and she is currently researching transformations of broadcasting.

Sue Thornham is an internationally renowned scholar and Professor of Media and Film at the University of Sussex. She has published widely on issues relating to gender, feminism, film and media. She is chair of the Media, Culture and Communications Studies Association (MeCCSA), and her recent book, *'What If I Had Been the Hero?' Investigating Women's Cinema* (2012), explores representation, narrative and identity in relation to female film directors.

Elke Weissmann is Senior Lecturer in Film and Television at Edge Hill University. She has published widely on television, in particular in the area of television drama and global television, as well as representations of violence. Her previous book is *The Forensic Sciences of CSI: How to Know about Crime* (2010). She is vice-chair of the Television Studies Section of the European Communication Research and Education Association (ECREA).

Andi Zeisler is the co-founder of *Bitch: Feminist Response to Pop Culture*. A long-time freelance writer and illustrator, Andi's work has appeared in numerous periodicals and newspapers, including *Ms.*, *Mother Jones*, *Utne*, *BUST*, the *San Francisco Chronicle*, the *Women's Review of Books* and *Hues*. She is a former pop music columnist for the *SF Weekly* and the *East Bay Express* and also contributed to the anthologies *Young Wives' Tales*, *Secrets and Confidences: The Complicated Truth about Women's Friendships* (both from Seal Press) and *Howl: A Collection of the Best Contemporary Dog Wit* (Crown). She is the co-editor of *BitchFest: 10 Years of Cultural Criticism from the Pages of Bitch Magazine* and recently finished a book about feminism and popular culture for Seal Press. She speaks frequently on the subject of feminism and the media at various colleges and universities.

Introduction

Renewing–Retooling Feminisms

Helen Thornham and Elke Weissmann

The feminist movement, we have been told, is history.[1] And if it does still exist, it has lost all its political currency because, as is evident to the commentators, it has had its effects on the mainstream and hence can be celebrated as an achievement. In contrast, this book suggests that the feminist movement is alive and kicking, still engaged with concerns and methodologies similar to those of the 1960s to 1980s and demanding its political place. Such a demand has become increasingly difficult to articulate in today's climate, where feminism is popularly represented as a movement with little connection to the general public, restricted to middle-class white women and even detrimental to certain sections of society such as independent retailers and small businesses. Indeed, the British Universities Minister, David Willetts, proclaimed that 'feminism has trumped egalitarianism' (see *Guardian*, 1 April 2011), suggesting that feminism was to blame for the disenfranchisement of the working classes, the lack of economic and social opportunities for certain sectors of society and a number of other social and economic ills. Not only does the false opposition between feminism and egalitarianism construct feminism as outmoded and outdated thus positioning feminism as something past and outdone; it also, of course, completely misunderstands feminism's political goals. This misunderstanding could be seen quite clearly in the representation of Hilary Clinton, for example, when she stood as presidential candidate against Barack Obama. Here we saw a reiteration of the popular critique of feminism as focused on a privileged class of white women who ultimately undermine the social power of non-middle-class and non-white men.

While it is worrying enough to see such misrepresentations and misconceptions rearticulated in diverse (and political) arenas, feminism has been constructed in problematic ways much closer to home. In the academy, feminism has been constructed as past – as *over* – and as separate from a constructed mainstream. Such a construction works in a similar way to those discussed above, insofar as it works to further relegate it to (historical if not social and cultural) margins. In the UK in 2011, the annual British Sociological Association (BSA) conference celebrated 60 years of sociology. While not explicitly relating to the discipline of feminist media studies, sociology has clearly played a major formative role in terms of methodological, critical and conceptual approaches not only to media but also to ethnography, notions of agency and authorship, narrative and representation. As part of these reflective celebrations at the conference, feminism was headlined and given a keynote address. On the final day, Arlie Hochchild (University of California–Berkeley) and Sylvia Walby (Lancaster University) spoke to the title of the session which explored the 'impact of feminism on 60 years of sociology'. Both speakers talked about the real and pedagogical impact feminism has had on the discipline, celebrating its radical influence to the extent that sociology itself can no longer be considered without the frame of gender.

Yet this plenary address, carefully included but scheduled on the final day and in itself an aside to the main attractions of the conference, details the contradictory issues at stake here. On the one hand, the levels of attendance point to a renewed interest in feminist issues, particularly by younger academics. The lively and engaged discussion after the talks detailed the depth of personal and political investment in feminism. Such levels of attendance point to the relevance and interest in feminism as politically, socially and ideologically relevant to the lives of the (mostly) female academics who attended. On the other hand, feminism was presented as something that had *happened*, that was over and that therefore could be celebrated. Further, its positioning within the conference schedule suggested that it continues to be located in, to use Charlotte Brunsdon's words, 'a girl zone' (1997, 169) – a separated and contained space, which may allow particular considerations and articulations, but nevertheless remains divested from the main event.

2

Of course, pedagogical practice in universities has done the opposite, embedding feminism into mainstream agendas similarly problematically. As Kristin Aune (in this book) details, the incorporation of feminism and gender studies into the metanarrative of media studies has led to what she calls the 'depoliticization of academic feminism', as students discover it alongside and embedded in other key movements and issues. Here the success of feminism is measured partly in terms of the impact it has had in terms of shaping other movements and partly in relation to the claim that all students engage with feminism in their studies. It constructs feminism as over, as 'just another approach'.

Angela McRobbie, reflecting on the 'gender mainstreaming' in universities (2009, 156), finds positive outcomes of the impact of feminism in the multinational and ethnic identity of her students, who are increasingly global in demographic make-up. At the same time, she argues that (in particular) Sylvia Walby's 'assumptions about the success of gender mainstreaming' are 'one-sided' (ibid.) and negate the rationale for feminism's integration – which emerges, not from sustained thought about pedagogy or ideology, but from what she calls a 'technocratic managerial strategy' (ibid., 155) that in itself is part of the 'prevailing logic of feminism undone' (ibid.). While we do attempt to elucidate some of these complexities below, our initial point in highlighting them is to suggest that they raise crucial issues about how feminism is represented, claimed and valued. The complex arguments and issues that are at stake in the relations and, inter alia, location of feminism (between disciplines, between spaces, between people, between experiences) also take on ideological and political resonance as positionalities and disciplinary/political/social boundaries become necessary to defend the importance of feminism *per se*. Ironically, of course, in the act of representing feminism as a definable, bounded movement or event that impacted *onto* and *outwards*, the generative, the personal and the problematic ongoing, lived and experienced relations of an inter alia feminism become somewhat understated.

By comparison to these approaches, then, this book is concerned with the lived, experienced, generative engagements and enactments of feminism. The book partly emerges from a one-day symposium in the UK during which two key issues became apparent. One issue was the embodied and lived feminism that researchers were attempting to articulate in their papers and which form and encapsulate our conception of feminism discussed below. The second issue related to the problematic representations of feminism *per se*, not only in popular representations but also as encapsulated in the wider use of the metaphor of 'waves', which suggest peaks and troughs, flows and dissipations, and is also, as our speakers suggested through its reference to the sea, profoundly gendered.

As suggested, then, the book emerges from the lived, political and ideological tensions between the personal and the political: from the very real frustrations caused by the fissure between how feminism is represented and how it is lived everyday by different generations of feminists. Indeed, encounters with feminism as representation suggest that the movement has become depoliticized, focused on individual choice and consumerism. Such representations are evident in newspaper articles, films, novels and dramas, such as *Sex and The City* or *Bridget Jones's Diary* (see Sue Thornham in this volume). These representations indicate that feminism has been 'taken into account' (McRobbie 2004, 255) while focusing on narratives about women who apparently 'have it all': the job, the money (hence consumer power) and eventually also the relationship (Arthurs 2003; see also Negra 2009; Tasker and Negra 2007; McRobbie 2009). Importantly, such representations of feminism have also caused an analytical turn towards a focus on representations of women, leaving many other issues of feminist media studies overlooked (Boyle 2005). At the same time, real experiences of feminists persist in challenging the social and political status quo and hence fundamentally continue in the line of what is called 'second-wave' feminism. This disconnect between representations and the lived experiences of political feminist engagement returns the problem of feminism eternally on itself as the need arises to critique these representations and offer new ones. As a result, feminism is constantly created as something that affects only women or is constructed as an exclusive problem for feminists (imagined as only female) and hence can be set aside.

The seeming disconnect between representations of women and lived experiences of political feminist engagement also spawned our own efforts and attempts to intervene. When we began developing the symposium on which this book is based, our initial emphasis was that of continuation. We wanted to show that contemporary feminism was still speaking from and to a position that was feminist – not relegated to any 'wave' or generation. We wanted to enable a dialogue between young academics, just starting out on their feminist careers, and those that were well established, in order to emphasize that there was no split within our movement. The symposium, held at the University of Reading in 2008, was a resounding success. Attended by over 70 delegates, from undergraduate students to some of the most established feminist academics in the field of media studies, the image that has remained most firmly lodged in our minds is that of the lunch break when delegates assembled in one room, sitting on floors and in smaller and larger groups, continuing the discussions from the previous seminars, animated and emphatically arguing with one another. It was these discussions, as well as the excellent papers that the delegates had presented, which manifested the interwoven structures of dialogue in feminist media studies and the movement more generally. Indeed, as we engaged with the (hi)stories of our movement, we realized that we were not simply or only talking about *continuation*; indeed, this notion – as our book explains – is both deeply problematic and inherently gendered itself. Instead we needed a conceptual framework that was multidirectional and that arced in a range of different ways – not just forward but backwards and sideways. These were multidirectional arcs,[2] sometimes fragmented, sedimented, contradictory and deeply personal and political. They were multiple and interwoven, and while the full range of the arcs from our symposium – or indeed of feminist media studies more generally – could not be represented here, in what follows we attempt to detail some of the themes which *are* represented in this book.

The first arc we want to outline reaches into the past and back to reconfigure and recontextualize past research in the present context. We find that in order to be able to contextualize our own current work, the feminism we want to speak to is still lacking a real location *within*. Feminism remains intangibly linked to disciplinary discourses but as stemming from an outside that does not really find – to paraphrase even earlier feminist thought – a place of its own (Woolf 2002/1929). This means that every time we discuss feminism, we need to 'return' to a particular point in order to progress. The arc is backwards and forwards, then, because in the very act of saying something contemporary, clarifications need to be made about the past. As many feminist historians and autobiographers remind us (Steedman 1992; Kuhn 1995; Clough 1992), however, the past is also a representation used selectively to support current debate. This is the argument of Christine Geraghty, whose own seminal work has often been used as an all-encompassing representation of a collective feminist intervention. As she argues here, however, contemporary representations do not account for the more rhizomatic, if not confused and uncertain, directions of past work. As she details, the point was to question, not to answer, and more importantly these questions are still pertinent and ongoing today.

The lack of a location for feminism is, of course, due to the multiple discourses and directions always operating within it. And in many senses feminism is always represented as located in the past, as a political movement, a moment in history, or as a specific impact. This is why Angela McRobbie talks about feminism being 'taken into account' (2009, 1), and the very fact it can be seems related to the representation of it in the past as done, as enacted and as, crucially, over.

Feminism is not over. Caroline Bassett in this volume argues that we need to retool, return to past understandings in order to radically intervene in future directions of media studies. Vicky Ball suggests we need to repurpose past methodologies in order to be able to fully critique media's place in society. For both Bassett and Ball and for feminist media studies more generally, this means that the process of going backwards is, in part, a process of gathering and remembering those tools in order to move forwards. In many ways, then, the arc backwards allows us to locate feminism as a discipline *within* and use its tools to theorize *outwards*. The notion of theorizing outwards also relates to the second arc represented in this book, that of the personal to the political (and vice versa).

This second arc is more familiar to feminist researchers and, in one sense, is explored through the notions of lived feminist identities and what it means to be a feminist scholar engaging in research and pedagogy. This is a lived and ontological notion of feminism, then, rooted in the complex identity of the scholar but emerging in various guises through the process of research itself. Many of the contributors to this volume start from a position of a personal engagement with feminism, theorizing their lived experiences outwards and towards the object of their study. Whether this is a tangible text or a more ephemeral dialogue, each contributor argues that the politics of feminism is alive and well in the spaces between researcher and researched. The arc from the political to the personal is, however, less publicly visible. In the wider context of neoliberalism and localism, which has proclaimed that there is 'no such thing as society' (Thatcher 1987) and which frames political engagement as essentially within economic parameters, politics seems increasingly disconnected from the individual in the social environment. This separation has been discussed by a number of seminal feminists, perhaps most notably Angela McRobbie, who argues that it has produced an 'intensification of power through imaginary tropes of freedom' (2011, xi). These are imaginary because they are rarely *experienced* in the everyday but are nevertheless powerful discourses because they are often *represented* through popular media. This power is also particularly imaginary for *women* because, as she suggests, the 'gender logic of neoliberal governmentality' may relocate power to the local and private (rather than the public and national), but 'these conditions of freedom are tied to conditions of social conservatism, consumerism and hostility to feminism in any of its old or newer forms' (ibid.). It also becomes clear from the chapters of this book that the relations between power structures and the individual discussed by McRobbie at a more macro level are also experienced at a more micro level by the contributors to this collection. Indeed, the connection between power structures and the individual can be seen most clearly in the alignment of the personal for a political project and in the rearticulation and reclamation of politics as much more than 'just' economics.

In the rearticulation of the personal and the political, contributors also return to the relationship between the public and the private, another key concern of feminism. In this volume Kristin Skoog, for example, points to the complex negotiations between the private and public that marked gender roles as they experienced modernization in post-war Britain. As so often, these negotiations primarily affected women who had historically been connected to the private, but whose skills and labour were urgently needed for public life. There is, then, significant political power at stake by blurring the distinctions between the public and the private – distinctions that conservative discourses continuously attempt to reaffirm, even in times when women's place in the public realm is accepted as reality (Weissmann in this volume).

The final arc reaches forward into the fantasies and futures of feminism. This can be seen most obviously through the focus on new media, but perhaps more importantly, the fantasies and futures of feminism are also felt in the rewriting of history and in the claim of authorship and agency embedded in such an act. The insertion of an alternative (hi)story is, in some senses, an attempt to stake a claim over an alternative future. As many of the chapters suggest, however, the act of narration is always already a fantasy of agency, an attempt to insert, disrupt and claim ownership over a past which remains intangible and continues to resonate in particularly problematic ways. The claim of agency and authorship also repeats a particular narrative structure, which is similarly problematic, relying as it does on a construction of the individual (neoliberal) hero who progresses linearly through space and time (de Lauretis 1984; Steedman 1992). Instead, in the contributions here, agency and authorship become untenable and give way to the collective, to contradictions, to grass-roots politics and to the embodied (Zeisler, Geraghty, McNeil, Kempadoo). What emerges instead is a simultaneous fantasy and disavowal of embedded agency and authorship.

The desire for agency also becomes enmeshed in an attempt to make a claim of empirical truth, but this act is also a move towards the individual, towards the grand claims of a patriarchal and colonialist history. In the end, it is the multiple, connected voices (the individual and/in the collective) and the grass-roots politics, complete with uncertainties and ambiguities, that re-emerge. The retreat from an assertive agency has been seen by some feminist as part of a 'third-wave' movement (Whelehan 2007, xv), but as Geraghty's chapter suggests, this ignores the probing uncertainties and different, often competing, approaches evident in 1970s activism. In this light, the contestations of certainty, the hesitant voices apparent in some of the chapters here, and the multiple and often competing discourses evident within feminism should be seen as a *continued* attempt to counter the neat solutions of narrativized (hi)stories.

There are a number of key themes to emerge from this collection, then. The first is the notion of retooling, explicitly articulated by Caroline Bassett, but nevertheless central to many of the themed sections and chapters. This is the need to find, locate and rediscover methodologies and politics in order to address contemporary issues: we need to discard the characteristic forgetfulness which has marked feminism. In retooling feminism, we are constructing a discursive framework, one which facilitates critical engagements with the contemporary. This discursive framework emerges from within the full spectrum of feminism's critical engagement of the past and is conscious of that spectrum. This is exactly connected to issues of authorship and agency, of finding a voice without falling into the patriarchal/colonialist/modernist trap of claiming an empirical truth or absolute knowledge.

The second theme relates to the notion of continuous dialogue rather than statement. The chapters aim to intersect, to question and to generate debate rather than provide clear solutions. This resonates with the attempts to engage with and represent the multiplicity of voices from which the feminist researcher always already speaks. Sonia De La Cruz's chapter, for example, examines the potential of video practice to represent and engage with feminist struggles. Importantly, De La Cruz situates her own place in narrativizing the experiences of women weavers in Guatemala in relation to and in communion with the other women involved: the women whose experience is relayed, the leaders of the weaver's collective and her students who accompanied her on the trip. Rather than offering a plan of action for future feminist video practice, De La Cruz's chapter opens up one experience as an exemplary moment that allows us to question who should own and who does own narratives of the past.

The aim of continuous dialogue also connects to the attempts of opening up areas of investigation, the third theme evident in this collection. In this respect, the place of pedagogy and the academy becomes of central concern. As the chapters by Sue Thornham and Kristin Aune both make evident, the academy remains a place where men and women often first encounter feminism, often as something apart or abstract from themselves. While this does not detract students from becoming active in personally and politically motivated ways, as Aune highlights, it does mean that the academy continuously contributes to the containment of feminism (see also Sue Thornham's chapter here).

Despite its containment, feminism in the academy also contributes to the opening up of avenues of investigation: Skoog, for example, draws our attention to a neglected afternoon radio soap opera and thus takes her place in line with historic feminist examinations of derided and overlooked genres that are gendered female (Ang 1985; Hobson 1982). Other areas opened up further for feminist critique are those of technological competency and expertise, which Helen Thornham and Angela McFarlane present as deeply gendered, and the role of scheduling in the attempt of broadcasters to control audiences' relationships with television content (see Weissmann's chapter in this volume).

In all of these chapters, the issue of (self-)reflexivity, the fourth theme of the collection, is equally evident. Roshini Kempadoo's chapter in particular makes this apparent through a complex weaving of textualities in her own writing. Using extracts from her research diaries, quotes from fellow artists, analyses of works by artists and her own video installations, which she places in relation to key philosophers and historians, her narrative always intersects, contextualizing not just her own work/words but those of others, too. This reflexivity also creates most strongly the sense of continuity and retooling. In their reflections on possible methodologies and avenues of investigation, the authors always also return to earlier feminist interventions and continue their probing into the possibilities of feminist futures.

Where Does Feminism Take Us? Scope of the Book

The collection as whole, then, aims to take part in the larger political project that feminism continues to be. Although emerging from a UK symposium, all the contributors to the book draw on theories and approaches from within and without the UK, thus extending the scope well beyond UK borders. The individual contributions speak from the messiness of personal experience and their complex relation to the social and political. The book's overall political project, however, is to indicate how the personal has been experienced as political even though this experience is constantly confronted with representations of a depoliticized personal and private realm to which feminism has been relegated. More importantly, it attempts to show that such an experience is inevitably linked to uncertainties but that these uncertainties can be fruitful for the political project. Thus, the book also counters the representations of feminism as waves or generations, with the second wave being presented as unified and clear of its political goals and the 'third' or 'fourth' wave – as some commentators (see Woods 2009) call the current resurgence in activism – as depoliticized, individualized and unfocused. Instead, we present feminist media scholarship as a continuous struggle to envision the personal as socio-political. Struggle, here, is meant literally: it is an effort that requires both our anger, as Ball makes clear, and the continuous uncertainty evident also in the documents stating the aims of second-wave activism, as Geraghty reminds us, and represented by the simple question 'is it?' scribbled into the margins alongside the official, recorded notes.

Notes

1. This notion remains popular even in the face of increasing recognition of the resurgent feminist movement, sometimes called 'the fourth wave'. Thus, despite a number of articles in the popular press such as the *Guardian*, *The New York Times* or *The Independent*, the dominant narrative about feminism in mainstream discourses remains one which is confined to the past – as the well-meaning inclusion of the suffragist movement in the history of Britain in the 2012 Olympics Opening Ceremony made particularly clear: here feminism was celebrated as something that had achieved political change. And while the impact of this change was again and again represented as having lasting significance today, it was noticeable that the movement that was celebrated was that of the late Victorian and Edwardian eras – eras of mythical importance to the British national imagination, but also eras firmly placed in the past.

2. It should be noted that we choose to engage in 'arcs' rather than 'waves' here. Indeed, as Imelda Whelehan has suggested, the 'wave' that is used as a 'prefix to feminism' 'implies that it describes a specific moment in history, and signifies a discernable transformation in [the] body of knowledge' (1999, 1). For the contributors and authors of this book, however, no distinctions were made between moments or bodies of knowledge. Instead, feminism is continually lived, enacted and produced in ways that don't recognize such demarcations and divisions.

The BFI Women and Film Study Group
1976–?

Christine Geraghty

The Women and Film Study Group was generated by a letter, dated 23 February 1976, sent out by three women working at the British Film Institute (BFI) and the Editorial Assistant at the Society for Education in Film and Television (SEFT) to around 35 women whom they thought might be interested. This led to a meeting in London on 3 April 1976, which was attended by 20 women who agreed to set up the group, which would meet monthly. By early 1978, the group had a core membership of around 10 women; it seems to have petered out in 1979/80.

The paper I wrote about this group for the conference on which this book is based had a particular purpose, which is repeated in this chapter. Terry Bolas has commented that 'it is surprising how little impact was felt at *Screen* during the 1970s as a result of the emergence of feminism' (2009, 279), and in drawing attention to the workings of the Women and Film Study Group, I wanted to acknowledge its part in the histories that Bolas outlines.[1] But I did not only intend to draw attention to the role of feminist approaches in the history of film and media studies in the 1970s and 1980s. The paper also sought to be useful in another way. At a conference that had been specifically designed to bring different generations of feminist scholars together, I wanted to speak across the generational divide and to provide an historical account that would relate to the lived experience of those of us in the 1970 and 1980s who were beginning to analyse film and television while at the same time speak to those for whom second-wave feminism was indeed history. I wanted to avoid the dilemma which Lynne Segal identified when she wrote that 'it is hard to avoid either idealizing or trashing the past, feeding the unruly envy between and within political generations' (1999, 1).

In this chapter, then, I give an account of the Women and Film Group, which I was involved with in the late 1970s. My aim is to record something of the history of that group and to reflect on how the group saw itself and its work through the fragmented documents that provide a record of its work. In doing so, I want to open up a particular instance of second-wave feminism that was perhaps more difficult and more fractured than the usual accounts suggest. Second-wave feminism has been accused of leaving a legacy based on 'a host of mystifications, imagistic idealizations and ingrained social definitions of what it means to be a feminist' (Walker 1995, xxxii). There has been a tendency to homogenize 1970s feminism in a way which pained second-wavers who felt that 'new narratives emerge as collective memories fade, writing over those which once incited our most passionate actions' (Segal 1999, 9). But the version of 1970s feminism offered by second-wavers was also homogenized, prioritizing a feminism which was radical, passionate, politicized and collectively organized. In offering this very specific example in some detail, I want to demystify some of our activity and avoid idealizations while at the same time indicating that acknowledging the history and achievements of the Women and Film Study Group in the late 1970s might tell us, in more detail, how work was done in that period and more generally how histories get written. As collective memories indeed fade and official histories get written, it seemed important to offer this particular feminist narrative a more stable form of telling.

One obvious but important point is that, at the time, I had little idea that I was involved in second-wave feminism though, as we shall see, the group had many of the features of second-wave activity, and at one point, the minutes record an invitation from Sheila Rowbotham 'to talk to her Sunday group about our work' (18 December [1976]). Nevertheless the group needs also to be seen within a context of general activity when feminist consciousness-raising groups, political and trade union action groups and special interest groups were all part of the cultural and political context. Some of these were specifically concerned with the role of women in, for instance, political parties and the trade union movement.[2] But the Women and Film Group was also associated with groups which were not necessarily nor directly engaged in feminist work but which were trying to develop frameworks for the study of the media, including questions of representation and identity with which we were concerned. These included groups which were linked, however problematically, to formal institutions of education, such as the working groups set up by the Centre for Contemporary Cultural Studies at Birmingham University; groups set up through other types of institutions associated with the study of film, photography and television, such as SEFT, *Screen* and the British Film Institute; and even less formal groups, often based on friendship, which got together to undertake the work of viewing, reading and discussion on a basis which is now impossible to trace. Such groups interacted (and disagreed) through the circulation of photocopied or duplicated papers which got more and more illegible as they were passed on; through meeting up at weekend schools, evening classes and the annual BFI summer schools; and through formal events, such as the SEFT AGM. In this context, the Women and Film Study Group is typical of a whole range of group activity, informed by but not necessarily associated with feminism, and as we shall see, its activities criss-crossed with a number of different groups. This intertwining of feminist activity with work to establish film and television studies as a proper object of study is important. Those of us working in film and television studies are perhaps particularly prone to nostalgia for what is now seen as the period of second-wave feminism, since this was also the period of the struggle, in which feminists played a significant part, to establish new methods for studying film and other media throughout the UK educational system. New narratives are perhaps necessary to avoid an easy nostalgia for 'those mythic times when people who were largely excluded from academic posts…sought to unlock popular creativity by changing how texts are taught' (Miller 2009, xi).

In this chapter, I adopt a particular approach to writing a short history of our group, but this writing has been informed by a number of other accounts. There have been a number of significant opportunities for feminists to reflect on the contribution of feminist thought and activity to the development of film studies, in particular two 'round table' discussions, hosted by two important feminist journals. In 1989 Janet Bergstrom and Mary Ann Doane asked feminist scholars to provide for *Camera Obscura* an account of their engagement with theories of the female spectator. Fifteen years later, in *Signs*, Kathleen McHugh and Vivian Sobchack asked pioneer feminist film and media scholars what feminism and feminist film theory meant to their current work. This second discussion offers a particularly good complement to what I am trying to do. In a reflective mode, these contributors take the opportunity to look back on their own pasts, comment on what was learnt and indicate how they have changed their views or positions. These are accounts based on knowledge and memory and offer a reflexive and thoughtful space which is in keeping with a feminist approach to the generation of knowledge. They reflect on the development of particular methods and approaches, sometimes suggesting ways in which feminist film theory has been or needs to be augmented in order to retain its capacity to generate new knowledge (Kuhn 2004, Doane 2004); sometimes admitting that it no longer informed their work (Spigel 2004, Williams 2004). A number of contributors start their essays by recording the difficulty they had getting going on their contribution; Doane records 'procrastinating more than usual' (2004, 1229) over writing and Williams entitles her contribution 'Why I Did Not Want to Write This Essay'. This is in part a concern about retreading old ground, but Laura Mulvey relates her difficulties to 'a break or fissure in the continuities of history [that] has come to separate a "then" of the 1970s, the moment of origin, at least in Britain, of feminist film theory and practice, from a "now"' (1989, 1287).

Something similar, which relates specifically to the Women and Film Study Group, can be found in the interviews Terry Lovell and I gave to Charlotte Brunsdon in the late 1980s and early 1990s, which she used for her 2000 book. Brunsdon asked us separately to recall our involvement with the group, and Lovell provides an important counterbalance to my account here. In particular, Brunsdon draws attention to the contextualizing work that Lovell does in terms of broader traditions of socialism and Marxism which she and others brought to the group.

The essays in *Signs* and Lovell's account both demonstrate the value of measured thinking about what can be learned, built on or acknowledged in the past. In developing this account, though, my sources led me to do something rather different. I recognize that it is not possible to bridge Mulvey's gap, but I do want to address it, using an approach which also seems to be in accord with feminist writing on media texts. In work on soap opera and melodrama, feminists have placed an emphasis on the communication of feeling as part of the work of representation; in *Women and Soap Opera* (1991), I argued that, while soaps might not present a particularly non-stereotypical or wholly positive representation of women, they did offer women in the audience the possibility of identification on screen with the feelings generated in their day-to-day lives.[3] In the same spirit, this essay does not aspire to the reflective mode described above but tries to give an account that is closer to the texture of the documentation I found, an account of what it *felt* like to be doing research on television in a feminist context in the late 1970s.

I have had access to the notes produced from 18 meetings of the group, along with some discussion papers, position papers, photocopies of articles to be read and correspondence.[4] This was material produced at the time for the group, and the lack of attention to dating and the poor duplication (printed via a stencil) confirms that it was not intended to survive as a record; indeed it is something of an accident that any of it has. As a result, perhaps the material has an immediacy which is the product of functionality rather than reflection. Reading it again, over 30 years later, I experienced the feeling expressed by a feminist historian of the US Women's Liberation movement: 'even when rereading her *own* diaries and letters she is amazed at their failure to match her current recollections of the events recorded there' (Segal 1999, 10, citing Margaret Strobel). This documentation reminded me of things I had forgotten, and it failed to record things I thought I remembered. In giving these fragments a context, I am also offering my interpretation of this material, although I hope the use of primary sources means that it is not entirely solipsistic. Other members of the group would have different accounts.[5] In the rest of this essay, I will outline some of the aims of the group as expressed at the first meeting, highlight some of its working practices and look at how its public interventions were made problematic by those practices.

Aims and Intentions

The notes of the meeting on 3 April 1976 record an interest in setting up the group with the following aims:

- to investigate available film theories and their relationship to feminism and to offer suggestions for defining feminist film theory;
- the need to produce accessible texts for use within the movement and within education;
- the need to investigate the relationship between theory and film-making practice.

Although this was ambitious, it is not a surprising set of aims for the time, and the notes amplify some of our intentions. The emphasis on accessibility and a later comment in these notes that 'theories are tools which should not be reified' hint at debates about language and address that were taking place in SEFT in the midseventies. None of the papers, however, indicate a specific attempt to make an intervention in the manoeuvrings around SEFT AGMs or the journal boards which Bolas describes. In addition, the intention of investigating the relationship between theory and practice was a common theme at the time and was reflected in the fact that the invitation to set up a group had been sent to a wide range of women, many of whom were not formally involved in higher education, and some of whom were engaged in film practice. At least one member of the core group had worked in the industry, and there were some links with independent film groups.

The assumption was that this would be a women-only group, but it did not set itself the aim of focusing on film-making by women. Indeed, the notes of 3 April [1976] record

> the danger of feminist film criticism being retrogressive by digging up forgotten women directors (do they necessarily make more feminist films than men) at a time when mainstream film theory is moving away from an auteurist approach.

Instead, the group decided, at least initially, that there was 'the need for shared reading', and members were asked to make suggestions about this.

A significant decision taken at the first meeting by this women and *film* group was to focus on television. This may have reflected difficulties in accessing film material in the days before the VCR became ubiquitous, but it linked also to the aspirations for accessibility and relevance. Later, a draft summary paper, written apparently for external use, explained the reasons for the choice:

> Our reasons for choosing this series were: that we wanted to deal with a cultural product which was current, within 'mass' experience and with a visual medium available to most women; some feminist work had already been done on film and we did not want to work on something (e.g. an earlier Hollywood film) we would undoubtedly have been isolating from its own context and which would not have been available to women now. We were also interested in the possibilities for feminist practice within dominant cultural forms and institutions. (Untitled summary of group's work [June/July 1978].)

Another summary paper, probably written earlier for the group and entitled 'Problems Our Investigation Is Faced With', puts it more succinctly: 'we need to bear in mind why we are analysing CS [*Coronation Street*] i.e. to discover how sexist ideology is produced in entertainment and story forms in order to be in a better position to challenge it and change it' ('Problems Our Investigation Is Faced With' [undated]).

Working Practices

The decision to study a popular television serial was not an easy or obvious move at this point. Television study had largely been concerned with serious television including the news (and football) and with authored single plays, although the BFI had published Richard Dyer's influential *Light Entertainment* in 1973, and *Screen Education* would publish a special issue on the cop series *The Sweeney* later in 1976 which the group read. In the light of debates in cultural/television studies about academic fans, it is interesting that the choice of *Coronation Street* was not based on whether we liked the programme or not. This is indicated in notes of the meeting of 26 June 1976, which record a detailed discussion of episodes of the programme with the comment that 'some of us realized that we enjoyed talking about CS although we didn't enjoy watching it'. The decision to focus on *Coronation Street* did cause the group problems. As early as November 1976, it was noted that some people were 'not especially interested in studying *Coronation Street*', and while the core group persisted with it, the choice may have led to others opting not to commit themselves to the group. The decision to study popular television also meant that the aim of working on the 'relationship between theory and film-making practice' was effectively translated into a desire to change the practices of mainstream television, which was certainly ambitious.

Having made a quick decision to use a television programme to test out theoretical insights, the group struggled with finding reading which might help us with thinking about television. The texts chosen (and this continued to be typical of the group) drew on debates that were taking place elsewhere ('We confronted realism first because ... of current debate in film theory that realist procedures in art can only reflect the status quo etc' ['Problems Our Investigation Is Faced With' (undated)]). But they were also intended to provide a framework for understanding *Coronation Street* as a realist text with an assumed appeal to a female audience. This led us to start with reading work by Lukacs and Brecht in order to work out the relation of realism to 'bourgeois/patriarchal ideology' (minutes of 5 June [1976]), which might contribute to the examination of progressive possibilities in a popular television programme like *Coronation Street*.

By the summer of 1976, other issues were being raised:

[W]e saw a need to move from a consideration of the realist aspirations of *Coronation Street* to a consideration of the relationship
between text and audience, and to the exploration of the processes
of identification and recognition. (Summary of work, prepared for
September 11 [1976] meeting.)

Inevitably, this meant a move towards psychoanalytic texts, dominant
in feminist work at the time, but the group wanted to take on a wide
variety of approaches, and discussion of Laura Mulvey's key article on
visual pleasure and an article by Alan Lovell, '*The Searchers* and Pleasure',
led us to conclude that 'we should not go on to demand some kind of
totalizing theory' (26 June 1976). 'The question of the relationship
between pleasure and ideology, and of the place of pleasure in popular
culture' (summary of work, prepared for September 11 [1976] meeting)
led us to discuss Richard Dyer's article 'Entertainment and Utopia'.
The need for adequate theories of pleasure, identification and ideological effects remains a persistent theme; as late as 29 April [1978] there
is a note that 'at the following meeting we'd like to have a read around
pleasure' and a reference to a paper written on the topic by one of the
group members.

There is no doubt that the group consisted of women with very different experience of the intellectual demands that the project made
and different levels of familiarity with the terms being used in the reading. Members of the group show generosity in leading debate about
theoretical work which they are more familiar with. But there is some
frustration at the level of understanding that could be achieved within
reading practices of the group. There are various references in the minutes to the problems of moving on to one thing before we had finished
another. In November [1976] there is a reminder that although there is
agreement to move on, we hadn't yet dealt 'satisfactorily' with Lukacs
and Brecht. After reading some psychoanalytical material, notes of the
meeting on 28 May 1977 record that it was 'generally agreed that these
texts were too difficult'. There was also the difficulty in reconciling the
typical reading of cultural debates of the time with more direct examples of women's culture, which led to some odd lists when reading was
allocated:

tasks (reading) AX: Hoggart BX: John Goode in Rights and Wrongs
of Women … CX: Sexual Divisions in Soc material plus Goode DX:

SDISM plus women's magazine stuff in the 30s Christine Ger:
Woman's Own/Woman (18 December [1976])

The idea from the start was that the group should operate as some kind
of collective. This set up expectations about commitment, attendance
and joint work which were challenging and difficult to live up to. Note
taking, posting out minutes and other information, recording visual
material, hosting meetings and introducing readings was meant to be
shared, though it is clear that the women who worked at the BFI took
on much of this group-support labour. The group met on Saturdays
for the first two years, moving to Friday evenings in 1978. There are
references throughout the minutes to the need for the meetings to be
better focused and various suggestions for how they might be chaired.
Attendance fluctuated, which affected what could be done; the notes
of the meeting of 3 April [1977] comment that the 'meeting [was] rather
a dead loss as not many came and the people who were presenting this
session's reading weren't there'. In February [1978] one member of the
group wrote a letter in which she reflected critically and constructively
on how the group had operated, suggesting that 'we have not organized ourselves for productive collective work'. This would have meant
meeting more often (as much as once a week, she suggested), an impos-
sibility for most of the group, all of whom were in full-time employment, a number of whom had children and many of whom were heavily
engaged with other activity in the women's movement and the trade
unions as well as with other BFI/SEFT work; a number also travelled
a long way to get to London for meetings. It was not just practical difficulties, though, and the letter writer suggests that the group had not
faced up to the model for collective work provided by other women's
groups: to do better collectively, '[we] would need to have a good *argument* between ourselves … we know we embrace a lot of different positions that might strain in different directions'.

Public Interventions

One of the difficulties that the group faced was that it was both a self-
education group and a campaigning group. The minutes show different
attitudes to this split focus among the group, which extended into how
invitations (some self-generated, some not) to speak or organize public events were handled. Certainly the minutes provide evidence of the
group struggling with its reading and theoretical framework while trying

to develop a version of its work so far which would stand up in public. This was further complicated when we learnt that the SEFT Potteries Group at Keele was also working on *Coronation Street*, which raised the possibility of joint activities. This was welcome since it extended the work of both groups, but it led into negotiations about how such events should be organized. Here I want to record some of the opportunities and problems posed by three public events.

The first public event took the form of a presentation to a day event on 'Images of Women in the Media' at the Polytechnic of Central London on 19 March 1977. This educational institution was a leading player in the establishment of Communications/Media Studies in UK higher education, running a pioneering postgraduate diploma in film studies and then an early MA in film and television. The conference heard from successful women journalists such as the editors of *Woman's Own* and the woman's pages of the *Guardian*, along with a female television producer. When the invitation was received, concern was expressed about whether our work was ready and about 'how to reconcile an attempt at undermining the media with an invitation to speak to women working in the media'. The group agreed to take part 'despite hesitations ... [it] might force us into getting something down on paper' (20 November [1976]). Notes of a meeting on 22 January 1977 record plans to cover 'production/audience details'; the 'rationale for studying *Coronation Street*'; changes in the programme over the years; 'the experience of our group'; 'our conclusions in relation to image [*sic*] of women'. We planned to show examples of episodes and allow time for discussion. It seems that the presentation was slimmed down and became an introduction of 'our work to date in relation to theoretical problems – particularly of realism – and to the representation (including stereotyping) of women in the series' (untitled summary of group's work [June/July 1978]). The group's anxieties over the event proved to be correct, particularly in terms of the interface between our work on representation and that of women working in the media. Discussion after the event recorded our disappointment at 'criticisms of our group's unhelpfulness to media women' made by one of the media professionals who, the group felt, was 'trying to make distinctions between the work of analysis and theory and attempts to work within the media directly', which we were trying to break down (3 April [1977]). A letter was drafted to send to her (it is recorded as ready to go on 28 May but is a future agenda item in October 1977), but there is no record of its content or whether it was sent. Our discussion in April noted, in addition, that this distinction was also made at a rather more pragmatic level in that the media professionals were paid to participate in the event while the group was not; we were not generally paid anything so this was probably considered in the context of differences in waged and unwaged labour, which was a key issue in feminist debates at the time.

The second public intervention that year took place at the Edinburgh International Television Festival. As with the PCL event, there was some wariness about this which centred on how far we could present our work in such a different forum.[6] Richard Dyer, then in a BFI-supported post at Keele University and involved with the Potteries Group, was the key point of contact for the festival organizers, and there was clearly some disagreement about how the session should be organized. In a letter to Dyer, the organizers thank him for agreeing to give a paper on 'Sexism and the Soap Opera' but ask,

> Would it be okay for just you to be on the panel – we're a bit afraid that if there are too many people on the platform there won't be enough time for a full discussion from the floor. (4 April 1977)

The group agreed to prepare material for this event 'as a collective' (30 April 1977). Two members of the group, Terry Lovell and Jean McCrindle, would present with Dyer. In the preparation period, the group continued to be 'doubtful about what our contribution would be able to achieve' (28 May 1977).

Nevertheless, this was our highest-profile event, and our members were on a panel which also featured *Coronation Street* producer Susi Hush. The paper 'Soap Opera and Women' was published in the official programme, which also gave all the names of the people who had contributed to the paper through the group at Keele and the Women and Film Study Group. The paper was deliberately provocative and included statements like 'Our interest in soap opera and what it could become does not mean that we do not find it at present largely contemptible' (Dyer, Lovell and McCrindle 1977, 37). As a later report in *Broadcast* suggested, this sentence was 'hardly likely to endear the group to many present' (C.L. 1978, 14). Press cuttings during the Festival indicate that the intervention by a number of academics at Edinburgh in 1977 was received with bafflement and a good deal of hostility, but not all of it was directed at our paper. Television producer Verity Lambert commented on 'the dense Marxist-feminist gobbledegook of a diatribe about "Soap Opera and Women"' but also found Raymond Williams 'almost totally incomprehensible' (*The Telegraph*, 5 September 1977).[7] Reading the paper now, I have a good deal of sympathy for Lambert, at least as far as our contribution was concerned. The uneasy shifts between textual work on representation and theoretical accounts of the capitalist system of production, not to mention a reference to the underlying battle with *Screen* over Althusser and realism, indicate the difficulties the group was experiencing in finding a focus. In a later summary of activity, we noted, in a massive understatement, that the paper 'provoked quite a stir' and, we thought, tongue in cheek, possibly some changes in the serial itself: 'the nearby factory, which we claimed was never shown except by its owner who frequented the pub, began to feature more ... the women are [at the time of writing] on strike, complete with picket line' (untitled paper beginning 'Early in 1976' [June/July 1978]).

The third event was a more traditional educational event in the context of the work the BFI and SEFT were doing at this time. The weekend school 'Understanding Popular Television' took place on 10/11 December 1977 and was organized jointly by the SEFT Potteries Group and the Women and Film Study Group, under the aegis of the University of Manchester's Department of Extra Mural Studies and with support from two Arts Associations and Granada TV. There were papers from three members of the Potteries Group and a collective paper from our group. This balance probably reflected the organizational responsibility across the two groups, though it is clear that the Women and Film Study Group, along with the paper, contributed to the preparatory work for the seminars, which some members also led. The papers were distributed in advance, so most of the work was done through the seminars, which focused on particular topics and reported back to plenary discussions. The minutes indicate that the group was consulted about various matters (there was early agreement that we did not want any discussion groups specifically 'restricted to women' (18 February [1977]), but there is again a fear about having to organize the material to fit the event rather than shape the presentation around our own concerns. On 28 May, the notes record that it had been suggested (by the Potteries Group) that the group should present a paper, 'Realism and *Coronation Street*'; there was concern that this 'did not encompass the most interesting work we had done on C.S. The group would prefer to offer a feminist perspective on C.S., perhaps entitled The Fictional World of Coronation Street'.

In the end, a paper entitled 'Women, Realism, Contradiction and Change in Coronation Street' was given at the weekend school; a copy is in the BFI archive. There are two separate, contemporary accounts of the weekend. The trade journal *Broadcast* published a sympathetic and detailed account but noted that 'of the seventy people present ... only three came from the industry – it's not a promising indication of the potential for a dialogue between the two groups'. The anonymized author suggested that such a dialogue could be 'fruitful and enjoyable' and that at least part of the problem lay with the broadcasters who 'all too often' ignored 'the fruits of the academic's contribution to broadcasting' (C.L. 1978, 15). This positive response may have been due to the efforts which had been put into developing an accessible mode of teaching; the second report provides backing for this. John Stewart, then a Regional Programming Officer at the BFI, felt that the event had attracted 'a fair number of "newcomers"' who were able to participate in the discussion since the teaching arrangements 'ensured that participants shared in a broad yet fairly detailed field of investigation' (1977/78, 69). He commented that a number of papers, including that by the group, 'were concerned with the re-presentation of a social world in *Coronation Street* and the relation between the fictional world of the serial and a social reality which actually exists' (1977/78, 70). He suggests that

> possibilities of progressiveness for the serial were discussed in terms of making it more adequate to the real, with less distortion or displacement of contradictions which exist in the real world and with fewer absences and less masking of parts of social reality. (1977/78, 70)

This does seem rather a limited account, one which focuses on the debates about realism, which had been a starting point for the group, though it does demonstrate how attitudes to realism operated as something of a litmus paper in assessing theoretical positions at the time.

The work done for and by this weekend school did contribute to the publication of the BFI's Television Monograph on *Coronation Street* in 1981, which included essays by two Women and Film Study Group members, along with contributions by members of the Potteries Group and an introduction by Richard Dyer. Both groups had disbanded by then, and the contributions to that publication, which itself had a complicated production history, were presented as individual essays.

A fourth event brought tensions within the group to a head. The group had agreed to do a paper at the 1978 conference of the British Sociological Association. The discussion at the meeting on 11 February [1978] was informed by a letter from one of the group's members, referred to earlier, who suggested that the group needed 'a sustained programme of reading, viewing and discussion' which was not possible while being 'always under pressure to produce for public display' (letter by group member to meeting of 11 February [1978]). In a draft statement to the BSA, pulling out of the conference, the group explained that it had tried to build a theoretical framework but was unhappy with how this had been expressed in its paper for the SEFT weekend school. The group had therefore decided to take a break from public activity in order to look 'specifically at feminist texts of relevance to our work' – Luce Irigaray's *Ideology and Consciousness* is mentioned, along with the CCCS's *Women Take Issue* (untitled document beginning 'Early in 1976' [June/July 1978]). There are two or three notes convening meetings after this, and the last properly dated document is a note to group members, dated 11 December 1979, which records that the group will meet in the coming year on the second Friday of the month. The only later document appears to be an undated note which convenes a meeting on Monday, 20 October, which I would date, but with no certainty, as being from 1980.

Conclusions

I would argue that, looking back from the present, all three of the events we participated in could be seen as successful and typical of the kind of extramural education activity that was characteristic of media studies work as well as feminism in the late 1970s. The events built on work which was still being developed; they sought out new audiences, including workers in the mainstream media, even though they got a hostile response; and they were the product of collaborative work between different groups. The papers at Edinburgh and PCL involved engaging with highly successful and often sceptical mainstream practitioners, while the SEFT weekend school was more careful than a number of other such events to make its theoretical debates accessible. More broadly, also, I think that the choice to focus on *Coronation Street* as a popular mainstream serial was vindicated and informed the development of a feminist engagement with television in the UK, which in the 1980s linked up with work on soap opera being developed in the USA. Certainly, soap opera became one of the texts of the emerging media studies curriculum, as I have discussed elsewhere.

But – and for this essay this is the crucial point – none of that was clear at the time, and I have shown how all three interventions were accompanied by disagreements and anxiety. The anxiety was not just about whether we could make these interventions effectively but also about whether such public interventions should be made at all. Certainly the fact that public interest in the group's work focused on *Coronation Street* was felt to exacerbate a problem which had been identified early on. A review note after six months recorded that '[a] central problem for the seminar has been that of working out the proper relationship between theoretical discussion at one level and analysis of *Coronation Street* at another level' (summary of work, prepared for September 11 [1976] meeting), and the minutes continue to show that the discussion of reading and the attempts to analyse *Coronation Street* in detail seldom came together coherently. A number in the group felt that the *Coronation Street* work was dominating at the expense of the more urgent work of understanding the complexity of women's engagement with popular culture. On 20 November [1976], well before any of the public events, there was discussion about how the group might work better for those 'who weren't interested in work on *Coronation Street*' and by April 1977, even as the Edinburgh and Manchester events were being planned, there was discussion about dropping the work on CS so as to 'spend more time on theory, especially in the area of psychoanalysis'.

In moving to a conclusion, I want to stress that this has been a personal account with none of the collective ambitions which marked the group's approach. In writing this I have also been aware of the complications of opening up the workings of this group and drawing specific attention to its difficulties. There is a danger, for instance, of implicitly setting up a contrast between the workings of the female Women and Film Study Group of the late 1970s and the apparently confident and assertive working practices of other groups, such as the *Screen* board and SEFT Executive, during this period. I suspect that most individuals involved in these activities did have doubts and second thoughts. And it is to the credit of the Women and Film Study Group that it was so careful in recording them even if it could not resolve them.

The debate between feminists about the legacy of 1970s feminism will continue. Once memory goes, we are sent back to paper records from which we have to construct our history. Inevitably certain records and articles are privileged in this process and the hesitancies and uncertainties smoothed over. My trip back into the archive indicates to me how uneven our knowledge was and how tentative our conclusions had to be. I am struck by the drafting and redrafting, the continual questioning, the extraordinary yoking together of Hilda Ogden from *Coronation Street* and the high priests of critical theory. I am struck by how painful it was to feel so uncertain and how little we actually resolved. I am reminded of Sheila Rowbotham's discussion of the difficulties of

articulating experience through the 'words of the powerful. ... There is a long inchoate period during which the struggle between the language of experience and the language of theory becomes a kind of agony' (1983, 32–3). In the end, though, what comes through to me in revisiting these papers is something less grandiose; it is the sheer doggedness of the engagement, the uncertain, puzzled, determined, hesitant voices of an endeavour which attempted to be both collective and individual and failed – and succeeded – at both.

One record in the BFI's Women and Film Study Group archive symbolizes this for me. One of the undated drafts, entitled 'Coronation Street – the Reasons for Study', argues that the programme is a chance to look at 'British mass culture' and 'a minefield of useful things to learn about what is going on in the media in Britain today and about representations of women in the media'. This seems to be something the group had agreed on after much work and discussion; it could certainly be used a written statement of the group's purpose. But on this particular copy in the margin, someone has written in ink 'Is it?' – a probing, hesitant question that indicates that even written records cannot be taken as read.

Acknowledgements

Particular thanks to Connie Balides, whom I first met at BFI Summer Schools in the 1970s, for her very valuable comments on an early draft and her ideas for taking it forward. Thanks also to the editors (and conference organizers) for their enthusiasm about the original idea and their supportive and helpful editing.

Primary source documents are indicated by date and/or title in the text. The British Film Institute's holdings can be found in Box 143 of its collection. I am grateful to Christophe Dupin for help with finding it.

Notes

1. Bolas is concerned with the history of the development of film and media studies in the UK, and although his book is a history of the Society for Education in Film and Television (SEFT), which published the journal *Screen* (1969–89), he also writes extensively about the Education Department at the British Film Institute (BFI).

2. I was at the time involved with NALGO (the white-collar local government and public services union) and in the early 1980s with the Women's Section of the Bermondsey Labour Party.

3. Work by Ien Ang, Christine Gledhill and Tania Modleski in the 1980s and 1990s offers particularly influential versions of this approach.

4. Much of the material is inadequately or inaccurately dated, and dates given in brackets indicate that I have tried to work out dates using the content of the document and other sources such as calendars. Despite this, the dating, particularly towards the end, remains stubbornly unconfirmed.

5. Although I have contacted and shown this work to some other members of the group, I have not attempted to make this a group project. And because I was not able to contact all members of the group, I have anonymized them except where their involvement is a matter of public record.

6. When I presented some of this material to a *Screen* conference in 2009, I was fortunate to meet one of the organizers of the Edinburgh event, Dr Jane Mills, now Associate Professor in Communication at the Charles Sturt University, New South Wales. She explained that, as a feminist, she had pushed for the panel and was very keen for soap opera to be seen as not just of concern to women. The request for only one person from the group was made in the context of not wanting to overwhelm other panel members; Jane recalls that she was extremely keen for the topics of all panels to be properly debated and not have sessions comprising little more than speeches from the panel members (which had tended to happen at the previous festival). There is no indication in the minutes that we knew that our invitation came from women working to shake up this male-dominated, industry-inflected event, and I don't recall knowing the background to any of this, though it is possible that other members of the group did.

7. The BFI Box 143 holds a collection of press cuttings on the 1977 Edinburgh Festival, including informative reports on the session by reporters from *Television Today*.

Section 1

Relaying Feminism

In their attempt to highlight how feminist media scholars continue the work of second-wave feminists, this volume and its preceding conference also had to engage with questions of how these new feminisms were constituted. Thus we asked the questions of how generations and/ or waves are perceived not just by each other but also by their environment and popular culture. Importantly, papers at the conference and the two chapters presented here highlighted the complexities of the discourses utilized in representations of the 'waves' and recognized both the perceived break from second-wave feminisms – particularly as it is presented by popular culture, which often assumes that feminism has become redundant – and the continuities that feminists experience within the movement.

In this section, both chapters engage with the struggle about language to describe the new feminisms and their relations to earlier ones. Are these generations formed by mother-daughter relationships? Are these waves that wash away previous activism? As van der Tuin (2009, 19) highlights, emphasis on generations tends to bring to the forefront conflict and rivalries between women which, in her eyes, constitute an 'unreal opposition'. Both S. Thornham and Aune here too reject the description and instead opt for 'waves', not because the term is without problems, but because it reminds readers more strongly of the energy and continuation of the feminist movement. Van der Tuin offers the metaphor of 'jumping' in order to connote that third-wave feminists both connect and break away from activisms of the 1960s and 1970s, while the latter move their positions to and impact directly on third-wavers. Similarly, both S. Thornham and Aune draw attention to how much of the work of current feminists continues in the spirit of and is at the same time different from the already existing second wave, with which it always also engages.

While the choice of the term 'wave' gives an indication of the complex relationship of the two feminist periods, the question of how feminism is relayed also allows the chapters to critically evaluate the continuities between the movements. Approaching the question on the one hand from the perspective of what kind of work needs to be done

(S. Thornham) and what activist work at the moment is being done (Aune), both chapters position a diverse range of feminisms and back-lashes to each other. As a consequence, the pervasiveness of particular arguments becomes evident, both within (the continued gender gap, the emphasis on violence, pornography, cultural representations and similar areas of activism) and without the movements (propositions of a redundant feminism and feminism being the root cause for women's unhappiness). Pointing to cultural representations of feminism, includ-ing its right-wing depictions by some academic men, both chapters remind us that believing popular culture about what kind of feminism we need or exist at any moment is to remain blind to the actual experi-ences of women and the reality of the feminist movement. Importantly, as both S. Thornham and Aune stress, the academy is a key place where both cultural representations and (the need for) feminist activism can originate.

Discussing feminism in the academy, Miriam David and Sue Clegg (2008) draw attention to the danger of having feminist language be sub-sumed into mainstream teaching, where it can become depoliticized and empty of its radical potential. In particular, they highlight how feminist rhetoric around the personal has been adapted by the academy in a neoliberal context which turns a blind eye to the social situatedness and specific embodiment which made the feminist critiques so radi-cal. Instead, neoliberal discourses of the personal emphasize individual agency as the sole producer of success and failure exactly because they do not acknowledge the realities of power structures in which the indi-vidual is embedded. In comparison to that, feminists such as Weber (2010) and McRobbie (2009a, 2009b) situate their analyses in their social and political contexts and use highly reflexive accounts of per-sonal experiences; a style of writing also adopted by S. Thornham and Aune. Their chapters furthermore provide complex critiques of the power structures within the academy and make visible their connec-tion to feminist activism.

S. Thornham emphasizes how the academy continues to be a place in which women encounter both real discrimination and discourses of feminist criticism. Using the examples of three campaigns developed for *Marie Claire* to 'rebrand' feminism as metaphors, S. Thornham highlights how feminist discourses within the academy are continuously undermined and instead replaced by others that 'efface history and material realities' while at the same time apparently taking feminism into account. Targeting in particular the arguments of post-feminism as well as those of the right-wing antifeminist backlash, which fix women and active feminism as known, S. Thornham shows that the discourses employed inside and outside the academy obliterate both women and feminism. She suggests that it is exactly the suggestion that feminism lacks reflexivity and mobility that makes the arguments so compelling while also misrepresenting the feminist movements and achievements.

While S. Thornham is particularly concerned about the misleading depictions of the second-wave, Aune highlights that there is also a danger of misrepresenting the third wave. Her chapter investigates the role of feminist teaching within the academy to the development of third-wave feminist activism and draws on both a wide-ranging survey with third-wave activists and her own grass-roots experiences of teaching feminist courses within media and cultural studies. Aune highlights that although many of the students might not originally call themselves feminists or articulate their feminist views in the classroom, the academy nevertheless plays a central role in originating feminist activism which in its scope, aims and indeed institutions is often close to if not the same as second-wave activism. Thus, where S. Thornham expresses concern about the limitations of the academy to offer spaces of feminist intervention, which she sees dwindling away, Aune provides a more optimistic reading of feminist potential within the academy. Considering the two different viewpoints taken here (S. Thornham adopts a macroview of the management and research culture within the academy, Aune a microview of feminist encounter in the classroom), their opposing assessments should be seen as complementary: while spaces for feminist engagement might be available in the classroom, the academic culture within a neoliberal context continues to contain these interventions to the spaces of the grass roots, where feminist activism even in its radical forms can be inspired, but can also be cited as an example of having taken feminism into account while evading the structural inequalities that still so evidently exist.

Rebranding Feminism

Post-Feminism, Popular Culture and the Academy

Sue Thornham

The introduction to an American anthology of 'feminist life histories', published in 2007, seeks to disentangle the various narratives that might be constructed to link the different generations of feminist scholars who are contributors to the volume. One narrative, write the editors, sees the relationship between them as a paradigmatic 'mother and daughter' relationship: a story of controlling mothers and rebellious daughters. A second 'assumes a linear, progressive understanding of history in the relations between generations', with feminism's 'third wave' manifesting a decided advance in theoretical and political sophistication on its predecessors. Finally, a third account focuses on the contrast between the collective struggles of the past and the individualism of today's (post-)feminist politics, a shift which it 'either celebrates or bemoans' (Aikau, Erikson and Pierce 2007, 2). While all three of these accounts hold resonances for me, it is a rather smaller and apparently less significant story that the editors tell on which I want to focus. What distinguishes older from younger feminists, they write, is the way in which they came to feminism. While older women became feminists as a result of personal experience or social activism, younger women's exposure to feminism came either through the academy, in the form of a university education, or through American popular culture (ibid., 1). It is the intersection of these two apparently very different fields which this chapter will address, together with the social, political and theoretical currents which unite and underpin them.

Rebranding Feminism

In November 2007 *Marie Claire*, the magazine 'for the intelligent, fashion-savvy thirty-something woman',[1] ran an article called 'Can we rebrand feminism?' 'With women still earning an average of £6k less than their male counterparts,' it asked, 'why is feminism still regarded as the unsayable F-word?' To 'declare yourself a feminist today', it explained, 'is to brand yourself frumpy, frustrated, strident, unsexy and man-hating'. Feminism, it concluded, needs 'a makeover' if it is to be rendered 'sexy again'. *Marie Claire* had therefore commissioned 'three leading [advertising] agencies' to 'rebrand ... the movement', and the proposed campaigns were to be judged by 'a panel of experts' (2007, 157).[2]

All three campaigns featured a poster image and a slogan. The first, which I will call Penis Envy, presented a novelty Penis Box. On one side was an image of a flaccid penis, overwritten with the slogan 'Get Ahead, Get a Penis'. On a second side were four further injunctions:

- earn an extra 30 per cent just by being a man;
- never be overlooked for promotion again;
- chair those important meetings, don't just make the tea;
- be taken seriously by your colleagues.

The agency explained: 'Sadly, feminism has become somewhat militant and aggressive. We wanted to bring some humour to the table ...' (ibid., 160). The second campaign, 'A pair of hairy legs', featured an image of a man's feet and lower legs, overwritten with the single word 'Feminist', and an asterisk referring the reader to an explanatory footnote: 'Anyone. As long as they believe in equality.' The agency commented, 'Feminism doesn't just need rebranding – it needs redefining.... If you go back to its roots, feminism isn't really about women. It's about human kindness ...' (ibid., 159). The final campaign, the one featured most strongly by *Marie Claire*, offered the image of a pink lacy bra in flames and below it the slogan, 'The underwear's changed, but have the issues?' The agency's pitch declared: 'Feminism has a huge image problem. It can be seen as antifamily and antifeminine and therefore irrelevant.... We wanted to unleash [women's] power rather than fight an illusory enemy – men. We've used an iconic feminist image, but we've updated it' (ibid., 162).

The version of history offered here, in which feminism was once sexy, feminine and fun but has more recently lost, or abandoned, these qualities, is hardly one which would be recognized by those earlier feminists it invokes.[3] It is, moreover, an account which is hardly new: the same claim has recurred regularly for the past 25 years.[4] Nevertheless, nestling between articles on 'What men really think about sex' and 'Swishing is the new shopping',[5] *Marie Claire*'s attempted 'makeover' of feminism presents us with views about feminism and its contemporary relevance which are widespread not only in popular women's magazines but also, for those of us who are academic feminists, in sites rather closer to home. In what follows, therefore, I shall take each of these ads as my starting point for reflections on the questions *Marie Claire*'s article provokes. First, however, I want to make four general comments on the article and its putative advertising campaigns.

The first concerns the rather obvious point that none of the campaign images actually includes a *woman*. Two of the images are of male body parts; the third, the lacy pink bra, suggests not so much a woman as a decidedly feminine and distinctly model-sized *girl* – at best, perhaps, a *post*-feminist. It is an absence which manages to erase the subject of feminism, women, even as it advertises its contemporary relevance. Yet it is one which also speaks of a genuine representational difficulty. For these advertising agencies and for *Marie Claire*, the idea of the female subject is so bound up with the concept of Woman as image that, faced with trying to affirm the first, the only way to prevent it sliding into the second is to omit the representation altogether.

The second point to be made concerns the notion of *rebranding*. Branding, as Naomi Klein (2001) has reminded us, effaces both the materiality of the product and its processes of production. Instead, what is sold is 'lifestyle': consumption patterns identified both with symbolic value and with notions of 'personal taste'. For women, such consumption is bound up with fantasies of self-transformation, in which femininity, as both appearance and identity, is both the process and the idealized outcome of this transformation. It is a process and an ideal – femininity *as* 'lifestyle', *as* mass culture, *as* consumerism – which feminism has been concerned, precisely, to critique. As Charlotte Brunsdon writes, 'Traditional first-world femininity is made strange by feminism – it is denaturalized, and therefore the multiple sites on which it is elaborated become areas for possible investigation' (2000a, 25). Effacing both the processes of its production and the material history of feminism, then, what *Marie Claire*'s 'rebranding' does is to reinscribe it within the very category – femininity – from which it has constructed a 'denaturalizing' distance and thus remove its critical voice.

Third, these 'rebrandings' are all, of course, reworkings of very traditional stereotypes of the feminist. They are highly self-reflexive but at the same time deeply ambivalent, offering an ironic reframing which is at the same time a *reinstatement* of the familiar image. All of them function to *fix* feminism at a considerable distance from the mobile and knowing reader which the ads themselves interpellate – the reader who *knows* these are stereotypes and, moving back and forth between engagement and detachment, connection and distance, can smile. Whoever this reader is, she – or he – is not a feminist.

And yet – my fourth general point – the article also asks whether 'the issues' have changed and concludes that they haven't. Feminism, it argues, 'is as relevant as ever'. The UK Equality and Human Rights Commission's *Sex and Power 2008*, which came out the following year, confirmed this conclusion. 'In 12 of the 25 categories for which figures are available', the report concluded, 'there are fewer women holding top posts'. Progress towards gender equality is either 'stalled' or in 'reversal' (2008, 3). In the remainder of this chapter, then, I want to use *Marie Claire*'s three advertising campaigns as a way of thinking in more detail about some of these issues.

Table 2.1. Missing women in senior positions 2008[6] public appointments

Women	Missing Women	Men
6,469	2,921	9,390
Directors in FTSE 100 companies		
24	436	560
Civil service top managers		
244	214	458
Members of Parliament		
125	198	323
Senior judges		
18	80	99

Penis Envy

This campaign poster contains two curiously interlinked elements. First, it is the only one of the three to reference statistical evidence of gender inequalities in employment. Second, however, its ultimate recourse is to a biological explanation for gender inequalities, however ironic in tone. It is the intersection of these two elements that I want to address here.

The fifth *Sex and Power* report, published in September 2008, produced figures for what it called 'missing women' – the number of additional women that we would find in senior positions were there to be gender equality. These figures (see Table 2.1) make depressing reading. If we use the same method to track the 'missing women' in UK universities, we find the above statistics (see Table 2.2).

To this we can add the information that, according to the *Times Higher Education Supplement* in July 2008, although women now make up 57.2 per cent of UK university students, they comprise less than half the UK research student population and are clustered in traditionally 'feminine' subjects and in less prestigious universities. If we probe further than *academic* staffing in UK universities, we find that in 2006/7, while women accounted for only 18.7 per cent of professors, they comprised 93 per cent of admin support staff.[8]

This concept of 'missing women' in senior positions, together with the need to explain them, is one that has figured strongly in recent years. Within higher education, it is the problem addressed, for instance, in the widely discussed speech by Lawrence H. Summers, economist and then-president of Harvard University, in January 2005. Although the speech did ultimately earn Summers's dismissal, it seems,[9] it is still worth examining, because the ideas in it have a recurrent life. Summers offered three 'broad hypotheses'[10] to explain these 'missing women'.[11] The first is 'choice': what Summers calls 'the 'high-powered job hypothesis', which argues that women choose not to apply for these jobs because of the long hours they involve. The second hypothesis is biology: what Summers delicately terms the 'different availability of aptitude at the high end'. The final hypothesis is discrimination, which

Table 2.2. Missing women in UK higher education 2008/9[7]

	Female	Male	Missing Women
Professors	3,270	14,265	**10,995**
All academic staff	77,745	101,295	**23,550**

Summers links to 'different socialization'. According to Summers, this last hypothesis is unlikely, for two reasons. First, 'if there was really a pervasive pattern of discrimination that was leaving an extraordinary number of high-quality potential candidates behind,...in the highly competitive academic marketplace, there would be more examples of institutions...working to fill the gap'. In other words, simple market economics render it untenable. Second, argues Summers, recent developments in 'the field of behavioral genetics' (together with his own observation of his two-and-a-half-year-old twin daughters) suggest that the effects of socialization on gendered behaviour have been overrated. In Summers's view, then, it is a combination of the first and second hypotheses (women choose to opt out of high-powered jobs, and there are fewer women than men at the very highest levels of intelligence) that is largely responsible for the employment patterns in higher education that we see. Much the same argument, notes Carla Fehr, has recurred – despite all evidence to the contrary – over the past hundred years. Thus in 1910 another eminent academic, Edward Thorndike, later to become president of the American Association for the Advancement of Science, made a very similar pronouncement. Since 'men differ in intelligence and energy by wider extremes than do women', he argued, 'eminence in and leadership of the world's affairs of whatever sort will inevitably belong oftener to men. They will oftener deserve it' (quoted in Fehr 2008, 106).

Summers's conclusions, then, provide a darker gloss on the *Marie Claire* advertisement, making its recourse to biology look rather less playful and ironic. For Summers, any notion that the terms of the 'high-powered job' might be alterable, that the private sphere might itself constitute a field of power relations, relations whose organization and structure produce the terms on which public roles can be occupied, is unimaginable. The public sphere of work simply is as it is. The 'most prestigious activities in our society', he asserts, 'expect of people...a large number of hours in the office, they expect a flexibility of schedules to respond to contingency, they expect a continuity of effort through the life cycle, and they expect...that the mind is always working on the problems that are in the job, even when the job is not taking place'. Self-evidently for Summers, women are less likely to want to do this. Investigating this phenomenon of women who have 'gone missing', however, Pamela Stone (2007) found that despite the fact that media coverage of women's decisions to opt out is saturated with what she calls 'the imagery of choice', behind this 'rhetoric of choice'[12] lies a 'reality of constraint' (2007, 112). In fact, she found, women suffer from a 'choice gap' in elite professions, caught between the competing pressures of the private sphere (to be an 'ideal mother') and the public sphere of work (being an 'ideal worker').

Finally and perhaps most important, it is clear that behind Summers's first hypothesis, choice, lies his second, biology: women *choose* to opt out because they are biologically programmed to. To pursue this argument further, I want to turn to another academic publication on the problem of the educated woman, James Tooley's *The Miseducation of Women* (2002). Women, argues Tooley, who is a professor of education policy, are being 'miseducated' not because their career aspirations remain unfulfilled but because, left to themselves, they *have* no such aspirations. What women actually want is 'babies, families' and 'reliable men to depend on'. 'The current educational landscape', he argues, is one inspired by feminism, but (or as a result) it 'is not conducive to women's happiness' (2002, 119). Reversing Betty Friedan's arguments in *The Feminine Mystique* (1963), he argues that today's women are being made to feel guilty for being 'fulfilled in their marriages, and families', because they are being taught (by feminists, who are the real oppressors of women) that 'they should be looking outside to the world of work for their fulfilment'. Evidence for his claims comes first from popular culture's Bridget Jones, for whom 'the feminine mystique [is] now unobtainable but infinitely attractive, her inner voice crying out for relief from her independence' (2002, 3). Second, it lies in the fact that despite the 'carefully crafted equality' which is the product of feminist educators, it remains true that '*as soon as girls ... are given any choice*, they select the traditionally feminine ... subject with renewed gusto' (ibid., 29, original italics).

Tooley's is, of course, a very familiar argument. What has shifted in his iteration of it, however, is that it is an argument now being made, not through statements about a woman's 'place', but through arguments around *choice*. Thus the figure of Bridget Jones, deployed by McRobbie (2009a) to illustrate ways in which 'post-feminist choice' conceals new forms of gender regulation, is mobilized by Tooley for the opposite argument: that in a post-traditional world, women, now free to choose, will make choices which reflect an underlying biological imperative. It 'only makes sense to speak of traditional spheres as oppressive', he writes, 'if we also accept that men and women are the same by nature' – and that 'seems increasingly unlikely'. Thus girls choose hairdressing rather than maths and science because 'maths and science ... do ... not fit in, in general, with their natural preferences'

(2002, 224, 232). In this argument, women, *offered* choice, individualization and social mobility, will nevertheless remain fixed on the side of nature, embodiment or what Lisa Adkins (2002) calls 'immanence'.

Hairy Legs

The stereotype of the hairy-legged feminist is, of course, another version of the idea of penis envy. The feminist, as *Marie Claire* points out, is seen as a woman who is both inadequately feminine – too ugly to get a man and therefore 'frustrated' – and inadequately masculine, hence 'man-hating'. She is both too masculine and not masculine enough. It is an explanation for feminism which has a long history. We can find it, for example, in Ferdinand Lundberg and Marynia Farnham's *Modern Woman: The Lost Sex* (1947). In a very similar way to Tooley almost 60 years later, Lundberg and Farnham argue that the 'modern woman' of 1947 has too much freedom and choice, and in choosing to work she is denying her femininity and thus making herself – and the rest of the world – unhappy. Like Tooley, too, Lundberg and Farnham place feminism in the past. It began, they write, in 1792 with Mary Wollstonecraft's *A Vindication of the Rights of Women* ('a severe case of "penis envy"') and lasted – rather imprecisely – until the early twentieth century. By 1947, although there are still women 'of feminist orientation', it is firmly in the past (1947, 177). The product of 'only a minority of women, differing from others chiefly in that they succeeded in articulating and giving an intellectual basis to their discontent and hostility', feminism has, however, left its mark on 'public policy in England, the United States, Germany (for a time), Russia, Scandinavia etc.' (ibid., 168). Feminism, then, 'has triumphed', but its fruits 'taste, to most women, like ashes' (1947, 178). Sixty years on, this is a message we find repeated both in academic arguments like those of Summers and Tooley and in 'post-feminist' popular culture. Here, as Diane Negra writes, 'choice' is 'encoded' in 'forms such as the resignation from work, ... or the formula of the ready-made family which leads a 'career woman' to discover that her truest vocation is stay-at-home parenting' (2009, 7). As Charlotte expresses it in HBO's *Sex and the City*, 'The Women's Movement was supposed to be about choice. And if I choose to quit my job, that's my choice. ... There's nothing wrong with having a husband' (2001, episode 4.7).

We can also point to a second recurring theme which the 'hairy legs' image suggests: that the best feminist, indeed the best woman, is a man. Films like *Tootsie* (1982) and *Mrs Doubtfire* (1993) rework this theme. In both of these films men 'perform' femininity out of necessity, to get work, in an economic context in which, as Yvonne Tasker says, 'white, male, middle-class incomes and job security' are seen as under threat, and femininity becomes an economic and professional resource for men (1998, 34). This notion of increased gender fluidity, or reflexivity, in the face of an increasingly 'feminized' workplace, is one discussed by Adkins (2002), in her analysis of professional service workers. The 'cultural feminization' she discusses has seen the transposition of 'feminine' skills into the workplace: from the huge growth in the service sector through to the 'people management skills' required of today's manager – what one chapter, 'Women and Management in Higher Education', calls 'a concept of feminine leadership that can be practised and enjoyed by both genders' (Kearney 2000, 5).

For Adkins, however, this increased mobility or flexibility of gender performance does not lead to a dismantling of gender hierarchies or an 'undoing' of gender, despite claims to the contrary. She suggests that the ideal worker of this new economy is in fact not so much a 'feminized' worker as 'one who can claim to possess a flexible or mobile relation to gender performance and hence to have taken up a reflexive stance in relation to gender' (2002, 58). And this ideal worker, she writes, is more likely to be a man. The *women* professional service workers she discusses were also reflexive about gender performance, but theirs was a performance enacted *within* the bounds of femininity. Eighty years after Joan Rivière's study, 'Womanliness as a Masquerade', which argued that 'womanliness' is 'assumed and worn as a mask' by the successful woman in order to defuse the threatening 'masculinity' of her position (Rivière 1986, 38), women still find it difficult – indeed dangerous – to 'take on' performances of masculinity. But if 'masquerading as a man [is] impossible' (McDowell and Court 1994, 745), when women *perform* femininity – deciding, as one interviewee said, to be 'more or less female' according to the circumstances (McDowell 1997, 198) – this is not *seen* as reflexive performance and hence rewarded, but rather viewed as a 'natural' attribute of femininity. Gender 'mobility' or 'flexibility', concludes Adkins, is a resource more available to men than to women.

Academics are not quite the professional service workers of the study Adkins references. Nevertheless I think we might point to several ways in which this *taking gender* – and *feminism – into account* does work in universities. At the institutional level, it works through equality policies and documentation: what Sarah Ahmed, in her study of the effects of the Race Relations Amendment Act (2000) in shaping a new 'politics of documentation', calls 'doing the document rather than doing the doing' (Ahmed 2007, 590). Echoing Stone's concept of 'the imagery of choice', Ahmed argues that equality documents 'become forms of institutional performance.... They are ways in which universities perform an image of themselves' and at the same time are seen as 'perform[ing] in the sense of "doing well"' (ibid., 594). The first comes to serve as signifier for the second, and both become 'something that can be ticked, measured, distributed and shared' (ibid., 595). We can argue that the equality guidelines produced for the 2007 UK Research Assessment Exercise worked in a similar way, so that gender equality issues are seen to be taken into account (in Ahmed's terms 'performed') in the mandatory allowances for maternity leave, a matter of female embodiment. Yet this is accompanied by the absence of any recognition for the 'feminine' academic roles – student support, learning and teaching, course and department management – which do make academics akin to the professional service workers of Adkins's study and which are more often performed – however reflexively – by women academics.

At the level of the subject discipline, this *taking gender* – and *feminism – into account* is evident in a 'gender mainstreaming' in which a feminist critique is, it is readily accepted, an *aspect* of each discipline but remains contained by that discipline rather than undermining its structures and boundaries by subjecting it to radical interdisciplinary critique. Thus an acknowledged gender reflexivity – the idea that we can all perform a gendered critique *when appropriate* – accompanies an actual remasculinization of knowledge to which the Research Assessment Exercise, with its disciplinary reification, has also contributed.

Bra Burning

Marie Claire's final advertising image offers us a paradigmatically *post*-feminist image. From its girlishness to its ambivalence of tone, it is an image which exemplifies McRobbie's argument that the post-feminist advertisement is one that, assuming 'some ironic familiarity with...feminist critiques of advertising', invokes generational differences in its interpellation of a younger female viewer who, 'educated in irony and visually literate,...appreciates its layers of meaning,...gets the joke' (2009, 16–17). This lacy pink bra, then, is not so much being burnt as *on fire*, and feminism is the object of the joke which we, as knowing readers who have *moved on*, are invited to share. I want to use this image to explore issues of fixity and mobility which post-feminism raises.

The reflexivity evident in this advertisement is typical of a number of recent ads aimed at young women. In Anne Cronin's (2000) study of a range of advertisements dating from 1987 to 1995, she divides her sample into 'reflexive' and 'unreflexive' ads. The first group she defines as ads which employ ironic or self-conscious forms of address, thus explicitly signalling their constructed nature and the *activity* expected of the 'knowing' reader in producing meaning. The second group is much more static, offering promises of 'self-actualization' through identification with an image. Unsurprisingly, she found the first group to be targeted at men, the second at women. More recently, however, as McRobbie (2004) has pointed out, some ads aimed at young women *have* employed a reflexive mode of address. A Special K Advert from 2003, for example, shows a woman standing in front of a mirror, holding a red dress against her near-naked body while her boyfriend looks on, thinking 'she does look great in that dress. Then again, she looks great without it'. Such an advert which assumes an educated and visually literate reader who will perform interpretive work in reading it, assumes femininity to be culturally constructed and bound up with 'to-be-looked-at-ness' (Mulvey 1989) and assumes a reader who knowingly and playfully – though perhaps a touch uneasily – adopts the feminine position. But as with Adkins's professional service workers, the identificatory positions this ad invites are reflexive images *within* the familiar repertoire of femininity. Returning to the Burning Bra advertisement for a rebranded feminism, we can see that, but now more explicitly, it is the feminine (or post-feminist) position which is seen to be mobile, reflexive and knowing, and the *feminist* position which is fixed and known.

In definitions of feminism produced by feminist theorists, one of the most striking characteristics we find is an emphasis on mobility and reflexive knowing. Recent versions of the mobile and reflexive feminist subject have included Rosi Braidotti's 'nomadic subject' (1994), Donna Haraway's ironic and utopian 'cyborg' (1991) and Teresa de Lauretis's account of the 'multiple, shifting and often self-contradictory' identity which is produced within feminist writing (1990). The feminist academic, as Brunsdon writes, 'produces herself' in the engagement with her subject, just as she produces a text for her area of study' (2000a, 4). She is both inside and outside her discipline, just as she is both inside and outside ideologies of gender (de Lauretis 1987).

Marie Claire's Bra Burning ad, however, places the knowing and mobile subject as outside – or beyond – feminism and refixes feminism as the known object. McRobbie has argued that this is a characteristic of the social and cultural landscape of post-feminism, and indeed, we can point to a whole raft of recent popular films aimed at young women, such as *Miss Congeniality* (2000), *Legally Blonde* (2001), and *The Devil Wears Prada* (2006),[13] which rely precisely on this device. But post-feminism, with its refixing of feminism as known object of the ironic, post-feminist gaze, is not confined to popular culture; I think that we can argue that something like it has happened in the academy, too. Women's studies has almost disappeared and with it what Nancy Miller called the academic 'signature' of women (1988, 76). It is unnecessary because there are now (regulated) feminist spaces *within* each discipline, and feminism has been *taken into account* in every mission statement, every equality and diversity document, within the university as a whole. Even in media and cultural studies, for which feminism was both a 'ruptural' and a foundational force (Hall 1992), feminism can be seen as placed, positioned within a subdivision, so that Brunsdon, for example, could write in 1997 that she 'turn[s] out to have been working in a girlzone' in which her work has 'had remarkably little impact on the wider contours of the discipline' (1997, 169).

From 'Rebranding' to 'Waves'

In a recent collection, *Feminist Waves, Feminist Generations* (2007), the authors discuss the problems inherent in thinking of feminism in terms of either 'waves' (they see themselves as 'third-wave' feminists) or 'generations'. 'Generations' or 'generational cohorts', they argue, suggest categories which are too rigid to encompass the range and variety of feminists and feminisms which they want to discuss. The concept of *waves*, however, seems more promising as a metaphor for 'the displacement and movement of theories, methods and ways of knowing that flow within a given generational cohort as well as across time and space'. Waves are connected, not discrete, and they 'are connected to multiple sets of waves called wave trains' (2007, 6). Waves, too, have their problems, however. As Hokulani Aikau comments, 'the water that composes a wave does not advance with it across the sea; each water particle ... returns *very nearly* to its original position' (2007, 235–6, original italics). The metaphor here takes on a more depressing aspect, at least for the individual who, like the water particle, is returned to the 'girlzone' of her discipline.

Aikau, however, wants to retain the metaphor despite its drawbacks, because of its sense of energy (waves are driven by currents), connectedness and mobility. And it is with this notion of mobility and its relation to feminism that I want to conclude the arguments of this chapter. De Lauretis writes of 'learning to be' a feminist, so that identity is 'an active construction and a discursively mediated political interpretation of one's history' (1990, 263). Our identities are formed and re-formed through experience, relationships, society, culture, history and language. Our sense of self is not illusory, but neither is it unchanging: it is a matter of constant (re)interpretation, of what she calls 'an active construction': an interpretation of ourselves in time. It is thus what the Italian feminist philosopher Adriana Cavarero calls the 'feminist impulse to self-narration' (2000, 61) that has generated the mobile and self-reflexive identity of 'feminist' of which de Lauretis writes.

This concept of feminist identity as learned reflexivity, however, is under threat, as I have suggested, from a number of related directions. It is under threat, first, from the very different kind of gender reflexivity which we see in the examples of contemporary popular culture examined in this chapter. This is a reflexivity limited to its functioning within what McRobbie (2009a) calls a 'post-feminist masquerade'. As with the 'intellectual woman' described by Rivière, who 'made sure of safety' by performing an exaggerated femininity (Rivière 1986, 37–8), the hyperfemininity of the post-feminist masquerade seems to ensure possession of both self-reflexive choice and 'normal' femininity. Such choices are, however, regulated by the norms of an acceptable femininity, their limits exposed by the penalties for straying too far towards either 'masculinity' or feminism. A feminist reading of the Special K Advert from 2003 suggests that behind the ironic and playful tone and the 'imagery of choice' associated with the consumption of fashion, lies a form of coercion barely concealed by the invitation to 'Stay Special'.

Second, underlying this concept of 'choice', it is under threat, as McRobbie (2009a) has suggested, from recent metanarratives of social transformation that assert that historical shifts in modernity have produced new and expanded opportunities for women. Thus young women now can, indeed must, plan 'a life of one's own' in place of the 'living for others' which traditionally circumscribed women's lives (Beck and Beck-Gernsheim 2001, 75). A new flexibility, or mobility, in gender identities therefore becomes an inevitable product of historical change rather than the outcome of political struggle, so that feminism, as what

Denise Riley calls 'the voicing of "women" from the side of "women"' (1988, 112), becomes pre-mobile, known, redundant.

Third, we can note the easy slide from the argument that processes of 'reflexive modernization' have meant that 'choice' has replaced social or ideological determinations in the construction of female identity to the kind of market logic employed by Summers. Here, 'choice' loses the more complex and ambivalent connotations of freedom *and* compulsion found, for example, in Ulrich Beck's concept of the 'disembedded individual' who is characteristic of modern society. Instead, it is collapsed into a neoliberal notion of *free-market* choice. In this argument (post-gendered) institutions like universities are rational agents which do not discriminate because to do so would be an irrational market choice, and women are underrepresented in them because they choose to be.

Finally, lurking behind this emphasis on choice, as we saw in the arguments of both Summers and Tooley, is a renewed recourse to *biological* explanations for gender inequalities. In this right-wing version of the modernization argument, in today's 'choice' society, in which gender restrictions no longer apply, the final explanation for the 'missing women' in our universities and elsewhere must rest with biology. Feminism thus becomes both deluded and dangerous. If we can only see beyond feminism's 'prim panopticon' to the 'truths' of evolutionary psychology, argues Tooley, we will see that many of the things 'which the education feminists find objectionable – male dominance of the public space, for instance – may have arisen out of *women's* desires for men of a particular sort and men responding to those desires'. Thus 'what the feminists attack as "patriarchy" is more accurately described as a society where *women's preferences* establish the "ground rules for men in their competition with one another"' (2002, 207, original emphasis).[14]

Conclusions

Describing the differences between their own first encounters with academic feminism and those of older women, the editors of *Feminist Waves, Feminist Generations* suggest that younger women like themselves have come to feminism, not, like earlier generations, through personal experience or involvement in social activism, but through either their formal education or 'exposure to American popular culture including films and television shows' (2007, 1). If this is the case, then in both of the spheres which the editors cite the feminism they will have encountered will have been one decidedly under assault, despite, or perhaps because of, its very taken-for-grantedness. In 1991 Tania Modleski wrote of the dangers of a *Feminism without Women*. More recently, she has been even more trenchant about an academic post-feminism in which, she writes, 'the very notion of female empowerment has been reduced to gobbledygook and announced as a fait accompli' (1999, 71). *Marie Claire* is not quite as sanguine as the academic post-feminists Modleski describes, recognizing that 'the issues' are unchanged and that 'feminism is as relevant as ever'. Nevertheless, like all makeovers, its 'rebranding' functions to efface history and material realities. Looking at the fetishized images through which its three advertising campaigns seek to provide feminism with a 'makeover', we can see that they succeed, rather effectively, in obliterating both women and feminism.

Notes

1. See the *Marie Claire* website, www.ipcmedia.com/brands/marieclaire.
2. The panel comprised the Women's Editor of the *Guardian*, the design director of a 'brand consultancy', an academic, Stacy Gillis, and a representative 'woman on the street' (a civil servant).
3. See, e.g., Jo Freeman's 1973 account of media treatment of the women's movement.
4. See Bonnie Dow (1996, 209).
5. 'Swishing' is apparently 'swapping instead of shopping'.
6. Source: *Guardian*, 4 September 2008.
7. HESA February 2010. See www.hesa.ac.uk/index.php?option=com_content&task=view&id=1590&Itemid=161.
8. See the *Times Higher Education Supplement*, 10 July 2008, www.timeshighereducation.co.uk/story.asp?sectioncode=26&storycode=402686&c=1.
9. Summers's speech was made in January 2005. He resigned Harvard's presidency in June 2006. See May (2008) for detailed discussion of the speech. The speech was widely reported at the time as 'spark[ing] an uproar' (*Boston Globe*, 17 January 2005). Summers was later appointed Barack Obama's Director of the White House National Economic Council.
10. The speech can be accessed at www.president.harvard.edu/speeches/summers_2005/nber.php.
11. In the context of his speech, these were women holding tenured positions in science and engineering at top US universities and research institutions.
12. Galinsky et al. (2003) found that while 75 per cent of executive men surveyed had a stay-at-home wife, 74 per cent of women executives had a spouse employed full-time.
13. See S. Thornham (2010).
14. Tooley is quoting here from evolutionary psychologist David Buss (1996).

Third-Wave Feminism and the University

On Pedagogy and Feminist Resurgence

Kristin Aune

The decline in undergraduate women's studies in the UK (a final cohort of students graduated from London Metropolitan University in 2008) has been much lamented by feminist scholars and teachers.[1] Its decline paralleled the burgeoning – even mainstreaming – of gender modules in arts, humanities and social science degree courses. Modules on gender, often taught from a feminist perspective, are common and popular with students, especially young women. The closure of undergraduate women's studies and the incorporation of gender into the academic mainstream are often portrayed as emblematic of the depoliticization of academic feminism: it is assumed that incorporation equals weakness.

This chapter will argue something different: that the 'mainstreaming' of gender modules can be celebrated as a sign of feminism's success in the academy and that in the twenty-first century, academic feminism can be effective in opening students' eyes to gender injustice and prompting their engagement with feminist activism. In other words, feminism is being relayed in the university today. For some students, studying feminism at university is a major factor in their becoming politically active feminists. The evidence for these assertions comes from two sources: a recent survey project investigating the resurgence of new forms of feminism in the UK and personal experience teaching gender modules to undergraduates on sociology and popular culture and media courses.

At the time of writing, feminist values and achievements are being challenged by neoliberal governments in response to the current economic crisis. Changes underway in UK higher education – where the cuts in government subsidy for degree courses (especially arts, humanities and social science courses) will have a disproportionate effect on female students – are likely to reshape the university experience in profoundly gendered ways (quite possibly undoing the progress achieved in previous decades). Higher education is in flux, and feminists in the academy have an important role to play in critiquing these changes and fighting for space to continue emancipatory work. Higher education's transformation is taking place during a period of renewed optimism about feminist activism in the UK, with mounting evidence that a younger cohort are re-engaging with feminist ideas and theorization of this activism as new generation or 'third-wave' feminism (Banyard 2010, Dean 2010, Redfern and Aune 2010, Penny 2011). This chapter engages with three connected areas: a) feminist generations or waves, b) learning about feminism and c) feminist teaching methodologies. These intersect in the university, and this allows students to continue to experience the academy as a place to encounter and engage with feminism and then perhaps to become politically active *as* feminists.

Young Women, Feminism, Post-Feminism and Higher Education

The pessimistic portrayals of the place of women's studies and feminist theory in the academy are perhaps understandable. In post-industrial societies today, young women are often depicted as having been co-opted by consumer capitalism and consequently possessing an uneasy relationship with feminism. Young women's position changed rapidly during the twentieth century. In late modern 'risk society' (Beck 1992), they have become 'unfixed' from traditional femininity (McRobbie 1994, 157–8), individualized as workers and consumers rather than, as previously, mothers, daughters or wives. Discursively, young women have emerged as a symbol of the late-modern social order. They are the workers of the new service economy, negotiating conflicting discourses that describe them both, as Anita Harris (2004, 6) indicates, as 'can do' girls who are achieving educationally, primed to smash glass ceilings and spend thousands on handbags, but also as 'at risk' of becoming out of control through binge drinking or teenage pregnancy. (These discourses are classed, of course, and to achieve 'can do' femininity, various forms of capital are required.)

Gender mainstreaming has occurred beyond academia, in the public and global arena, as political institutions (notably the UN and EU) have committed to making women's interests central to their decision making. There is an ongoing debate as to whether this represents feminism's success, as Sylvia Walby (2002, 2005) argues, or whether, as McRobbie (2009a, 155) fears, 'Gender mainstreaming in effect replaces feminism', becoming part of a cultural consensus that feminism is no longer necessary.

The term *post-feminism* is frequently invoked to understand the contemporary culture in which feminism is taken for granted yet simultaneously undone and rendered no longer necessary (McRobbie 2004; Tasker and Negra 2007). Particular attention has been given to ideals of femininity advocated by post-feminist media representations and the way in which popular cultural post-feminism acts as ideology which interpellates (Althusser 1971) young women, calling them to create themselves in relation to these ideals (Negra 2009). Post-feminism is the dominant discourse younger women draw on in forming their sense of self, constituting 'a new site of female subjectivity' (Genz 2006, 344) in Western cultures. Post-feminist femininity amounts to a new norm that the young woman is compelled to 'cite... in order to qualify and remain a viable subject' (Butler 1993, 232). Gill (2007b) has described this 'postfeminist media culture' as a 'sensibility' in which femininity is seen as 'a bodily property' (in other words, women are equated primarily with their bodies); there is a 'shift from objectification to subjectification', with women obliged to present themselves as sexually empowered; women are encouraged to monitor and discipline themselves in adherence to the 'makeover paradigm' common in popular culture; individual empowerment is held up as a good; and ideas about so-called natural sexual difference are experiencing a renaissance.

Importantly, feminism is viewed as something that young women disavow in the post-feminist climate (McRobbie 2009a). Young women's post-feminism – their 'I'm not a feminist but...' attitude – is often understood as rejection of feminism. In fact, disembedded from the gender patterns of their mothers and grandmothers, as McRobbie puts it, young women are traversing new and challenging ground. And their response to feminism is complex. In an academic context influenced by post-structuralism, young women may find it harder to take up the identity 'feminist', since they are suspicious of labels that con-note a singular identity (see Karlyn 2006, 62). In the British context, a range of public figures have depicted feminism as 'dead', outmoded and of no interest to a younger generation (see Redfern and Aune 2010, 1–17, 217–20, for examples and refutations).

But these pessimistic accounts of young women's denial of feminism are problematic where they do not recognize (or even permit) young women's challenge to post-feminism's hegemony. They fail to acknowledge the ways in which young women resist post-feminism; they do not recognize that some young women *are* feminists and are engaging in feminist political activism. This neglect is perhaps most visible in McRobbie's work, where British young feminist activism is not even mentioned, and US third-wave feminism is briefly dismissed as individualistic, consumerist and 'anti-feminist' (McRobbie 2009a, 156–9). In the context of higher education, McRobbie's 2005 lament in the *Times Higher Education Supplement* about students' lack of involvement in political activism or protests against sexualized culture could be countered with the observation that some feminist students *are* involved in political groups, and, at the time she was writing, there were a number of young feminist activist groups campaigning on precisely the issues she mentions as being neglected.

Equally, as well as failing to recognize young women's engagements with feminism, these negative accounts betray problematic assumptions about what constitutes 'proper' feminism. Assumptions about what social movements *should* look like to qualify as social movements are prevalent. For instance, in an interview in the collection *Third Wave Feminism: A Critical Exploration*, Elaine Showalter explains that she finds it difficult to believe that there is or could be another women's movement after second-wave feminism. For her, third-wave feminism is simply 'another way of talking about the contemporary moment rather than calling it post-feminism' (Gillis and Munford 2007, 292). For Showalter, movements need clear, agreed goals and recognizable leaders, so if these are not present (or, we might argue, not viewed to be present by observers), there is no movement. In Showalter's account, it is not possible to call even significant numbers of 'third-wave' feminist activists a feminist movement.

Then there is the problem of 'feminist purism', which, as Dean (2008) identifies, accords greatest respect, via attaching the label *radical*, to particular kinds of feminist activism: those which are autonomous and do not collaborate with state institutions. Hence, organizations like the Fawcett Society and Women's Aid are found wanting, since they work with state organizations.

There is also a dismissal of activism addressing media and cultural representations. Cultural activism – which includes such examples as scrawling 'this is sexist' on men's magazines featuring naked women, feminist blogs, feminist knitting and craft groups and festivals promoting feminist and queer art or music – is often considered not to be 'proper' activism. Natasha Walter first argued this in *The New Feminism*, where she wrote: 'to believe that feminism's rightful place is in the cultural and personal arena ... [removes] feminism's teeth as a strong political movement' (Walter 1998, 9; the 2010 publication of *Living Dolls* saw her change her mind about this). Harris (2008, 1) has helpfully critiqued these ideas, arguing that 'young women have new ways of taking on politics and culture that may not be recognizable under more traditional paradigms, but deserve to be identified as socially engaged and potentially transformative nonetheless'.

In the UK, many of today's young female undergraduates are the first generation of women in their family to attend university. In the last forty years, there has been a sevenfold increase in students entering higher education, due to the expansion of the universities, the change in status of the former polytechnics post-1992 and government agendas. This has had the most significant consequences for women, who are now over 50 per cent of first degree students[2] and who, especially in the newer universities, are from a wide range of backgrounds.

Concern about young women's disconnection with feminism has been applied to female students by McRobbie and others. Feminist media studies scholar Rebecca Feasey (2008) has bemoaned her students 'inability to see the links between feminist debates and their own lived experience'; instead, they readily 'revert to populist descriptions and first hand accounts of their romances, relationships and friendships far removed from the literature in the field.' But these first-hand accounts are, surely, important, for they are part of the raw material feminist theory makes sense of. If this is not explicitly articulated in the feminist classroom, that doesn't mean that it is not happening outside it or in the minds of students loathe to express, or nervous of voicing, their views, as students begin to think of what the connections might be between feminist theory and their own relationships and media pleasures.

While not wanting to deny these accounts – to be sure, many of the students taught by feminists do not use the 'F word' to describe themselves – it is important to look beyond them to see the ways in which students *are* engaged, personally and academically, with feminism, to see the ways in which feminism is being relayed and reformulated within a new generation. The chapter will turn to this shortly.

Woodward and Woodward's (2009) book, while not a formal study of students' engagement with feminism, contains observations which resonate with my experiences of teaching young women from predominantly working-class or lower-middle-class backgrounds in a post-1992 institution. Sophie Woodward comments on the way, despite reluctance to use the 'F word' because of reactions it might generate from others, that feminism does resonate for students and in different ways according to their own locations (e.g. in relation to ethnicity or class). The feminist classroom can be a vibrant space where gender debates extend into their personal and social lives in the university, too. In a later section I will go on to discuss my experiences in my own feminist classrooms, but before that the discussion turns to evidence from a recent research project on new forms of feminist activism in the UK.

Reclaiming the F Word: The Resurgence of 'Third-Wave' Feminism in the UK

Since around 2000 there has been an apparent resurgence of feminism in the UK, predominantly among younger people (mostly women). In 2008/9 Catherine Redfern and I carried out a survey (online and in paper version) of people involved in these new forms of feminism. We received 1,265 completed questionnaires.[3] The new manifestations of feminism include new conferences (such as the FEM conferences, Ladyfest festivals, Feminist Fightback conference and the Feminism in London conference); national issue–based campaigns (on a range of issues including street harassment, childcare, pornography, religion, rape and media representations); local groups in cities, towns and regions; Internet activism (including blogs, webzines, Facebook groups, Twitter, YouTube videos) and, more recently, new student feminist groups in universities.

The constituency of these groups is predominantly young: of our survey participants, three-quarters were under 35, with 62.3 per cent in their twenties or younger. In addition to these new groups, younger women have joined older 'second-wave' groups such as the Fawcett Society, Rape Crisis and the Women's Environmental Network.

Notwithstanding the problems with wave or generational metaphors – does 'wave' wash away the achievements of earlier generations? Does 'generation' erase feminist bodies and labour that do not fit into neat time periods? Do feminisms outside western Europe and North America adhere to these constructions?[4] – I believe that the extent of this activism makes it justifiable, in an anglophone context, to use the term 'third-wave feminism'. I use the term 'third wave' to describe a mostly younger cohort of feminists who were not old enough to be involved in women's liberation in the 1960s and 1970s and became active in the 1990s in the USA and from the 2000s in the UK. For me, *wave* is preferable to *generation* because it implies continuity and resurgence rather than a clean break between two distinct generations. In the USA, third-wave feminism occurred from the 1990s, aims to be diverse, includes men and transgendered people and has challenged some of the more structural approaches of second-wave feminism (notably radical feminism). In the USA there has been conflict between second- and third-wave feminists, with some second-wave feminists believing that third-wavers are individualistic, apolitical and too concerned with popular culture rather than issues like violence and poverty. But in the UK, generational conflict is largely absent, and third-wave feminists' concerns and analytical frameworks are similar to second-wave feminism's, with strong support for radical and socialist strands of feminism (Redfern and Aune 2010).

Our survey does not provide an accurate representation of post-2000 feminism; for one thing, two-thirds of respondents completed it online, and online survey participants tend to be more educationally privileged. Nevertheless, as the only survey research that has been done on the UK third wave, it is indicative of aspects of this feminist movement.

Survey participants were highly educated: 90.2 per cent possessed or were studying for an undergraduate or postgraduate degree, and 41.5 per cent had or were working towards a postgraduate qualification. Thus higher education has played a role in nearly all these feminists' lives.

For a small number, the significance of higher education for their feminism lies in the new feminist student groups that have formed in the last few years in some UK universities. These are important, in a context where the 2010 student occupations and protests against the Conservative and Liberal Democrat coalition government's rise in tuition fees led to claims that students were becoming newly politicized. These groups, however, preceded the new student protests and focused on a range of issues disproportionately affecting female students, notably student debt and poverty, harassment, violence and stalking, and a sexualized student culture.

Academic study of gender and feminism are, however, much more significant for the development of third-wave feminism. Almost half those questioned (46.3 per cent) said that they had undertaken some academic study of feminism or women's studies.[5] Those who responded affirmatively were asked what this was. A number mentioned studying gender during A-level sociology, history, politics or English literature. Many more cited university qualifications, mostly degrees and post-graduate qualifications. The range of courses cited was wide, but most were in humanities and social sciences. Some were single or joint honours degrees or postgraduate degrees in women's studies. Others studied feminist or gender-related optional modules within their degrees. Some chose feminist topics for their assignments or dissertations. The selection below gives a flavour.

> Two undergraduate modules – one on Feminist Cultural Studies, one on Sexuality and Society. Enjoyed both far more than my actual degree which was in Philosophy! (female, 25, south east)
>
> Women's studies as part of my BA degree; did PhD on Irish women's writing; teach & research women's literature (female, 53, midlands)
>
> Have an undergraduate degree in sociology and my PhD concerned the forensic medical examination of sexual assault victims (male, 28, Scotland)
>
> As part of my sociology degree I undertook a Gender Studies module, but also completed my dissertation on the impact of the Civil Rights Movement in America on the role of the black woman, and most of my sociological studies were based around gender, for example in psychiatric treatment, religion etc. (female, 36, London)
>
> Study of women's suffrage in school history classes (female, 18, south west)

We asked whether they had always called themselves feminists and if not, why and when they started to.[6] Of the 47.1 per cent who had taken on feminism later, by far the most common inspiration was positive experiences during education (often at university), and the second was reading feminist books (sometimes while at university). Other sources of inspiration included Internet feminism, having friends or parents who were feminists and, less commonly, negative experiences in a relationship or workplace.

The stories pinpointing university as the spur to feminist identification emphasized four aspects: academic study, reading feminist literature (sometimes as part of academic study), making friends who were feminists and being involved in feminist groups or student union activism. The stories below are illustrative of the sorts of things these participants said:

I was raised by a strong & inspiring single mother, who probably wouldn't identify as a feminist, but certainly gave me many of the tools I needed to think and act like one. There was definitely a time during my early years at university when I heard the word 'feminism' for the first time, and started to learn about the history of it & realize how incredibly relevant this was to my life – from learning about feminist performance artists in my studies & arts practice, to contextualising & finding ways to tackle the chauvinist men I was often serving in my bar jobs! Historically too, I had only to think of the limited opportunities that were open to my mother and grandmother, compared to myself, and had it not been for feminism, I wouldn't have been at university at all articulating these thoughts! (female, 27, north west)

It wasn't a sudden realization – more a gradual coming to consciousness. I think I first started thinking about the position of women in our society in my first year at university. I remember being in one of the typical student clubs one night, dancing (i.e. gyrating) to graphic, misogynistic hip-hop with some of my female friends and realising just how sexist the implications and aspirations presented by this music actually are. I can't remember why but I decided to buy Ariel Levy's *Female Chauvinist Pigs*... and it all seemed to click. I don't necessarily agree with everything she says, but the subject matter really resonated with me. I guess that's when I became a feminist. I set about buying a few more books, including some of the older 'classics' of the genre, and exploring feminist groups on the internet. It's the latter approach that I've actually connected with the most; I like the community provided by groups such as the F-word, especially seeing as many of my friends either fail to understand or are indifferent to my feminism. (female, 23, south west)

Through my undergraduate studies I became interested in issues of gender, and consequently feminist theory and politics. Another pivotal moment when I would have defined myself as feminist was producing a performance of *The Vagina Monologues* for a women's domestic violence charity in my second year of university. (female, 26, London)

I was 18 and looking for books on lesbianism in the university library. I came across Audre Lorde's *Sister/Outsider* and took it out because the author was a lesbian. It also introduced me to feminist thought. (female, 32, Wales)

The evidence from this survey demonstrates that academic feminism can be effective in making students aware of gender injustice and prompting their engagement with feminist activism. For some, studying feminism at university is a vital step on the way to becoming politically active feminists. The demise in undergraduate women's studies should not be read as evidence that feminism has disappeared from the curriculum even if it means that the possibility of prolonged study of the subject has vanished; instead, it has spread out into a wide range of modules and assignment topics within undergraduate and postgraduate degrees. Moreover, the demise of undergraduate women's studies does not mean that the link between theory and activism, much touted by women's studies academics as one of women's studies' distinctive features, has been lost. Learning about feminism during a Sociology degree, say, can and does inspire students to work for feminist organizations or fund-raise for women's charities.

Teaching Women and Popular Culture

So far, I have used the results of a study of third-wave feminism to argue that feminism is alive and well in the university. The second piece of evidence for this claim comes from personal experiences teaching on sociology and popular culture and media programmes in a 'new', or post-1992, university, where I have worked since 2005. These programmes attract a broad cross-section of students, predominantly young women, most from working-class or lower-middle-class backgrounds and mostly the first generation in their family to attend university. Although young white students are in the majority, there are a significant number from other ethnic backgrounds, as well as students returning to education after working or bringing up children.

I co-teach (with a male colleague) a first-year module called Feminism and Society, which provides an introduction to the sociology of gender from a feminist perspective. I also teach a second-year module, Gender and Work: Feminist Perspectives, and a third year module, Women and Popular Culture. The first two were designed by a predecessor, while I devised the Women and Popular Culture module in response to student interest in this topic.

I will confine discussion to Women and Popular Culture, but it is worth saying initially that in an early session of Feminism and Society, when surveyed anonymously on paper about their attitudes to feminism – specifically, whether they would call themselves a feminist and what feminism means to them – normally about a quarter say that they are feminists. The Gender and Work module covers topics including how work is defined (and the implications of this for women's non-remunerated work), the so-called feminization of the labour market, emotional labour, masculinity, work and identity, globalization, ethnicity and gender at work and balancing work and family. The module provides room for classroom and online discussions about students' experiences of work. With virtually all students undertaking paid employment to support their studies, often in 'flexible'/precarious work, including work in bars, restaurants, retail, lower-level administration and personal care, discussions are often occasions for students to articulate dissatisfaction with their perceived exploitation in a part-time, casualized labour market. For many students, academic feminism speaks directly and relevantly to their situations.

Women and Popular Culture takes an interdisciplinary approach, drawing mainly on sociology, cultural studies and media studies, mostly from a feminist perspective. The module explores the relationships between femininity, popular culture and feminism. It is assessed by one essay (with students allowed to design their own question) and a student-led seminar in which students work in small groups to lead a half-hour section of the class towards the end of the semester.

The module is informed by feminist pedagogy, so it is important to outline what this means and how I apply it in my teaching. As feminists entered the academy in the 1960s and 1970s, they wanted their teaching methods to break with the masculine model in which the male lecturer stands at the front and talks at the students in an authoritative fashion with little interaction. Freire (1970) called this the 'banking' model, within which students are passive receivers of the teacher's authoritative wisdom.

Many feminists began to operate with these principles:

- to strive for egalitarian relationships in the classroom (to minimize power relations between lecturers and students);
- to try to make all students feel valued as individuals (to know all the students' names, to provide individual tutorial and pastoral support, for instance);
- to use the experiences of students as a learning resource (Welch 2002; see also Culley and Portuges 1985).

Within the expanded and marketized higher education sector, it has become harder to work like this. Moreover, post-structuralism has challenged the notion that we can address women as a coherent group. It has made us see the fractured, constructed and diverse nature of identities, and many question whether feminist pedagogy is now possible. Is feminist pedagogy 'in ruins'? Gaby Weiner asks. But like her, I believe feminist pedagogy is possible – or rather, that 'the fragmented nature of feminism ... suggests that pedagogy needs to be pluralized, since one pedagogy cannot speak for (or represent) all feminisms' (Weiner 2006, 87).

We can learn from feminist post-structuralist pedagogies and should first and foremost, as Hughes (2002) argues,[7] enable students to deconstruct the dominant discourses which they speak and which speak them. The post-structuralist contention that pedagogy is performance is also important: we may not be coherent subjects, but we can at least perform learning (Gallup 1997; Felman 2001). Jyn Lyn Felman recommends feminist teachers create the class as a performance through which they learn to understand and deconstruct power relations: 'In the patriarchal model the goal is to master the subject matter and the class, while in the feminist performative model the goal is to provide all participants with mastery of the power dynamic itself' (2001, 211).

But it is not necessary to employ a purely post-structuralist feminist approach, and the beauty of contemporary feminism is that it can (and does) draw on and select from the wealth of feminist history and theory without being wedded to one particular approach. It can simultaneously endorse radical feminist critiques of patriarchy, socialist critiques of capitalism, antiracist challenges to hegemonic white feminism and post-structuralists' attention to seeing discourses as generative of oppression and constraints for those who do not conform to gender norms. As Woodward and Woodward put it, discussing the importance of cross-generational dialogue:

> ... feminist ideas at different moments are constitutive of the present, as part of the stratified deposits that make up the common sense of contemporary feminism with which it is in dialogue ...
>
> ... feminist ideas can move forward and across intersecting fields in a process that challenges linearity so that we are also not stuck in an oppositional impasse. (2009, 163–4)

Practically speaking, I operationalize feminist pedagogy in various ways:

- devising the module in line with student interests;
- moving the classroom furniture so that rows facing the front were replaced by a circle where students faced each other;
- encouraging discussion, both through structured activities and unstructured dialogue;

- allowing dissent to be voiced without toeing a 'feminist party line';
- taking the role of a co-learner as well as a lecturer with overall responsibility for the class;
- allowing students to devise their assessment topics;
- introducing a 'pass/fail' piece of group work in which students run a half-hour segment of the class that explored women's interaction with popular culture; this enables them to develop leadership skills and shifts the balance of power within the classroom;
- using theorists from a variety of feminist perspectives (second-wave and third-wave) and which address the new, post-feminist context of young women's lives;
- inviting PhD students engaged in 'third-wave' feminist research from other universities to lead sessions on their research topics;
- recognizing multiple feminist perspectives (e.g. asking the class to provide an intersectional reading of a TV makeover show) and challenging any notion of there being 'one true' feminist perspective (there were a number of students with a strongly radical feminist perspective who tended to influence the class in that direction, and I had to emphasize to quieter students who held a more liberal view the validity of their viewpoint too);
- cultivating connections between students and between lecturer and students as people, including several social gatherings after the class.

How successful is this? Does this module – and can feminist modules more generally – encourage students' positive engagement with feminist ideas? In most cases, it does. For the four years I have taught it, I have included three questions probing this on the module questionnaire students complete at the end of the semester (along with requests that the student rate the module out of 5 and for positive and negative points about the module, to enable me to improve it for future years). These are a) how has the module contributed to your own engagement with popular culture? b) would you consider yourself a feminist? and c) what does feminism mean to you?. The module scores consistently highly, with students awarding it averages of 4 or 4.5 each year and making very positive qualitative comments.

Responding to the question about their engagement with popular culture, students commented that the module increased their knowledge and understanding of popular culture and feminism; inspired them to engage personally with feminism; helped them see the relationship between cultural representations of women and the position of women in society; and helped them think more about the popular culture they engaged with.

The second question was about whether they considered themselves feminists. Of 57 who completed questionnaires, 22 students (just over a third) responded affirmatively without qualification, 11 responded with qualified yeses, 12 were unsure or said they didn't use the term but believe in some feminist principles, 3 responded with a qualified no and 7 with a clear no; 2 didn't answer. Therefore, a clear majority did identify, to some degree, as feminists. Interestingly, some commented that their views had changed as a result of studying feminism at university, in that they had become more positive towards it or begun to call themselves feminists. Some examples of responses are below:

All the time!

Yes but I am scared to tell people in case I can't back it up!

After completing numerous modules at university I would consider myself a feminist. I am very interested in feminist topics and equal rights.

I didn't when I first began uni. After modules such as this one, I have definitely endured a much more feminist perspective in life.

Post-feminist maybe, but I wouldn't make any sweeping statements and talk about it.

I wouldn't claim myself as a feminist, but believe I am more willing to maybe say one day that I could become a feminist.

No, but with some aspects taken on and used in my life.

Since this is not a systematic study, it does not 'prove' that studying feminism makes students feminist. Also, people selecting a gender-related module would be more likely to have feminist views in the first place. But what these questionnaires and my teaching experiences show is that students are interested in discussing popular culture from a feminist perspective and that they believe feminism offers important insights into popular culture and society.

When placed alongside the results from our survey of participants in new forms of UK feminism, some of whom became involved with feminism after encountering it at university, a picture emerges of a process where feminism is relayed and absorbed and aspects of it are taken on (albeit in modified and heterogeneous ways) in students' lives during and after the feminist module has finished. To claim that students are disengaged from feminism and that they reject feminist academics' attempts to relay feminism to them is not an accurate reflection of what occurs in students' minds, conversations and lives or in the feminist classroom itself. That feminist academics in the twenty-first century can offer feminist modules that are popular and well attended and that provoke personal engagement with not only the subject matter but with feminism as a personal philosophy is surely evidence of feminism's success, not its failure. The students in our classrooms are part of the future of feminism. To be sure, the future of feminism in higher education is not secure, and in an increasingly market-driven context it must be continuously fought for, by academics, staff and students. The involvements and investments of students in feminism, as outlined in this chapter, give us cause for hope and reason to learn from them, let their concerns shape our own and be optimistic about feminism's future.

Acknowledgements

Thank you to the editors and Alexa Athelstan for their helpful comments on a draft of the chapter.

Notes

1. For examples of this in the print media, see Lakhani 2008; McRobbie 2008 also discusses this. While women's studies no longer exists as a single honours undergraduate degree, gender studies is offered as a joint degree at several universities and as a single honours degree at one. At postgraduate level, gender and women's studies taught courses and research degrees continue to recruit well.
2. HESA statistics for 2009/10 indicate that women constitute 56.6 per cent of first-degree students.
3. The survey was distributed in hard copy and online to people involved in manifestations of feminism which had formed in the UK since 2000, with a request that it be passed on to individuals involved with their activities. These included four conferences, events or festivals; over 50 local and national organizations; and web-based groups. All those who identified as feminist or pro-feminist were asked to complete the questionnaire and were assured confidentiality and anonymity.
4. For debates about these metaphors, see Looser and Kaplan 1997, Henry 2003, Graff 2003, Aikau 2007 and Gillis et al. 2007.
5. The question asked was, 'Have you ever undertaken any academic study on feminism or women's studies?' with 'yes' or 'no' given as the options to tick.
6. The question asked was, 'Please tick the statement which best reflects you: a) "I can't remember a time when I wasn't a feminist"; or b) "There was

definitely a noticeable time in my life when I 'found' feminism".' The follow-up question said, 'If you ticked "There was definitely a noticeable time", please explain what sparked your interest?'

7. Christina Hughes (2002) contends that feminist pedagogies have four concerns: [i] subject position as sexed, raced and classed; [ii] construction of knowledge; [iii] which voices we hear and listen to; [iv] authority. The overarching one is to enable students to deconstruct the dominant discourses which they speak and which speak them.

Section 2

Lived Feminist Identities

As Teresa de Lauretis reminds us, 'the work of narrative ... is a mapping of differences' (1984, 121). For de Lauretis, the differences she discusses – between fictional characters and mythical places, between the spatial and temporal, between subject and object – ultimately work to produce a hero who is gendered male 'regardless of the gender of the text-image' because, as she suggests, the 'obstacle, whatever its personification, is morphologically female' (ibid., 118–19).

In a similar vein to de Lauretis's work on fiction, the contributors to this section are also engaged with modes of narrative. However, by comparison with de Lauretis, they each attempt to turn her gendered dialectic on its head, seeing the terrain on which they locate their stories – the obstacle to be navigated – as gendered male, through the construction of it as a canon of scholarship concerned with class and the everyday (the 'scholarship boys' of Maureen McNeil's narrative), memory work and history (Kempadoo) and traditional representative practices of documentary production and ethnographic practice (De La Cruz). By comparison with de Lauretis, who writes about fiction, however, the chapters in this section all detail a different narrative form: the autobiography. This means that shifting de Lauretis's dialectic of male-subject and female-object around is not as simple as first appears, not least because the joint venture of authoring each story and being a character *within* it produces a range of tensions, which we detail below. It is also not simple because the discursive formations which collectively work to construct narrative, authorship and autobiography and which they attempt to write against or intervene in are deeply and profoundly gendered.

The notion of intervention into, or disruption of, existing structures is, of course, a long-standing feminist act. Indeed, what becomes increasingly apparent from this section is not only that the tensions around narrative relate to wider concerns of feminism and are consequently deeply implicated in the chapters here. It also becomes apparent that these tensions are lived, experienced and negotiated every day and are both deeply personal and profoundly political. They are worth outlining here, then, not least because they resonate and draw on wider feminist concerns, with issues relating to authorship and narration, but also because they continue to be central concerns for feminists and continue to shape both research itself and how it is subsequently storied, narrated and *made to mean*.

The first tension relates to the notion of autobiography *per se* and the potential interventionist spaces it may facilitate. As always-already one step removed from the more public, masculine claims of history, autobiography occupies a potentially interventionist space simply by virtue of its being apart from the metanarratives of history. Indeed, the contributors to this section are all aware of the potential this positioning allows, each occupying a position as *counter* in order to critique a broader discipline.

McNeil, for example, writing in response to what she describes as the 'glib pronouncements of post-feminism' and the 'misery memoirs' that have become the mainstay of popular culture, (re)positions and (re)claims a core body of feminist autobiographies in order to argue for their resonance today. The three texts she draws on are positioned as responses to the 'scholarship boys' (such as Hoggart and Seabrook) and are used by McNeil to reinvestigate the relationship between class and gender which, she argues, has become increasingly difficult in today's climate.

Kempadoo writes about her own work as an artist in response to what she calls the 'authoritative interpreters of archives and history'. Her chapter details a range of feminist art works, including her own, which each reinterpret and rewrite colonial histories through the active and generative creative of what she calls a 'contiguous archive'. This is a lived practice – an act of dialogic creation – working to construct the past (and the archives from which art work draws), not as closed statement, but as insistently open exchange.

De La Cruz, the last author in this section, writes reflectively about filming the collaborative documentary *TRAMA Textiles: Weaving the Life of Guatemala* (2008). This video is in itself a counterproject insofar as it is a small-scale, collaborative project between San Francisco State University's Broadcast Electronic and Communication Arts Department and the women-led TRAMA textile co-operatives. Her chapter, which is centrally concerned with issues of representation, is clearly positioned as counter to discourses and power relations of colonialism and post-colonialism.

At first glance, then, autobiography can be claimed as feminist, because it constructs both the text and the author as interventionist – disrupting and (re)writing a long 'tradition of writing and reading'

(Clough 1992, 27). Indeed, in the face of a long tradition of *writing*, Kempadoo and De La Cruz offer different modes of representation, which, they argue, is better suited to their projects. However, as many feminist theorists have argued (and the contributors to this section detail), autobiography is much more than 'simply' interventionist; it is also a *tool*, used to explore (and potentially mask) a particular relationship. This relationship is not the obvious relationship between author and event (as with history), however, but rather a much more personal relationship between the lived and imagined *author*. As Clough suggests, the very act of claiming authorship is both creative and imagined, not least because in order to claim authorship, the writer needs to initially construct *herself* in a particular way:

> For a woman to write as a woman, she must write self-productively – that is, autobiographically – so as to create herself as a writer as she writes. (1992, 77)

Creating oneself as a writer allows authors to tell the story in a particular way, using narrative tools now available to them. They can, to quote Carolyn Steedman, put things 'in order' (1992, 49), and this ordering, as she suggests, produces a causal configuration: not only does it establish structure; it produces a hero, who can logically and rationally order these events/things. The irony of this ordering is, of course, that the hero re-emerges as gendered male: 'he is the active principle of culture, the establisher of distinction, the creator of differences' (de Lauretis 1984, 119). In the face of a single (gendered) hero, however, the contributors to this section all argue for a multitude of voices. Indeed, even when they insert themselves into the narrative they recount (as with Kempadoo and De La Cruz), the result is to enmesh themselves problematically into the weave (to borrow an image from De La Cruz), rather than elucidate a single narrative thread. Kempadoo, for example, worries that in the act of (re)searching absences in the archives, she actively contributes to their disappearance – becoming implicated in the very process she seeks to expose. De La Cruz also implicates herself, wondering to what extent she replicates the power relations of the colonizer, not only through the representation of the TRAMA women in the final video but also through the process of mis/identifying with them.

The anxieties that these accounts detail not only relate to issues of representation, they also relate to a fundamental anxiety about *authorship* and the uneasy relationship each contributor has with and to it.

Perhaps this is because, as Clough details, the claim to authorship is constructed through the creation of an *imagined* Self, which each contributor simultaneously constructs and rejects. This struggle – which is also a struggle between a desire *to* story (and claim agency) on the one hand and the modes of representation (i.e. the text) on the other – is a long-standing concern for feminism. Indeed, not only is it evident in the chapters in this section; it is also a key issue for the seminal writers McNeil draws on. As McNeil suggests, Jeanette Winterson (1985), Carolyn Steedman (1986) and Annette Kuhn (1995) each experiment and explore what McNeil calls 'storytelling devices'; merging imaginary and 'real' characters, visual images and written text and writing rhizomatically rather than chronologically. These works, as McNeil highlights, are playful, personal and deeply political, not least because they are centrally concerned not only with issues of representation but with their own status as author and their sometimes conflicting relationship with the story (or stories) they tell. Seen here, Steedman's question 'why do I want to tell my story *in this particular way?*' (our italics; Steedman 1992, 44), becomes doubly pertinent. It is a question not only about representation; it is also a question that (re)directs us to the relationship between author and text – between lived and imagined self.

The contributors to this section, then, all argue against what we might call a monolithic narrative, a singular story or an individual hero. Yet each contributor, through practical and critical contribution, not only *authors* her own work; she also claims *authorship* through the act of writing/creating and through the reworking of these stories for a political feminist purpose. Rather than argue these positionings ultimately resolve the tensions detailed here around authorship and narrative – or worse, return us to the gendered discourses of narrative and representation – we want to suggest that the chapters that follow (and indeed the chapters throughout the book) are read as evidence of a struggle with these issues. We should read claims of authorship less as statements of intervention and more as 'traces of desire' (Clough 1992, 77). And the 'perforated' narratives (ibid., 125) that emerge should be celebrated for the anxieties, the tensions and concerns that are storied. Indeed, if autobiography is always-already counter to the central and metaclaim of history, then we want to suggest, in keeping with Clough, something far more profound: that in reading these chapters and in engaging in and with the tensions, it is the centre, the meta, which potentially no longer holds (ibid., 137).

Classy Subjects

Maureen McNeil

Recent flippant dismissals of feminism and glib pronouncements about post-feminism have cast a shadow over the achievements and insights of feminism since the 1960s. Likewise, the marginalization of 'class' as a category of social analysis and the glitter of consumerism and complacency about the polarization of economic resources make it difficult to see class relations. In current circumstances, in which it has been increasingly difficult to think about either gender or class, let alone consider their interrelationship, I find it helpful to (re)turn to a very distinctive cluster of feminist texts which insightfully explored this nexus.

This chapter identifies a striking strand of autobiographical writing on gender and working-class lives that emerged in a set of extraordinary texts published between 1985 and 1996 in Britain. It begins by situating and introducing this remarkable cluster of books, first, by considering the social, political and cultural background that influenced and shaped the lives and writing of the authors of these texts. It offers an introduction to three of these texts, highlighting some of their most striking features. At the core of this chapter is a set of commentaries on the ways in which these authors offered not only distinctive perspectives on gender and class, but also challenged both the conventions about the writing of working-class lives and the assumptions about those lives in twentieth-century Britain.

Post-Second World War British Culture: In Search of Working-Class Culture

From the late 1950s into the early 1970s there was evidence of a new interest in working-class culture in Britain. Michael Young and Peter Willmott's *Family and Kinship in East London* (1957), an anthropological study of a working-class London community, was a key publication which both registered and fuelled this interest. Tracing what he characterizes as the 'discovery of working class culture' (Critcher 1979, 16; see also Johnson 1979, 41) in Britain during this period, Chas Critcher (1979, 13–14) assembled a list of key sociological studies which he describes as having 'in common a concern with the effects of social change on the working class' (1979, 14). D. H. Lawrence's *Lady Chatterley's Lover* (1961), which was written before this period but published in a storm of controversy during it, evidenced a rather different kind of curiosity about working-class culture – through its literary representation of class relations and sexuality. Moreover, a new mode of theatrical realism, which came to be labelled 'kitchen sink' drama, offered British theatre audiences depictions of working-class life (exemplified in John Osborne's *Look Back in Anger* [1957]) in the late 1950s and 1960s.

The flourishing interest in British working-class culture was sustained, to some extent, by a curiosity about worlds very different from the ones some of these writers and many of the readers and the audiences they attracted inhabited. Indeed, many of the key texts which sparked such interest were written by authors who did not themselves come from working-class backgrounds but who were fascinated by the differences they perceived within Britain. Hence, most of these texts represented British working-class lives and culture through the eyes and with the voices of outsiders, and some of these encounters were rather voyeuristic.

While the British theatrical, academic and literary worlds were turning their attention to 'other' lives – outside the upper and middle classes – some young men were making their way into higher education as the first members of their families to enter universities. Educational reform, grammar schools and post-Second World War expansion of opportunities for university education (including for those who had done wartime military service) created new opportunities for some working-class young men. This expansion of educational possibilities, in turn, contributed to the emergence of a fresh wave of publications on British working-class culture. Written by a generation of young men who came of age in the 1940s and 1950s, these publications provided some striking accounts of working-class culture, informed by the authors' own personal experiences of it in Britain.

Scholarship Boys: Authentic Accounts of Working-Class Life in Britain

The most influential of these texts was Richard Hoggart's *The Uses of Literacy: Aspects of Working-Class Life, with Special Reference to Publications and Entertainment*, which was published in 1957. Hoggart's book would become a founding text for British cultural and media studies. However, it was first and foremost an autobiographical depiction of life in working-class Leeds. Hoggart was clearly an insider – familiar with the ways of the community and culture he set out to depict and analyse. Much of the early credibility of his account derived from his insider status. A quarter of a century later, another autobiographical text, which took its inspiration from *The Uses of Literacy*, written by another working-class lad appeared. Jeremy Seabrook's *Working Class Childhood* (1982) announced its origins and its concerns explicitly in its title, and substantially, it positioned itself as an autobiographical account of working-class life in the tradition of Hoggart's publication.

Hoggart and Seabrook were part of the wave of British working-class young men who benefited from the extension of educational opportunities in the second half of the twentieth century. When they wrote about working-class life, it was not outsider curiosity or voyeurism that impelled them. Much of their writing was autobiographical, rendered through first-person narration. Their representations claimed and realized legitimacy deriving from their direct knowledge and experience of working-class life. In the preface to *The Uses of Literacy* Hoggart explained that his book was 'about changes in working-class culture during the last thirty or forty years' and that '[w]here it is presenting background, this book is based to a large extent on personal experience' (1957, 9). He then went on to explain that this was to be supplemented by 'the findings of sociologists where they seemed necessary as support or qualification of the text' (ibid.).

Authenticity was a key feature of the autobiographical books produced by Hoggart, Seabrook and other working-class British writers of their generation. Reflecting on the appeal of *The Uses of Literacy*, Richard Johnson concluded that '[i]t was surely the fact that working-class culture was described intimately, from within, that made the book so powerful' (Johnson 1979, 59). These texts were evocative; they put into circulation a powerful set of images of working-class communities in Britain.

While the authenticity of these portraits of working-class life was lauded, the specificity of their viewpoints garnered little attention. In fact, these were accounts of white, working-class men of a particular generation, and there was often a regional specificity to their portrayals. Nevertheless, these authors seldom commented about their gender or ethnic identity. Interestingly, Hoggart did register some concern about the validity of his account, as he mused: 'A writer who is himself from the working-classes has his own temptations to error, somewhat different but no less than those of a writer from another class' (1957, 17). However, as his misgivings were about the possibility that his emotional engagement with working-class culture might distort the objectivity of his account, he did not reflect on the ways in which his gender, ethnic, or regional identity might have influenced his perspective.

In the period demarcated by the appearance of Hoggart's and Seabrook's books, British working-class novelists, playwrights and intellectuals were beginning to make their mark in the literary world, academia, theatres, radio and television. For example, as well as publishing a number of novels and plays about working-class life, the Yorkshire novelist and playwright David Storey collaborated with Lindsay Anderson in converting one such play – *This Sporting Life* (2000/1960, 1963) – into a film. Likewise, the Welsh working-class playwright Dennis Potter produced a very distinctive sequence of television dramas. In a rather different realm, Raymond Williams emerged as one of the foremost British literary critics and social-political commentators of the twentieth century.

Authenticity was the watchword of the autobiographical writing produced by this cohort of British working-class 'lads'. For the first-time in British history, working-class writers were offering accounts of working-class life that were gaining wide circulation. Assumptions about class and culture came under scrutiny, new images of working-class life were generated, and class barriers in education and other domains were challenged.

Scholarship Girls: Different Stories of Working-Class Lives in Britain

The authors who are my primary concern in this chapter were of a different generation and different gender from the wave of scholarship boys considered above. Nevertheless, they were influenced by the interwar generation of British working-class male writers who had forged new representations of and fresh perspectives on class in the UK. Although they sometimes explicitly took issue with their work and, as I shall argue, for the most part, produced rather different kinds of autobiographical writing about class relations, these women were often in dialogue with these male predecessors.

Like their male counterparts, the female working-class writers which I will consider here benefited from the expansion of higher education after Second World War. In addition, feminism, which from the late 1960s into the 1980s was a vibrant social movement in Britain, had a profound influence on the lives and writing of these women. Hence, there was a consciousness, indeed, a *self*-consciousness, not only about class, but also about gender and sexuality which pervaded their writing.

The key figures in this post-Second World War cluster of autobiographical working-class writers in the UK includes Annette Kuhn, Jo Spence, Carolyn Steedman, Valerie Walkerdine and Jeanette Winterson. What makes this group of writers so fascinating is that each found very distinctive ways of writing about class and particularly about their working-class lives which challenged the conventions of such autobiographical writing. They forged very striking explorations of the interrelations of class and gender and, in some cases, sexuality.

The next sections of this chapter consist of brief introductions to three key texts from this cohort of writers. These provide 'tasters' indicating the richness of this seam of writing. I then offer a set of reflections about what seems so extraordinary about these texts, with particular reference to their conceptualizations of class and gender.

Landscape for a Good Woman: A Story of Two Lives *(1986)*

As the subtitle suggests, Carolyn Steedman's *Landscapes for a Good Woman* revolves around two life stories. The 'two lives' that are represented and analysed in this book are those of Steedman and her mother: these are the intertwined stories of two working-class lives – one originating in Burnley in the 1920s, and the other beginning in South London in the late 1940s. Steedman frames these as 'case studies', and the stories of these lives are concentrated in 'Part Two: Exiles' and in the brief introductory and concluding sections focused on her mother's death. (The book has three main sections, together with an introduction and a conclusion.) Parts One and Three are titled 'Stories' and 'Interpretations', and in these Steedman considers the cultural and theoretical resources available for telling and interpreting these two, entwined life stories. Her opening pronouncement is clear and jarring: 'This book is about lives lived out on the borderlands, lives for which the central interpretative devices of the culture don't quite work' (Steedman 1986, 5).

From the outset, Steedman contests the way working-class (particularly British working-class) people have been represented. She deplores the 'extraordinary attribution of sameness' (1986, 11), 'the psychological simplicity' (1986, 12) and the 'uniformity and passivity' (1986, 12) that she sees as features of such representation. She identifies three reasons for such problematic treatment: the first being that the conceptualization of emotional and psychological selfhood derives 'by and through the testimony', not of working-class people themselves, but of those 'in a central relationship to the dominant culture' (1986, 11). Furthermore, she assesses 'the sons of the working class, who have made their earlier escape from this landscape of psychological simplicity', as having invested heavily in 'accepting and celebrating it' (1986, 12). Here she seems to be alluding to some of the writing of the 'scholarship boys' (her term) cited previously. Marxism is highlighted as the third negative influence, since she assesses that it has fostered interpretations of mental life as crudely determined by material circumstances and of class consciousness as mechanistically produced.

Steedman's text is in dialogue with the work of the British 'scholarship boys' of the preceding generation considered above. As her comments about those who 'escaped' reinforcing and, indeed, relishing rather static images of the working class suggest, this is mainly a critical dialogue. References to Seabrook's 'iconography' and Hoggart's 'landscapes' (1986, 6) come early in the text, as Steedman notes that these could not accommodate her mother. She particularly takes issue with their conventional picture of '"our mam"' (1986, 92), based on women who did not go out to work (Steedman's mother was employed). Nevertheless, she does invoke the insights of one 'scholarship boy' – Raymond Williams – both by citing some of his reflections on the difficulties in writing about working class life (1986, 20) and through her employment of his concept of 'structure of feeling'.

Family Secrets: Acts of Memory and Imagination *(1995)*

While stories are the primary concern of *Landscapes for a Good Woman*, pictures or visual images are the pivot of Annette Kuhn's *Family Secrets: Acts of Memory and Imagination* (1995). However, Kuhn is also interested in stories, particularly those associated with memory. Visual images – specifically, photographs and film images – are the prompts for Kuhn's investigation of memories and stories. Like Steedman, she presents her book as a set of case studies. Her case studies are of key biographical moments that are evoked by particular visual images – photographic or filmic – pertaining to Kuhn's own biography, and they are grounded in reflections on class and gender and her exploration of how memory works.

Kuhn sets out to 'unravel the connections between memory, its traces and the stories we tell about the past' (1995, 3). She acknowledges her experimentation with a specific method for analysing memories developed as a form of feminist consciousness raising about women's relationships to their bodies, which was articulated in the German feminist Frigga Haug's and her colleagues' 1987 publication, *Female Sexualisation*. While Kuhn cites Haug et al. (1987) as an important influence on her own project, she explains that she has 'drawn freely' on the specific 'protocols' for memory work which were developed by Rosy Martin and Jo Spence (1987) 'for their phototherapy and family album work' (1987, 6–7). These are set out as a set of procedures and questions to guide users in analysing photographs which have emotional resonance.

There are six case studies which follow the introduction, each of which articulates memories associated with specific visual images pertaining to Kuhn's own biography – particularly her childhood and early family life. Her own memory work and reflections on popular memory are supplemented through references to a broad range of theoretical commentaries deriving from psychoanalysis, film studies and cultural studies.

Kuhn registers her appreciation of *The Uses of Literacy* as having offered an 'account of popular culture and the working class' which 'touched' her 'for the first time' in her life 'with a profound recognition of something shared but previously unnamed' (Kuhn 1995, 99). While she effusively acknowledges how important Hoggart's book was for her, she assesses that it 'skirts dangerously close to nostalgia, the pitfall of the uprooted' and contributes to 'a working-class romance that has become almost distressingly familiar' in representations of that class in the UK from *Coronation Street* to the films of Terence Davies (Kuhn 1995, 102). She also observes that, whatever Hoggart's achievements in articulating aspects of British working-class life and culture, the 'scholarship girl' must find her own distinctive voice. Indeed, Kuhn most closely identifies with and borrows from the work of other scholarship girls – notably, that of Rosie Martin, Jo Spence, Carolyn Steedman and Valerie Walkerdine, each of whom has forged distinctive perspectives on class and gender.

Oranges Are Not the Only Fruit *(1985)*

Oranges Are Not the Only Fruit (2001/1985) is the only novel considered in this cluster of writings by post-Second World War British scholarship girls. It is also the most popular and most lauded of the three books examined in this article. It won the Whitbread Prize for best first novel in 1985. It was also made into a widely acclaimed, although controversial, BBC three-part television drama series, which was broadcast in 1990.[1] This book is generally regarded as an 'autobiographical fiction' or 'autobiographical novel' (Douglas 2001, 809). It fits with the other two books, not only because of its identification as autobiographical, but also because of its striking handling of issues of class and gender and because of its vivid rendering of working-class lives in Britain.

Oranges revolves around the experiences of a young woman – the heroine and narrator, Jeanette – growing-up in a very conservative, evangelical working-class family and community in a Lancashire town in the 1970s. Winterson's book foregrounds issues of sexuality more intensely than the other books considered here. A key thread in the narrative traces Jeanette's growing awareness of her sexuality – her lesbianism – and her dealing with homophobic hostility in her home environment. Jeanette is scorned and punished by her mother, the church and the community because 'she loved the wrong sort of people' (1985, 125) and because, in her mother's terms, she was subject to 'Unnatural Passions' (1985, 7).

Jeanette's story is laid out on a biblical grid, and the chapter titles correspond with those of the first eight books of the Old Testament. Despite this grid structure, as Winterson has emphasized, 'Oranges['] ... interests are anti-linear. It offers a complicated narrative structure disguised as a simple one ... that you can read in spirals' (Winterson 1985, xiii). While Jeanette's story is the spine of the book, reconstructed, alternative versions of fairy tales and legends ensure the spirals.

It is the humour in Winterson's first novel, which has guaranteed *Oranges'* popularity and critical acclaim. This feature is clear from the opening of the book:

> Like most people I lived for a long time with my mother and father. My father liked to watch the wrestling, my mother liked to wrestle; it didn't matter what. She was in the white corner and that was that. (Winterson 1985, 3)

The unorthodox handling of religious tropes and unromantic, antisexist versions of fairy tales add to the book's humorous appeal.

So, for example, Jeanette continues her introduction of her mother (moving on from her identification with wrestling, quoted above) and explains her own origins with the observation that

> [s]he [Jeanette's mother] had a mysterious attitude towards the begetting of children; it wasn't that she couldn't do it, more that she didn't want to do it. She was very bitter about the Virgin Mary getting there first. She did the next best thing and arranged for a foundling. That was me. (Winterson 1985, 3–4)

Likewise, one of the many new twists on fairy tales which the novel provides is the princess turning down the prince because she is too busy, trying to make a deadline (Winterson 1985, 45).

Stories Replace Authentic Accounts of Working-Class Lives

The three books introduced above provide vivid accounts of working-class childhoods in post-Second World War Britain. However, unlike their scholarship boy predecessors, these authors do not offer straightforwardly autobiographical accounts, nor do they stake claims to authenticity. These three books are each, in their own distinctive ways, powerful explorations of and experiments with storytelling about class and gender.

In all three of these books there is a disavowal of the unified, authentic autobiographical voice. Jeanette, the fictional character, is the main (but not exclusive) narrator of Winterson's semi- or somewhat autobiographical text. Kuhn employs a third-person account at various points in her text – a device which is linked to the method of memory work which she delineates in her introduction. Steedman does employ the autobiographical 'I'. However, she is continually interrupting her own storytelling, stepping back from what she describes as 'the compulsions of narrative' (Steedman 1986, 144). She opts instead, as she explains at the end of her book, for a call for a recognition of 'what has been made out on the margins', and yet, having come to this recognition, she opts to 'refuse to celebrate it' (ibid., 144).

Indeed, autobiography as a form and practice comes under Steedman's scrutiny as a problematic and slippery vehicle that has not served working-class subjects well. Citing Kathleen Woodward's memoir *Jipping Street* (1928), she insists that this working-class author 'did not write an autobiography but rather a psychic reconstruction of childhood at the turn of the century' (ibid., 74). Likewise, she claims that Kathleen Dayus's (1982) book presents 'a story that lies outside the literary framework of working-class autobiography' (ibid.). In addition, Steedman alludes to two further celebrated moments of gendered and classed disjunction around the conventions of autobiography: Mayhew's encounter with the watercress girl in his observational study of mid-nineteenth-century London life and Freud's encounter with his client, Dora. She interprets these as primarily stories of 'middle-aged men who, propelled by the compulsions of scientific inquiry, demanded stories from young women and girls; and then expressed their dissatisfaction with the form of the narratives they obtained' (ibid., 130).

Rather than offer a conventional autobiography or biography, *Landscape for a Good Woman* undertakes a review of some of the conceptual resources available to tell the stories of modern British working-class subjects. Steedman's close reading of key literary and historical renderings of working-class figures (from those embedded in the writings of historians such as William Mayhew to those cast in literature by authors such as D. H. Lawrence) demonstrates the shortcomings of such storytelling. The failure to attribute psychological depth or complexity and the lack of attention to diversity and specificity are some of the problems she identifies in the stock imagery of the British working-class. Moreover, as I will discuss in more detail below, she is equally dissatisfied with dominant social theories (including psychoanalysis, as well as popular psychological and sociological theories) which she insists emanate from circumstances of class privilege and which are, accordingly, inadequate in providing the tools for analysing different, less privileged lives.

If textual analysis and the interrogation of theory are the modes through which Steedman investigates the resources for telling stories of working-class lives, Kuhn chooses methodological experimentation and visual analyses as her route. She uses particular photographs and film images as the prompts not just towards autobiographical storytelling; these also trigger reflections about the parameters and challenges around such narrativization.

Despite being something of a hybrid text (see below), Winterson's book is generically a novel. Although there are obvious connections between Jeanette Winterson's life story and that of the book's narrator / main character, who happens also to be called 'Jeanette', the generic form proclaims that it is fictional rather than factual. In form, it thus eschews authenticity. Moreover, like Steedman and Kuhn, in this book Winterson espouses a wider interest in the kinds of stories that are told about gender, class and sexuality. The text is a thick assemblage of playful encounters with and ingenious transformations of biblical stories, fairy tales and literary narratives centred on these issues. The play with these and their juxtaposition make readers aware not only of their constructed nature but also of that of the 'originals' recast. Hence, Winterson offers her own form of problematization of conventional modes of storytelling around gender, class and sexuality, and this unsettling is often realized through humour.

Stories of Class, Gender and Sexuality: Revisioning and Resourcing

The three autobiographical texts considered here not only challenge the conventions about representing working-class lives; they actively interrogate and experiment with the forms of such representation. Hence, while providing their own stories about class, gender and sexuality, they also analyse the way such stories are told. In their different ways, they investigate and experiment with the resources for telling stories about working-class life, foregrounding the handling of issues of gender and sexuality.

As noted above, Steedman provides a set of critical commentaries on the currently available theoretical resources for such storytelling, highlighting the inadequacy of available frameworks, ranging from those provided by psychology and psychoanalysis to feminist theories of patriarchy in fleshing out working-class lives. Grappling with the entanglements of class, gender and sexuality both in her own experience and in that of others, she poses a set of thorny questions about the interpretative frameworks designed to illuminate their restrictions. These questions emerge from specific stories which do not fit with dominant interpretative frames. Hence, with reference to theories of reproduction and mothering, she asks, what about women who refuse to reproduce or mother? Likewise, reflecting on her own mother's desires and frustrations, she prods at assumptions about 'class consciousness' by asking how they deal with envy. Having recounted an episode in which her father was reprimanded for picking bluebells and her watching 'the park-keeper snatch the bluebells' from his hands (1986, 76), she reflects on his social powerlessness. She notes the disjunction between this powerlessness and the renderings of patriarchal power within psychoanalytic theory.

This critical mode extends into a consideration of working-class 'figures' (a term she borrows from Hoggart) as they have been rendered in celebrated historical and literary texts. She finds these equally unsatisfactory:

from Mayhew to Lawrence and Orwell, she uncovers stick figures, with little or no attribution of complexity, subjectivity or depth. She identifies the problems with these renderings: as representations which not only pathologize and marginalize but which cast working-class people (particularly women) uniformly and which dehistoricize them.

It is the denial of subjectivity and specificity in all their dimensions (ignoring fantasy, desire and the operation of the unconscious) in working-class lives that propels her critical overviews. She is concerned that, wherever she turns, she finds recurring patterns of representation of working-class subjects, which deny or pre-empt 'a particular story, a personal history, except when the story illustrates a general thesis' and 'an unconscious life, and a particular and developing consciousness of the meanings presented by the social world' (1986, 11). In sum, Steedman concludes that '[t]he very devices that are intended to give expression to childhoods like mine and my mother's actually deny their expression' (1986, 9).

Highlighting the roots of psychoanalytic and related sociological theories of the family in bourgeois life, she concludes, 'only with extreme difficulty can it be used to present images of a world that lies outside the framework of its evidential base' (1986, 77). While she draws attention to their problematic origins and the consequent inadequacy of much of the theoretical repertoire available for understanding working-class life, she does not refrain from employing theory in her own analysis and storytelling.

Like Steedman's text, *Family Secrets* is by no means a conventional autobiography. Structured as a set of discrete and somewhat disparate essays, there is no attempt to provide a sequential life narrative. As noted previously, in some of the essays there are shifts into third-person narration from the first-person mode which is the conventional vehicle of autobiographical writing. Eschewing these conventions, Kuhn pursues other routes to provide fuller accounts of working-class lives.

Kuhn's core concern is with memory, which she tackles as a vital, if unwieldy, resource for storytelling about class and gender identities. As indicated above, she turns to the memory work method developed by Frigga Haug and her colleagues in undertaking her own collection of personal memory projects. For Kuhn, visual resources, particularly photographs, are crucial prompts in her assembling her stories about class and gender. *Family Secrets* is richly suggestive in its reflections on memory and its workings, particularly on how it may be triggered by specific visual images. But, like Steedman, Kuhn mobilizes an eclectic range of theories in her readings of photographs and other visual materials; psychoanalytic, cultural and film theory are resources which inform her analysis of class and gender relations.

Oranges Are Not the Only Fruit is a playful text. The narrativization of Jeanette's life is continually interrupted, and the text is interspersed with interludes in which fairy tales and legends are reworked in distinctive, alternative renderings. The conventions of gender and hierarchy, which are mainstays of the conventional versions of these stories, are thereby exposed. Indeed, in Winterson's versions these conventions are challenged and disturbed.

Winterson's book shares with those of Steedman and Kuhn a concern with the modes of storytelling. Not only does the form of *Oranges* unsettle the generic distinction between the autobiography and the novel; questions about the fact-fiction distinction and destabilizing reflections about storytelling itself erupt and disturb the narrative flow.

> Of course that is not the whole story, but that is the way with stories; we make them what we will. ... Everyone who tells a story tells it differently, just to remind us that everybody sees it differently. Some people say there are true things to be found, some people say all kinds of things can be proved. I don't believe them. The only thing for certain is how complicated it all is, like string full of knots. It's all there but hard to find the beginning and impossible to fathom the end. The best you can do is admire the cat's cradle, and maybe knot it up a bit more. History should be a hammock for swinging and a game for playing, the way cats play. (1985, 91)

In effect, Winterson's text, like the others reviewed here, emphasizes the crafting of history and life stories while extending the repertoire of resources for such crafting. *Oranges* raids and transforms the conventional tales of class and gender relations embedded in the Bible, fairy tales and legends. *Landscape for a Good Woman* and *Family Secrets* critically investigate a range of cultural, social and political theories to enrich their storytelling about working-class life. Feminist sensibilities inform and shape these explorations and experimentations, which highlight the interactions of class and gender formations.

Class Mobility

In post-Second World War Britain, the scholarship boy and the scholarship girl were the symbols of class mobility and the promise of a more meritocratic social order. The very notion of class mobility is often taken to imply a replacement of one class identity by another and a consequential leaving behind of working-class affiliations – a simple matter of betterment. Reflecting on his own class mobility, Richard Hoggart characterized his positioning as a 'double relationship', and he explained bluntly: 'I am from the working-classes and feel even now both close to them and apart from them' (Hoggart 1957, 17). However, even Hoggart's grappling with doubleness is rather flat and reductionist, and it fails to convey the complexity of the living of class mobility.

The three books considered in this chapter emanate from experiences of class mobility, but perhaps more significantly they provide vivid pictures of key moments in that process, of its lived, psychosocial dimensions. Kuhn tackles this most explicitly in a chapter titled 'Passing'. The title refers, in the first instance, to her passing the eleven-plus examination, and the chapter recounts the consequences of this for Annette and her family. Within the arrangements of British education at this time (which are outlined in this chapter of the book), this 'passing' ensured Kuhn's entrance to grammar school, and it made her into a 'scholarship girl'.

However, the title also denotes the more generalized social activity of inauthentic self-representation and its consequences. Kuhn recounts that the grammar school 'never ceased feeling strange to me, and I always felt an outsider there' (Kuhn 1995, 87) and that it was 'impossible to give a name to my own feeling of not belonging' (ibid., 88). She details both the devices she employed in attempting to pass and the endemic forms of insecurity ('the most craven fear of exposure' [ibid., 93]) which resulted, noting that 'I knew very well that I was not one of them...and that my difference was something to be ashamed of' (ibid., 91).

The iconic spark for the chapter is a photograph which has disappeared but which Kuhn remembers vividly. It is a picture of her in her school uniform, which was several sizes too big for her, purchased by her mother to ensure that it lasted her entire school career. The ill-fitting uniform becomes a metaphor for Annette's class unease, as she explains:

My clothes did not fit, I was different: and, being born of inferiority, this difference was the source of the deepest shame, the most craven fear of exposure. Would my cover be blown, and the terrible truth of what I truly was be revealed? Would I be stripped of my shoddy disguise and shown up as an impostor, passing for something I was not? (ibid., 93)

However, Kuhn makes it clear that the class unease was not just a feature of her school life. Her school life becomes 'a bone of contention' (ibid., 89) in her family, and this builds into a confrontation with her mother, who declares, 'You're leaving that school! You can't rise out of your class' (ibid).

Kuhn looks back on the dilemmas and difficulties of her school years, dispelling illusions about cost-free social mobility. For Kuhn, '[c]aught between two ways of belonging, between milieux which demanded entirely different kinds of conformity, the scholarship girl stood at risk of losing all sense of what she was or might become' (ibid., 95). She foregrounds the price of class mobility and the forfeit demanded by equality of opportunity, explaining that '[t]he meritocratic ideal of equality of opportunity would have us forget this, would have us believe that by virtue of getting an education a working-class child becomes something else; that you cannot be working class and at the same time be educated and civilized' (ibid., 97).

In *Oranges*, the central narrative – Jeanette's story – is also a story of social mobility. The restrictions of her working-class community are vividly portrayed and symbolized in her mother's insistence that 'oranges are the only fruit'. Literally and metaphorically, Jeanette's trajectory involves her tasting 'other fruits', through exposure to other life possibilities, both in terms of class and sexuality. In the final scene of the novel, involving an encounter between Jeanette and her mother, after she had emptied her 'War Cupboard' of its store of tinned pineapple, her mother acknowledges: 'oranges are not the only fruit' (1985, 167). This is far from a trivial acknowledgement. This statement is the marker of class transition in the novel: signalling that Jeanette is moving into other worlds – out of the constrictions of her Lancashire evangelical working-class community. Jeanette is mindful of the significance of this moment, registering her mother's concession as philosophical. She is then represented as leaving her home in a reflective and almost melancholic mood:

> I thought about the dog [the family dog] and was suddenly very sad; sad for her death, for my death, for all the inevitable dying that comes with change. There's no choice that doesn't mean a loss. (1985, 167)

Jeanette's sober assessment can be read as an appraisal of the cost of social mobility.

Winterson and Kuhn convey profoundly embodied and psychologically complex images of class mobility in which class, gender and sexuality are all in play. There is no room for nostalgia (in the style of Hoggart or Seabrook) in these renderings. Yet these moving, detailed stories flesh out the cost and complications of such social movement.

Conclusions

This chapter has explored the background to and the features of a unique set of writings by post-Second World War British feminist scholarship girls. In framing the texts examined in this chapter with reference to the work of the 'scholarship boys' that preceded them and highlighting aspects of the setting for their emergence, I have portrayed their authors as looking over their shoulders and as influenced by their particular historical context. Nevertheless, in many respects, these were forward-looking, even prescient, texts.

Landscape for a Good Woman, *Family Secrets* and *Oranges* are books that revolve around the recognition of the power of storytelling and its significance for feminism. They constitute feminist-informed investigations of the conventions and restrictions of a particular kind of storytelling, and they offer alternatives to them. Such interrogation and experimentation has proliferated since the mid-1990s, as feminists have pursued related questions about the conventions, restrictions and possibilities of storytelling in a wide range of fields: from the natural sciences (Haraway 1989) to the history of feminism itself (Hemmings 2011). Indeed, critical exposition of and experimentation in storytelling have become key and versatile feminist methodologies.

Moreover, Kuhn, Steedman and Winterson creatively unsettled the established repertoire of representations of British working-class life. Strikingly, it was the mother-daughter *relationship*, rather than the *figure* of the working-class 'mam' or matriarch, which came centre stage in the texts considered in this chapter. This focus ensured a more complex and dynamic set of perspectives on working-class lives and on the interactions of class and gender, leaving little room for either class-based nostalgia or family romance. Subsequent generations of British feminist 'scholarship girls' (see Skeggs 1997, 2004; Skeggs and Woods 2008; Tyler 2010) have picked up these cues in undertaking their research on more recent British working-class lives and culture, inspired by the work of Kuhn, Steedman and Winterson.

As indicated above, the three texts examined in this chapter have an uneasy relationship to autobiography as a genre. This is not surprising, given the gendered history of this literary form (Smith 1987; Felman 1993; Swindells 1995; Cosslett, Lury and Summerfield 2000). Nevertheless, each of these texts is a refreshingly vibrant piece of working-class life writing. These texts have, once again, been extremely influential: steering feminists away from complacency about this genre but also exposing the need for good feminist *work* with autobiography (Cosslett, Lury and Summerfield 2000).

I began this chapter by observing that, in Britain and other parts of the Western world, these are confusing times for clear thinking about class, gender and sexuality. 'Telling your own story' is now an overworked cliché, enacted through multiple media. The 'misery memoir' is a titillating, popular, moneymaking genre, yet discussing class remains difficult and is often tabooed. Journalists, novelists and polemicists now celebrate and incite women's capacity to 'flaunt their (hetero) sexuality', while gender inequalities abound.

Amidst these confusions, I find myself (re)turning to the texts discussed in this chapter. As I have suggested, they are the products of a particular era of the British welfare state, of British educational provision and of British feminism. Despite this, these tales still have considerable resonance today. They speak eloquently about: 'lives lived out on the borderlands … about interpretations … about the stories we make for ourselves, and the social specificity of those stories' (Steedman 1986, 5). Nevertheless, *Oranges*, *Landscape for a Good Woman* and *Family Secrets* are by no means comforting texts in these troubling times. Indeed, they abound with stern reminders which have pertinence today, including the following:

> While fully aware that femininity is a fabrication, as far as the world is concerned – and indeed as far as I, too, am concerned – I am still a woman, and live with the very consequences of a particular gender label. (Kuhn 1995, 1)
>
> There's no choice that doesn't mean a loss. (Winterson 1985, 167)

These are texts of their time, but they are also texts for this time. They challenge and they continue to disturb assumptions about class, gender and sexuality. They remain powerful and refreshing reservoirs for reading and telling stories about how lives are shaped in and through these key social relations. Speaking eloquently of negotiation, borderlands and power, these books have much to offer contemporary feminists.

Notes

1. The series was directed by Beeban Kidner and appeared on DVD in 2005.

Imagining Her(story)

Engendering Archives

Roshini Kempadoo

Diary entry January 2009, London UK.

Research of artist Donald Rodney (1961–98) inevitably begins online. As an important artist from the Caribbean diaspora associated with Britain's BLK Art group in the 1980s and someone whose art was dominated by his physical condition, I was keen to refer to his perspective in using technology as a way to extend his practice beyond a physical presence and life. I learn of the acquisition of Rodney's papers by the Tate Archive in 2003 and hyperlink to the Tate website. In Book 31 (1989–90), for example, Rodney creates black ink sketches as silhouettes of icons that are repeated and returned to throughout the sketchbook. They appear as recurring signifiers many of which are familiar popular icons, such as the Hiroshima mushroom cloud or the First World War memorial statue of a soldier with his head bowed and resting his hands on his rifle (assumed to be inspired by the monument at Clitheroe Castle, Lancashire). Online is a veritable feast of Rodney's material, including a related interview by the Tate with curators and artists about Black History Month. Hyperlinks refer to Donald's project Autoicon (1997),[1] commissioned by Iniva, which in turn leads to further digital archives of work and texts.

In April 2009, I arranged a visit to the Tate archives. The librarians and archivists showed us the physical space which holds the vast collection of documents and related material they select, collect, and preserve as material considered significant to British art history. The collection is daunting, hard to fathom and yet impressive. Tate staff provided an introduction with a display of some physical documents. This included, as a stroke of serendipity, a couple of Donald's sketchbooks. Their size and physical appearance reflected Donald's haphazard and brilliant thoughts of day-to-day encounters. I leafed through the pages – they evoked contradictory feelings of nostalgia and loss on the one hand and sheer excitement on the other for the way in which Donald's creations were apparent junctures between historical instances and his ironic, imaginative and embodied practice. Here in the archives were inscriptions that fantastically commented back on our notion of history and facts. The visceral experience of the sketchbooks here in the archive confirmed Donald's legacy of creativity and thinking.

Authoritative interpreters of archives and history are most often historians, anthropologists, curators, sociologists, cultural theorists, professional and amateur genealogists and collectors, or political and community activists. Such scholars and individuals are awarded authority and negotiated access to archive material by their caretakers, including librarians, conservationists, archivists, private collectors and family members. As researchers they painstakingly and meticulously endeavour to write and publish public narratives associated with the 'facts' of the matter, as evidenced by the written documents, photographs, illustrations, locations and buildings – monuments, and institutions that constitute archives. Their accounts rely on accuracy in reprinting records and documents as closely reproduced to the original version as possible. As authoritative interpreters they (and the material) carry the burden of representation to present accurate reference to *"That-has-been"* (Barthes 1984, 76).

Such historical accounts become history in turn; they are physically located alongside and fully integrated into the continued archive process and practice. They maintain continuity and process and are 'put to work' as vital material for museums, galleries, libraries; they are collected and displayed *as history*. Such interpretive texts are 'officially validated' then, not only because they exist in the public domain. They are also validated through the process of adding them to the archives. Examples of this include the *Regina Anderson photography collection* of African American photographs from the 1920s and 1930s in the Photographs and Prints Division, Schomburg Center for Research in Black Culture, New York Public Library or the *Farm Security Administration (1935–44)* photographs held at Getty Images and the Schomburg, featuring significant photographers including Gordon Parks (1912–2006), Dorothea Lange (1895–1965) and Bert Hardy (1913–95).

While some interpretations become 'history', others become counter-memory, not least because the very process of inclusion defines the parameters for *exclusion*. Despite emerging from a similar responsive interpretation, counter-memory work is rarely given the same status as the more public histories discussed above. Instead, they are assigned the lesser status of autobiography, or cultural memory – concerned with processes (Steedman 1986, 1992) or relations and denying the characteristic trait of history: closure (Steedman 1992, 48). Perhaps this is why, as Marianne Hirsch and Valerie Smith note,

> much of recent feminist scholarship touches directly or indirectly on questions of cultural memory [in which] gendered politics of decolonization, exile, migration and immigration have given rise to questions about the archive and about the transmission of memory across spatial and generational boundaries. (Hirsch and Smith 2002, 3)

Cultural memory is clearly a counter-method used by women artists of diasporic and post-colonial heritage discussed in this chapter. Taken together, their work reimagines and evokes characters, identities, events and lived experiences of people and places that might have existed historically. Like Rodney's *Autoicon* project created for his afterlife, such works pose questions of what may have been present or what may be absent from historical narratives as they relate to women's lived experiences. They are counter-memories not only because they offer an alternative voice or perspective or make visible something that was not visible before; they are also counter because they focus on the relations between lived experience and characters, identities, events that constitute a past. As George Lipsitz suggests,

> ...counter-memory is a way of remembering and forgetting that starts with the local, the immediate, and the personal...[it] starts with the particular and the specific and then builds outwards toward a total story. Counter-memory embodies aspects of myth and aspects of history, but it retains an enduring suspicion of both categories. Counter-memory focuses on localized experiences with oppression, using them to reframe and refocus dominant narratives purporting to represent universal experience. (Lipsitz 1990, 213)

Such works are dramatic, provocative, contentious, humorous or simply wildly bizarre but always highly imaginative responses to material. Including my own interactive work *Amendments* (2007; see Kempadoo 2008) and those by other artists, including Erika Tan, Stacey Tyrell, Nicole Awai and María Magdalena Campos-Pons, such works not only offer counter-interpretations through their representation and engagement with the material itself; they also counter the very process of constructing history.

Creativity in the Contiguous Archive

Contiguous archive[2] is a living practice that conceptually frames the interconnectivity and interdependency between material objects, their locations and their historicization through both interpretive and creative responses. Contiguity of archive material and practices explores historical material objects and locations *adjacent* to and *in constant dialogue* with interpretative and creative material created and inspired from it. Connectivity, interdependence and acts of transmission emerge from complex relational dynamics between practices such as remembering and forgetting, material as evidence or art works created as fiction interventions – conscious or unconscious acts evoking anxiety or pleasure. In turn, the material (archives, history and memory) are perceived from the divided post-colonial perspective of what Amitava Kumar refers to as the '"there and now" of history. At home in neither one discipline nor one country ...' (Kumar 2000, x).

The term *contiguous* suggests a form of connectivity and integration between the various components, then, conceived in the interstices of colonial/post-colonial locations, past- and 'presentness', temporary and permanent, process and form, factual and imaginary. The archive is conceptualized as a living reflexive practice of collection and consignment that cannot be distinguished from the researchers' and artists' experience, creativity and process of encountering them. My argument is that they are not bounded in the same way that history is constructed. The activities associated with archives emphasize notions of contact, proximity, adjoining and constant reference to each other. They emphasize a *relational* system embedded in the practice revealing the dynamic involving researcher, the artist, the material and the places in which they are found. The notion of archives therefore incorporates an experiential and spatial exploration of the landscape, terrain and persons associated with the interpretative and responsive accounts of the materials and the spaces from which they exist. This concept places emphasis on analysing the visual material beside and in conjunction with aural and spatial representations, recordings, creative and written accounts.

The contemporary art works that partially constitute the *contiguous archive* are for the most part conceived and created in response to, or in contestation with, a European/Western-centred framing and not associated with hegemonic narratives. Like novels dating to the nineteenth century, these art works contain sensibilities nourished by post-colonial, racialized and diasporized life experience. Not only are they concerned with reimagining particular oppressions, but they 'identify as well a use of the past that speaks to present day intellectual concerns with time, history, subjectivity and fragmentation' (Lipsitz 1990, 215). They are concerned with the simultaneous dimensions of colonial and post-colonial matters and emerge from the fragmented nature and survival of archives in the post-colonies and contemporary works that emerge from them.

The concern for reimagining particular oppressions also marks such art works as deeply gendered. They address the notion of *absence* from history through the creation of fantastical imaginings as narratives about and by women, which speak to the literal absence of material in existing archives. They are also gendered through specific techniques, which I call *techniques of contiguity*. These demonstrate the ways in which women artists consistently draw on a multiple range of aesthetics associated with disrupting or intervening in conventional linearity of narration and time, in order to create work involving digital networks and multimedia. The work detailed in this chapter is also gendered through the insistent focus on informal, everyday and personal objects, which become central to offering a different narrative. Finally, gender emerges in relation to the terrain of non-European spaces, which are conceptualized by artists through the relationship between the landscape and its visual referents and between material and its related location.

Taken together, these art works (in which I also locate myself) detail a substantial body of work, which offer counter-memories through a range of devices and practices. Seen as part of a larger post-colonial and feminist project, the archive is utilized in order to facilitate a discursive openness that interrogates the authority of a hegemonic historical narrative. As a consequence, I argue that what is important is not only understanding what the art works mean *per se* but also their contiguous nature – how they create and sustain a continuous dialogue.

Absence in the Archives

The Trinidad *Guardian* newspapers from August 1935 in the National Archives of Trinidad and Tobago (Port-of-Spain, Trinidad 2002–6) were instrumental in shaping the fictional framework of my art work *Amendments* (2007).[3] *Amendments* is a multimedia art work of montage, sound, imagery, writing, music and voice. It is a single screen projection, which allows two users, playing dominoes on the table in the gallery space, to experience various Caribbean and Trinidadian 'characterizations'. The characterizations relate to the narrative of a woman as the central character whose story is told through relatives, friends and

Figure 1 Roshini Kempadoo (2007):
Amendments (screen still)

others. She is in some way a mythical and enduring figure that is present in past, present and future narratives.

Amendments (2007; see Figure 1) comments on the colonial material and spaces of the archive, using the game of dominoes to present past and present social spaces in the Caribbean and Trinidad. The art work responds to the notion of absences and loss, which was literally and conceptually felt in the process of researching and displaying the art work. As I turned the pages of the newspaper in the archive, the literal physical disintegration of the paper in my hands conjured up and symbolized Trinidad's colonial past *sous rature* (Derrida 1974), or 'under erasure', and in a state of decay. I became acutely and disturbingly aware that I was actively contributing to the physical disappearance of this historical material. Ironically, this historical period was also symbolic of the last decades of colonialism, also under erasure, and one could detect a political anxiety in the material itself – in the newspaper reports and accounts about the general and widespread unrest.

The notions of absence and loss were also, as suggested, encapsulated in the material itself through my use of a Caribbean and Trinidadian woman. Indeed, the normative history of emancipation and liberation is usually configured through the black male body, and the presence of women mostly of African and Indian descent in both colonial and post-colonial Caribbean history has been overlooked. This absence has prompted other women artists to seek alternative histories, alternative practices of research and alternative forms of storytelling to contribute to cultural memory – memory work that involves fictional, non-linear and feminist perspectives.[4] It is through this process that the *contiguous archive* places emphasis on contemporary practices of rereading and reimagining the female voice and perspective.

For me, the notion of contiguous archive meant that I pursued material relating to historians, curators, publishers, artists (various persons whose names I researched, in addition to family friends and acquaintances). I made several visits to Boissiere Village and the Santa Cruz valley to visually and sonically record a sense of the space, architecture and persons living there. This included recording ambient sounds and photographing in and around the Stollmeyer cocoa plantation in Santa Cruz, interviewing women who once worked on the plantation and researchers recovering local family history, photographing the houses and views in Jagan (the village adjacent to, and whose land is mostly owned by, the Stollmeyer plantation). I gathered together a range of cross-disciplinary material made up of images I had created and digitized copies of documents and photographs I had collected from the period of the 1930s to the 1960s.

Such methods produce a less public, less official perspective. Instead, it is a woman's viewpoint that is staged, one markedly absent in the more public historical texts. Equally it was through the montage of Trinidadian Creole conversations, gestures and visual/sonic references that I was able to evoke a locally specific sense of what may have occurred during this period – implementing a 'what if' scenario. This method resonates with the work by the artist, critic and poet Ramabai Espinet, who has developed a Caribbean feminist approach of the *Kali Pani*, or 'black water' (Espinet 1993, 44), in order to conceive of the independent Indo-Caribbean woman. It is this sensibility I am aiming to invoke from the historical documents. For Espinet, the spirit is associated primarily with the figure of Kali, to connote the indentured woman's independence and autonomy. As she suggests,

Kali embodies the other, undomesticated side of woman-the-creator-and-the-destroyer merged into a powerful female force. Kali has no domestic underpinnings. She is of the world, alongside males, ... she harnesses tremendous sexual energy and procreative power. Kali is an OTHER, outside the domestic sphere. (Espinet 1993, 44)

Techniques of Contiguity

Using digital techniques to create art works – whether embedding interactivity through triggering devices or hyperlinking or using multiple-screen installations – has, I argue, further facilitated forms of critical engagement with hegemonic narratives and popular media saturated spaces. My art works such as *Amendments* (2007) and *Ghosting* (2004) and that of others, including the video work by Erika Tan *Persistent Visions* (2005), are able to extend contradictory and contested discourses and develop more complex relationships with the audience/viewer/user/participant. Artists concerned with rearticulating historical and oppositional experiences have created critical interventions of bytes and bits into an apparent universalizing digital media space to convey heterogeneity, pose contradictions, appear ironic and contain fantastical, imaginative and melancholic narratives. They have insisted on strengthening the connection between digital media space and the racial, socio-political and psychic relationships perceived as belonging to the 'real world'.

Erika Tan's three-screen video work *Persistent Visions* (2005),[5] for example, is created through the reuse of film archive material from the British Empire and Commonwealth Museum comprising government films, Christian missionary footage, amateur and various broadcast and educational material. The silent video work appears as a collage of images, which Mashadi and Flores propose as 'ambivalent in its own constitution and seemingly self-effacing in its potential confrontation against the colonial...' (2009, 7). The work was exhibited in the NUS and Vargas museums (2009–10) in Singapore and the Philippines, respectively, as installations set within and among the hosts' archaeological and historical paintings – a form of displacement and questioning of the institutional status and archival practices.

Multimedia and multiple-screen work, such as Tan's installation, encompasses a temporality that fluctuates between past, present and future accounts and events. These create a hybrid space, articulating a fluidity of movement between territories, nations and locations and towards the slippery and contradictory moments in memory and in historical accounts. Factual, normalized histories are consequently problematized through an imaginary network of narratives. As Teren Sevea notes,

> Tan invites viewers to position themselves vis-à-vis the footage and 'tell' or 'be told' new stories. Using silent footage and the technical process of producing seemingly moving images from still ones... Tan invites readers to actively participate in this process of creating new meanings or stories from silent (or perhaps, silenced) archival footage. (Sevea 2009, 26)

Tan's research and art work emerges as a critique of institutional and established archive practices of colonial material as much as it celebrates the post-colonial moment. In creating the piece, she enacts and performs a critical engagement with the archive precisely in the process of researching, conceptualizing and technically creating the work. In her interview with Shabbir Hussain Mustafa for the catalogue of the exhibition, Tan describes the physical experience of engaging with the archive. Her approach alludes to the feminist archive methodologies that Steedman (2001), Laura Ann Stoler (2008), Roberta McGrath (2002, 2007) and Antoinette Burton (2006) have theorized, referring to the 'relational toiling' experience which includes

> the convoluted physical access to the archive offices, the smell of the place, encountering actual material, watching hours of silent footage often in fast-forward, ... being out of my depth, 'discovering' 'hidden' 'secrets', finding systems to remember what had been watched and what might be interesting to use for the work; and eventually leaving the physical structure of the archive, tired, grubby, head aching from too much screen time only to find that images continued to play and replay, creating loops of nostalgia, indignation, shock, delight, recognition, and even alienation. *Persistent Visions* is in a way my own personal compilation of images that *stuck*. (Mustafa 2009, 12)

Tan's title *Persistent Visions* (see Figure 2) refers both to the general association with cinema's mechanism and indirectly to the seminal text *The Persistence of Vision*, by Donna Haraway, who advocates an embodied approach to vision – arguing that the feminist 'situated' gaze of partial vision embeds our moral responsibility of 'how we learn to see' (Haraway 2002, 678). 'Vision', Haraway argues, 'is *always* a question of the power to see – and perhaps of the violence implicit in our visualizing practices. With whose blood were my eyes crafted? These points also apply to testimony from the position of "oneself"' (2002, 680). Seen here, the

Figure 2 Erika Tan (2005): *Persistent Visions* (screen stills) (reproduced with the kind permission of the artist)

'relational toiling' experience that Tan describes above is also embedded with power: the very act of creating art works is an intervention into a hegemonic structure such as history and, as Haraway reminds us, into visualizing practices *per se*.

Indeed, it is from Tan's physical encounter that she develops a critical technique to her research practice – as Stoler proposes – *along the archival grain*. She exposes institutional practices of the search/ indexing process in which she finds the 'neutral' keywords, such as 'parade', 'cricket' or 'picnic', elicited better results than her own initial keyword searches of 'native', 'slave', black', and 'indigenous' (Tan 2009, 14). Seeing indexing as an intrusion, Tan conceptually develops a technique of exposing what she describes as 'patterns' in the content of material. Instead of seeking the 'untold' individual stories, Tan perceived the entire archive as a collection. The resultant three-screen video work of multiple repetitive footage demonstrates the 'bringing together' function of the archive (Tan 2009, 18). Drawn from what she has recognized as a pattern to the film-making technique of the colonial amateur footage, she systematizes each film into a rhythmic form of four parts: 'film leader, arrivals and shots on moving platforms, encounters, rapid sections of film splices, slower sequences and finally leader again' (Tan 2009, 19). In this way she develops her own classifications and key terms as a critical intervention to the vast collection and systematic amateur recordings of colonial life belonging to this archive.

The Informal, Everyday and Personal in Archives

Contiguous archives of historical material and artistic works also discern tropes and genres of material that might define and resonate with feminist and post-colonial concepts of history and cultural memory. The personal photograph, for example, becomes central here. Indeed, as Stoler has argued, following her analysis of family album imagery from the Netherlands Indies of the late nineteenth and early twentieth centuries, the colonial project also contained 'an investment in knowledge about the carnal, about sense and sensibility as [a] commitment to "the education of desire"' (Stoler 2002, 7). The *mise-en-scène* of desire, intimacy and sensibility is the domesticated, familial space and the types of family-focused imagery associated with these spaces of the casual snapshot of family celebrations, family portraits, holiday films and photographs. Patricia Holland (2000; Holland and Spence 1991), Victor Burgin (1982, 2004), Christopher Pinney (1997), Steve Edwards

(1989), Gillian Rose (2010), Deborah Willis (1994) and others have long established that visual material drawn from personal collections (I define personal and private collections of family documentation as *informal archives*) encompass the aesthetics, function and purpose of family life and family myths. Reflecting the portrayal of 'family values' to evoke intimate and domestic spaces is particularly relevant to the notion of critique of official historical narratives.

Stacey Tyrell's series *Position As Desired* (2001), exhibited as part of the show of the same name (in 2010 at the Royal Ontario Museum, Toronto), explores her personal family archives and history evoking – in particular, a daughter's longing to imagine her mother's earlier life as a young woman of Caribbean descent growing up in the UK and Canada. Tyrell's photographs are partial sightings, detailed views of her mother's photo album, framed as fragments of images juxtaposed alongside the colours and textures of others. Her photographs provide glimpses of the types of photographs that make up the album. These are visual registers of the rites of passage, including photo-booth photographs taken by adolescent teenagers who 'muck around' to explore their identities, formal studio portraits as 'markers' of children growing up and colour snapshots of young women confirming friendships, sexual similarities and differences and establishing their presence in the local town. It is these kinds of personal pictures that Holland reminds us 'are deeply unreliable, but it is in this very unreliability that their interest lies'. As she argues, 'to *reread* private pictures … is to revalue the undervalued and to bring into public discourse meanings which have hitherto been concealed in the most secret parts of the private sphere' (Holland 2000, 122).

Position As Desired illustrates the way in which Tyrell values the personal and private archive as a way of creating her photographs. One photograph centres on a micro and scrutinized view of an album page. The bottom two-thirds of a snapshot of four women sitting in front of a house predominates in the photograph's composition. Our sense of what we imagine is represented here, our a priori knowledge and convention of reading suggests that this album page contains photographs from the late 1960s, judging by the colours of the snapshots and the dresses worn by the young women pictured. We do not see their faces or feet but rather a row of bare legs in minidresses. Her mother's legs among her three friends' ones (presumed to be European), perched on the wall in the sunshine, arms linked as friends embrace, their knees together, their demeanour reflecting a consciousness of good upbringing, yet relaxed, self-confident (see figure 3). This fragmented image hints

Figure 3 Stacey Tyrell (2001): *Position As Desired* (reproduced with the kind permission of the artist)

at the period of the late 1960s and 1970s, in which voices of complex and contradictory radical thinking, student culture, antiwar protests, women's liberation and civil rights were prominent. Holland argues that snapshots always contain a 'hint of disruption' and 'a reproach to dutiful lifestyles' (Holland 2000, 151). Tyrell's photograph also alludes to the feminist critique of the photographic family album (and 'the family' itself) as not fully able to reveal the absences and gaps 'between the enrichment and proliferation of ideal images of family life and the complexity of its lived reality' (Holland 2000, 151). As Tyrell notes,

> [t]here are areas of the past that we, living in the present are never intended to know. In every family and family album these gaps exist both physically and emotionally, consciously and subconsciously. But it is up to us, the viewer, to form our own narratives. (Tyrell 2010)

These images are equally concerned with the gendered subculture of being a young black woman in suburban Canada. Her mother's signification in the photographs and her daughter's restaging of her presence as women of the Canadian/Caribbean diaspora are an alternative to Gilroy's observation of his own lived experience as the 'transitional' generation of black Britons, where

...we were not so much a lost generation as a lucky one. An unusually eloquent, militant and musically rich culture oriented us as slave-
descendants, as diaspora subjects and as world citizens.

That fortuitous alignment encouraged us to employ vernacu-
lar wisdom in order to defend ourselves, identify our interests and
change our circumstances. We were bolstered by a cosmopolitan
movement for democratic change and energised by the intensity of
a very special period in the cultural life of the black Atlantic. (Gilroy
2007, 248–51)

Colonial/Post-colonial Space and Location

The physical traits associated with non-European landscapes are
embedded representations in the art works explored in the chapter
and in the notion of the contiguous archive. Much of the terrain associated with post-colonies still bears the legacy (economic, social, cultural,
physical) of having been plantation economies, providing evidence of
the period when African and Indian labour was a valuable commodity
to the West (Scott 2010).

In her exhibition at the Smith College Museum of Art (USA) entitled *Sugar: Maria Magdalena Campos-Pons* (2010), Campos-Pons talks
about her new commission, *Sugar/Bittersweet*, in which she reimagines the legacy of sugar and the sugar cane field. The 'sugar cane field'
comprises a gridded layout of wooden carved stools, each containing a
spear positioned upright from the stool – African artefacts acquired for
the installation. As if threaded by the spears, multiple single-coloured
stacks of cakes are moulded in the shape of beads. The solid, smooth
shaft of beads is made in four shades of colour associated with refining
sugar cane and created out of a range of different materials. The 'pris-
tine' white beads and those she describes as having a 'mulatta' hue are
made of glass associated with making crystallized sugar, symbolic of the
pinnacle of 'refinement' and taste. The deeper brown beads are made
with sugar found in street markets in Colombia, where it is popular and
reasonably priced to cook and preserve with. The black treacle beads
are made with molasses, a sugar by-product used for making rum and
most often fed to animals – considered to be at the other end of the
scale of the refining process, sticky, crude and bitter in taste.

This racially implied sugar cane field at once creatively inhabits the
mythology of Africa so central to the formation of Caribbean cultures
and its 'imagined communities' (Anderson 1983). The field signifies

masculine power through the mechanistic rigidity of the plantation factory. Campos-Pons also perceptively situates the field as both a danger to the slave as a brutalizing space to work in and a perceived threat to the success of the plantation by the 'field negro' as the rebellious, potentially violent slave. As she says of her installation,

> [s]ugar constructs power. Sugar constructed power that allowed people to sit and rest – on both sides. Some sat on his stool of power, complicit with that trade, and somewhere in between was this accumulation of sorrow and pain. (Video interview of Maria Magdalena Campos-Pons, 2010; http://scma.smith.edu/archived_exhibitions/sugar/video.html)

The physical and perceptive transformation of the terrain to create the plantation landscape coincides with what Thompson considers the 'tropicalization' of the other parts of the landscape during the eighteenth and nineteenth centuries. This, she suggests, was 'imaged for tourist consumption' (Thompson 2006, 5). Referring to Henri Rousseau's paintings among others, Thompson suggests that visions of tropical landscapes were engendered through a complex visual history of fantastical and imaginative constructs that 'conformed to … exoticized and fantastic ideals of the tropical landscape. The picturesque denoted a landscape that seemed like the dream of tropical nature' (2006, 21). The post-plantation landscape and economy, particularly for island terrains, including much of the Caribbean region, have been transformed and are now used and perceived as idyllic holiday destinations, with tourists mostly travelling from the North American continent.

As a counter-discourse to connotations of the picturesque, the 'tropical' and the colonial plantation space, post-colonial scholars and artists have re-presented, reinterpreted and reimagined the terrain of the South. Most noticeable has been the consideration of the terrain as integral to Creole discourses, as explored earlier in this chapter, including writings by Antonio Benítez-Rojo (1996), Édouard Glissant (1989) and Françoise Vergès (2003). Through fictional prose, poetry, critiques of historical literature and documentation,[6] they examine the particularity of the islands' physical locations, the oceans they emerge from and the continents they are closest to.

Benítez-Rojo conceives of the population of the Caribbean as 'people of the sea', in which Creole practices are defined in relation to three words – plantation, rhythm and performance. He sees a configured rhythm in the 'people of the sea', one that corresponds to the ocean

Figure 4 Nicole Awai (2006): *Bikini Beach: Maracas* (reproduced with the kind permission of the artist)

currents: 'a detour without purpose, a continual flow of paradoxes...' (Benitéz-Rojo 1996, 11).

The concept of the sea, then, is simultaneously deployed to signify both the brutal historical system of slavery and to reconstitute identities and dignity from out of such denigration. Perceived for its complexity, mystery, danger and unpredictability, among many other imaginings, the sea becomes an overwhelming and monumental rhythmically recurring visual and aural trope particularly associated with the work by diasporic artists as well as artists from the South and the post-colonies. Nicole Awai's Bikini Beach (2006) series (see Figure 4), a selection from which was included in the exhibition *Infinite Island: Contemporary Caribbean Art* (2008) at the Brooklyn Museum, New York, is a case in point.

As the title of this particular photograph, *Bikini Beach: Maracas*, suggests, a bikini is the central focus of the photograph, taken at Maracas, the most popular beach in Trinidad, on the north west coast of the island, which on the weekend becomes culturally a comparable location to Santa Barbara or Venice Beach in Los Angeles – in other words a place to 'hang out', 'lime'[7] or 'look cool', particularly for young, upwardly

mobile Trinidadians and exiled Venezuelans. Awai is one from a generation of artists whose own more complex migratory relationship
between the Caribbean and the USA includes 'temporary sojourning
and circulatory "visiting"' (Conway 2001), meaning she lives and works
in both Trinidad and the USA. The photograph at once seems to evoke
a historic interrelationship between the USA and Trinidad, evoking a
wry smile at the popular 'kitchy', 'skimpy', polka-dot swimwear. The
title of the piece and the central focus of the 'discarded' red polka-dot
bikini in the photograph immediately evoke titillation and the risqué
notion associated with a range of individual and popular references:
our own teenage memories and sexual encounters on holidays or week-
ends; of the fantasy and sexuality that Trinidad carnival proposes each
year; the explicit sexual signifiers of ragga soca,[8] such as the bikini-clad
women on the CD covers; the beach-party film genre associated with
a number of 1960s Hollywood films, of which *Beach Party* was one; the
historical relationship that Trinidad has to the US Army (1940s–70s)
and the popular representation of US GI's, who were based there as a
location of strategic military importance to the USA and an important
oil resource. The photograph positions the viewer on the beach – as
if lying or sitting on the sand with a view of the sea in the distance.
We are implicated and seduced by the artist. The sea is perceived as
a known threat to us and the photographer, with the red warning flag
on display to the right of the frame; yet this threat is safely contained
and does not encroach into the beach scene of the couple stretched
out, where Awai has positioned us. The sea, contained within a bay
area, remains a 'constant, benign' border in the frame; its surf is there
but harmless. This beach has not been airbrushed; it is not perfectly
sunny and visually does not resonate with an idyllic beach scene of
the 1960s Hollywood film from which its name derives. It is represented as slightly unkempt and messy, the weather slightly overcast,
and contains uncomfortable coconut twigs poking out of the sand and
unseemly rocks exposed in the left of the frame. The intense orange-
red hue of the bikini, preoccupying and dominating our field of vision,
is echoed by the small red flag.

The photograph reflects a more individual memory and imagination through the use of the family archive. Inside the bikini is a family
photograph of the artist aged five, with an older male relative or family
friend 'wearing a similar bathing suit on the same beach in Trinidad'
(Awai 2007, 48). The family photograph that lines the bikini portrays
Awai as central in the tinged, sepia reddish–bleached photograph
reproduced on the fabric. The relative's head appears to have been

cropped by the elastic trim of the bikini. Awai's place in the photograph is separate, positioned close but not touching the adult. Her arms are self-consciously folded in front of her while his hands are by his side. There is little indication of warmth or intimacy between adult and child. The two subjects appear as if reluctantly posing for the photograph, as if the photographer cajoled them into capturing the moment. Awai knew she 'had to take the bikini "on location" back to those beaches in Trinidad. ... The statement felt more complete – the place within the place ... creating the permanence of the event and the resonance of "place"' (Awai 2007, 113–14). The family photograph set within the intimate pleats of the bikini lining display discomfort, estrangement and anxiety. As women often associated with being the keepers of family albums, this photograph is likely to be familiar to us as a scene or intimate family story that may have gone unspoken or denied.

Awai's photograph of Maracas from her series Bikini Beach is associated with representational space, as Lefebvre proposes, a concept of space that is 'directly *lived* through' (Lefebvre 1991, 39). Her photographs as *representational spaces* compound and add to our sense of and a priori reference to the 'tropical' beach scene of the Caribbean. As contemporary visual signifiers – embedding familial memories literally into the space, the photograph 'overlays physical space, making symbolic use of its objects' (ibid.). Awai creatively reimagines the space to add to and to *translate* the scene based on a directly lived-through autobiographical experience of the beach and her swimwear.

Conclusions

In my art work *Amendments* the central woman character is remembered by Eunice, her long-time friend and ally. She recalls their friendship and the time they were together – while taking in the washing one evening on All Souls' Day in Trinidad. The audience hears Eunice speaking Trinidadian:

> It wasn't all fussing, fighting an' feuding
> We had some good times
> Remember dem dance we use to go to, an d-night when King Radio bring out Sedition Law.
> how the chorus go? 'Dem go licence we mout dem nah wan we talk'
> HiYiYi, dat was when d-cuban did afta yu,

dat man coulda dance Eh!
Ah wonda wuh happen to he?

Amendments (2007), text by Marc Matthews

Eunice evokes a period of political disturbance and civil unrest in Trinidad during the 1930s, when the colonial government depended on the law of sedition as one way of curbing political disturbance, speech and action – what was considered insurrection and incitement. She refers to the lyrics of the song created by the musician called King Radio during a time when calypsonians emerged as astute political observers, commentators and critics – with their 'fingers on the pulse' of the politics of the time. As Gordon Rohlehr (1997) notes, the calypsonian reflected the political mood and articulated canny, political commentary in the 'language' and style of the general population. On the other hand, 'in 'true Trini style', Eunice refers to ways in which the party, or the *fête*, is associated with carnival and sexual encounters. These may also be perceived as integral to the woman's lived experience and considered as spaces of liberation and freedom.

Amendments, like the other art works discussed in this chapter, offers a relational encounter with history, articulated here though a hybridized and Creole female voice. This evocation contains specific local historicity, experienced by the viewer aurally and visually as an animation playing in the present moment. Eunice is visualized (some of the time) by an actor staging the act of remembrance. This gendered re-enactment of the archive locates and positions an often absent figure in the archives – that of the black woman. Further, she is located through a performance, which as Carol Boyce Davies argues, is overlayered with gender, class, sexuality and cultural history.

> If following Judith Butler, the category of woman is one of performance of gender, then the category of Black woman, or woman of color, exists as multiple performances of gender and race and sexuality based on the particular, cultural, historical, geopolitical, class communities in which Black women exist. (1994, 8–9)

The processes and practices of constructing contiguous archives are not only necessary in order to locate absent voices then; they are also political, social and cultural interventions into the public validation of what we call history. Seen in this light, contiguous archives become ideological, framed as feminist and post-colonial interventions into histories. More importantly, and unlike history, they are open, dialogic and generative. They resist the closure endemic to historical texts, and as a praxis for enquiry, action and creativity, produce new meanings and interpretations. It is the feminist and post-colonial frameworks, then, that construct contiguous archives as interventionist, not least because this means they resist closure and are always susceptible to new meanings, new creations and different contestations.

Acknowledgements

The author would like to thank Nicole Awai, Maria Magdalena Campos-Pons, Erika Tan and Stacey Tyrell for their inspiration and for allowing the work to be reproduced for this article.

Notes

1. Donald Rodney's art work *Autoicon* (1997) makes reference to Jeremy Bentham's autoicon as a way of creating a multifaceted record of his body. Bentham's dream was of integrating the dead with the living. His body was preserved and stored in a wooden cabinet acquired and kept by University College London since 1850.
2. I conceptualize the term *contiguous archive* as part of my thesis on archives in Trinidad; see *Creole in the Archive: Imagery, Presence, and Location of the Plantation Workers of Two Plantations, Nearby Villages and Towns in Trinidad (1838–1938)*.
3. This multimedia art work was created and launched at Matrix East Research Centre, University of East London, as a prototype for a larger installation (Domino Effects, 2010).
4. Contemporary Caribbean feminist historians and cultural theorists, including Reddock (1987), Mathurin (1995), Mohammed (1998), Shepherd (1999, 2002), Boyce Davies (1994) and Puri (2004), reread archive material in order to resignify the presence of the Caribbean woman.
5. Erika Tan's *Persistent Visions*, a silent three-screen video work (24"), was commissioned by Picture This in collaboration with the British Empire and Commonwealth Museum.
6. In a series of selected thoughts, positions and concepts written during the 1960s and 1970s in *Caribbean Discourse: Selected Essays* (Glissant, 1989), Glissant explores the notion of Creolization from a Martinican context. His writings address the particularity of Martinique as a French department and the way in which creative expressions of language, performance, music, novels and poetry form the basis of exploring Caribbeanness. Vergès (2004) explores historical documentation in 'India-Oceanic Creolizations: Processes and Practices of Creolization on Réunion Island,' as a way of

perceiving Creolization as a spatial-symbolic practice firmly based in the French department of Réunion and the plantation. Benitéz-Rojo (1996), in *The Repeating Island: The Caribbean and the Postmodern Perspective*, explores the Caribbean imaginary using historical literature from the Spanish-speaking islands as a way of addressing Creolizing practices.

7. 'Lime' is a Caribbean (and particularly Trinidadian) term for hanging out and socializing. In the *Dictionary of Caribbean English Usage* it is associated with '[a]n unorganised social gathering to pass the time away in chat and banter' (Allsopp, 1996: 349).

8. Ragga soca is a fusion of Jamaican ragga and Trinidadian soca associated with Trinidadian singers, such as Machel Montano, from the late 1990s. It is a term coined by soca pioneer Kenny Phillips. For further information, see www.nalis.gov.tt/music/music_raggasoca.html.

Weaving the Life of Guatemala

Reflections of the Self and Others through Visual Representations

Sonia De La Cruz

The casualties of Guatemala's devastating civil war fought from 1960 through 1996 gave birth to *TRAMA Textiles*, a 100 per cent worker-owned association comprising more than 400 weavers from 17 different cooperatives in five different regions of the western highlands of the country. The indigenous Mayan women of the cooperatives proudly continue the ancient textile art of backstrap loom weaving that has maintained their cultural traditions and community ties for centuries. Traditionally, the designs of weavings reflect elements of creation and nature that express indigenous cosmovision;[1] and in the pre-Columbian era, women weavers were often buried with the weaving tools they utilized throughout their lives. In the aftermath of the civil war, the indigenous women of the highlands have redefined the use of their weavings as one that aims to principally support their families, although its practice continues to be an important cultural custom that is passed on to new generations of women.[2] In an effort to make a living, preserve their cultural traditions and empower their community, the women of TRAMA Textiles, in collaboration with a student film crew, produced a video that functions as an engagement tool to highlight the association's current plight.

I locate this account as a feminist autoethnography in order to situate my perspective in relation to the cultural complexity of Guatemalan indigenous people and history. This autoethnographical approach also allows a discussion about issues of power and representation that emerged during the production of this visual project and provides a distinct perspective about the dynamics of identity and accountability of visual representation. I present this self-reflexive narrative through autoethnographical vignettes that acknowledge the subjectivity of the text and recognizes my role(s) within this experience as outsider. This analysis is also informed by theories within development communication that emphasize a communicative praxis rooted in Freirean thought (1970), which values dialogue as an avenue for individual and communal consciousness and power.

I argue that the creative praxis or participatory strategies within the development of the video serve the reflexive spirit of this ethnographic work; particularly because they helped mediate tensions that arose during the process of collaboration and helped uncover the different power relationships that emerged among the people involved. I argue that the power over visual representations in this project entailed the acknowledgement of the self as a way to discern the different decision-making processes that transpired. This article examines how as individuals we might portray others when we do not belong to their particular reality. Furthermore, it questions how we go from our own lives, engrossed in our own concerns, to retaining a profound sense of responsibility for those we are representing. And how does the use of video function as an engagement tool for collaborative work and thereby give voice to people?

TRAMA Textiles: The Past Is Shaping the Future

For us, the Spanish word *trama*, meaning the weft or binding thread, is interchangeable with the word *comida*, food. Our weavings clothe us, warm our families through highland winters, and carry our babies on our backs. They unite our people from generation to generation and sustain us as much as any food.

from the TRAMA Textiles website

It is necessary to account for the social, political, economic and cultural aspects of the lives of the indigenous women of Guatemala to recognize the complexity of their history. The atrocious violence of the civil war spanning 36 years was ignited by the inequitable distribution of income and land between the upper class and indigenous people and resulted in a brutal history of ethnic genocide and discrimination coupled with the elite's unwillingness to entertain peaceful organizing around civil reforms and economic rights (Pessar 2001). This civil war brought about a number of attacks in which local villages were destroyed and thousands of civilians were killed. Men of indigenous descent became the primary victims of military and guerrilla attacks, and many disappeared or were murdered during the turmoil (Clouser 2009). As a consequence of Guatemala's civil unrest, the women of various Mayan communities came together to support each other and to find a way to survive. It was in realizing the benefits of unity and collaboration that, in 1988, TRAMA Textiles was formed.

TRAMA Textiles is an association of women for artisan development in backstrap loom weaving. It is a worker-owned weaving cooperative that aims at creating work for fair wages to honourably support families and communities affected by the Guatemalan civil war. As a tradition that is transferred from one generation to the next, the art of weaving continues to be a distinct part of indigenous people's past and present way of life. The weaving looms are warp yarns stretched between two sticks or end bars that are attached by a backstrap around the hips of the woman on one end, while the other end is affixed by a rope to a tree or post (Figure 5). The women of the association consider

Figure 5 Backstrap loom weaving

their *tramas* to be the binding thread that unites them, and through the practice of weaving, the women can provide sustenance for their families while preserving their culture and history.

Currently, the 17 cooperatives that are part of TRAMA Textiles are located throughout five regions in the western highlands of Guatemala They are Sololá, Huehuetenango, Sacatepéquez, Quetzaltenango and Quiché. The weaving patterns of each cooperative vary, thereby identifying the particular location where the weaving has been produced. In the city of Quetzaltenango, the association has a weaving school that is open to the public and a store where the *telares*, or textiles, are sold. Textiles are a long-standing symbol of respect to the weavers' ancestors and are a significant trait of cultural identity. The women of TRAMA Textiles consider their art of weaving a form of healing, particularly with those women who remain affected by the memories of the civil war and the loss of their loved ones. Weaving is mostly a communal act, so the women of TRAMA Textiles often come together to weave and talk about matters related to the community or maintenance of the association.

Scope of the Collaboration

The video entitled *Trama Textiles: Weaving the Life of Guatemala* (2008) was produced for the association of women weavers, and it offers stories of the women's past while highlighting their vision for the future of the association. Although the logistical details of the project will stay at the periphery of this chapter, I would like to note that this work has been produced to aid the marketing goals of TRAMA Textiles, which aimed at promoting the weaving work they perform. The project was produced in collaboration with the women of the association, along with the instructors and student crew[3] who were conducting video-based community service.[4] The germane idea behind this collaboration was to create a space of trust, mutual respect and understanding among all participants.

The participatory practices of collaboration meant involving the women in the various phases of production. In the pre-production phase, the women of TRAMA Textiles spelled out the goals for the association and provided the specific objectives for the video, which were defined as creating awareness about the association and promoting their weaving work. Throughout the production phase, the women participated in conducting interviews, shared their experiences as interviewees and gave their opinion about the direction and the type of content that should be included in the project. During post-production, the participation of TRAMA Textiles was limited, mainly due to the production crew's return to the United States. However, before the crew's departure, some of the women recorded the narrative for the video's voice-over and provided their feedback on the structural back-bone of the video. The final version of this work was completed in San Francisco, California, and copies of it were sent to the association for their use.

As of this writing, the association is led by Amparo de León de Rubio and Oralia Chopén (Figure 6), president and vice-president, respec-tively. Both Amparo and Oralia acted as mediators between the dif-ferent communities during the video's production; primarily because some of the communities we visited are monolingual, speaking the Quechua, Kiché or Kachiquel language. For this reason, Amparo and Oralia at times took up the roles of interviewers and translators, while the accompanying professor[5] and I acted as Spanish-speaking transla-tors between Amparo, Oralia and the students (see Figure 6). My roles

Figure 6 Amparo (left), Oralia (middle), with a student from the USA

in this project included that of director, executive producer, organization liaison, video production instructor and translator.

In Pursuit of a Reflexive Methodology

This work is located within feminist ethnography in that, in the most obvious sense, it centres on the female voice(s) of the women of TRAMA Textiles as well as my own. Through the analysis, I hope to offer a way to understand the power differentials that emerged between us, particularly when utilizing visual methods for representation. Arguments about the validity of visual methods for offering direct and uncontaminated views of subjects have been criticized. David Buckingham (2009) argues that such methods 'need to display a degree of reflexivity to understand how it establishes positions from which it becomes possible for participants to speak' (635). Moreover, Holly Wissler (2009) has suggested that representations that have been mediated through the ethnographer's experience and personal reflections contribute to ongoing concerns of ethics of representation in visual productions. The particular creative practices of visual work can render a way for understanding different power relations, but only if researchers acknowledge the responsibility of accounting for their voice and perspective within the experience. In practicing feminist writing, I am mindful of what Gayle Letherby (2002) observes as a methodological and epistemological position regarding feminist research, which acknowledges that 'researchers are not intellectually superior to their respondents and they have the responsibility to providing accounts of their research process so that readers can have access to the procedures that underlie the way that knowledge is presented and constructed.'[6] Ellis and Bochner (2008) further describe how, through the autoethnographic experience, 'we can look more deeply at the self-other interactions [which] display multiple layers of consciousness, connecting the personal to the cultural' (cited in Subedi and Rhee 2008, 1071). In conducting autoethnography, we place ourselves within the social context as a way to mediate and reflect on lived experiences. These experiences 'move from a broad lens focus on individual situatedness within the cultural and social context, to a focus on the inner, vulnerable and often resistant self' (Boyle and Parry 2007, 186). Therefore, the autoethnography concentrates on the examination of the interactions, dynamics and conscious experience of the author in relation to the participants and environment involved.

While developing this project, I aimed at validating the voice of the women of TRAMA Textiles by observing a communicative praxis between all collaborators, particularly in relation to indigenous women who continue to challenge their political subjectivity and self-determination. Feminist scholarship holds a strong political value in that there is a desire to give women a voice in a world that defines them as voiceless:

> It is transformative in that it is concerned with helping the silent speak and is involved in consciousness raising. (Dervin 1987, 109)

Indeed, for the TRAMA Textiles project, there is an emphasis on 'communication as dialogue, communication as social practice, and communication as a social right' (Richards et. al. 2001, 8). In turn, successful communication and collaboration depends on the active participation of all individuals involved in any given project. Participation in this analysis is embedded in the communicative praxis between the participants and researcher. I use praxis in the liberating approach that attempts to eliminate the separation between participants and researcher, while generating mutual collaboration in order to create a 'fruitful dialectic for the construction of knowledge, which is systematically examined, altered, and expanded in practice' (Huesca 2002, 502). This can help foster a more genuine dialectical relationship with participants as it opens channels for dialogue and personal interaction (and reflection), since it aims to legitimize the experiences of those seeking empowerment.

Writing from a First-Person Perspective

The following accounts are drawn from different moments I experienced during the production of this video. Since this is an introspective exercise that involves the 'carving out of pieces of narrative, that are selected, edited and deployed to border the argument', the project can be approached as 'sites of identity production' where a postmodern sensibility can elucidate the construction, articulation or resistance to particular traits (Fine 1994, 22; Vickers 2007), such as ethnicity, class and culture. This chapter allows me to offer different realities, positions or ways of knowing, whether linguistically or culturally based, which acknowledge the history and realities of people's lives, particularly when they are markedly different from one's own personal, political and intellectual perspectives.

The act of self-identification in an autoethnography insists on the recognition of one's own identity to clarify our position within the work, as well as serve as a way for acknowledging other voices that are presented in the narrative. Here, identity should be understood as '…increasingly fragmented and fractured; never singular but multiply constructed across different, often intersecting and antagonistic, discourses, practices and positions. They are subject to a radical historicization, and are constantly in the process of change and transformation' (Hall and Gay 1996, 4). So I think of identity as being fluid and multiple and tied to the ways in which individuals make sense of their own lived experiences. In the act of situating myself within this text, I confess that although I feel familiarity with some of the ways of life of Central American nations, especially Guatemala, I do not live nor have lived the realities of the indigenous women.

On that account, I am compelled to reflect on my own identity(ies), although nervously, as a way to offer the reader the reflexive view that I engage, the understanding that this is a subjective text and that my introspection hopes to help break the silence of voices that are at the periphery of the mainstream, like those of the women of TRAMA Textiles. First, I want to give some thought to the instructive roles I performed in Guatemala and then comment on my standpoint. As producer and director, I made the final decisions about the construction of the video and saw the project to its completion. As instructor, I taught students various production techniques; I emphasized the importance of teamwork and the need to be conscious observers. My hope was that the student crew would have a better finger on the pulse of their lived experiences and reflect on them while working on the video. This, I believed, would contribute to understanding the spirit of collaborative work and would develop an honest engagement with the women of TRAMA Textiles. Personally, I am a woman of Mexican descent. I grew up in Mexico and come from a working-class family. At present, I find myself part of a middle-class culture of the United States and part of a privileged community of academe, constantly vacillating between the English and Spanish language. I am inescapably reminded of my colour or ethnic heritage, which often drives many of my day-to-day interactions. I feel as a woman living in the *borderlands*, a concept Gloria Anzaldúa (1987) has qualified as one that is constituted in the here and there, that ultimately constitutes who I am now. A sort of physical 'being' in one space and place at a time but enacting different strands of the self that connects me to multiple aspects of my Mexican(ness), woman(ness) or self(ness), which incessantly moves me across multiple borders.

Self-Reflexive Vignettes

This analysis presents three autoethnographical vignettes that deal with different moments of the experience of producing this video; each reflects on issues related to the accountability of visual representations, power relations, dialogue and creative practices. To construct this piece, I draw from interviews, field notes, journal annotations, many hours of video footage and photographs collected during the 28-day period. The act of revisiting the many images brought memories and emotions of the time spent in Guatemala, which led to deeper reflection on the overall experience. The analysis consisted of looking for patterned regularities in the data in order to evaluate standards, interpret connections between the culture-sharing group, discover how issue-relevant meanings emerge and see how they connect to larger theoretical frameworks (Wolcott 1994). My reflexive approach, then, intends to 'go beyond the emotion that is inexorably tied to those memories, towards understanding, something that would have been more difficult at a time closer to the events shared' (Vickers 2007, 224). The following vignettes contained in this chapter are not constructed in a chronological manner; rather, they describe moments relevant to its theoretical foundation.

First Vignette: Juana's Story

During an afternoon at the weaving school, I was sitting in the courtyard being taught how to weave by Amparo, while Oralia was spinning yarn. It had been a relatively slow day at the school, so the three of us engaged in leisurely conversation. We shared details about our family and personal lives, and during the conversation, I realized that there was a great difference of experiences, beliefs and customs among us. Even though Mexico and Guatemala have similar social-cultural traditions, our experiences had shaped our lives in distinct ways. I had believed that I could anchor myself in these cultural similarities and thereby create greater common ground among us. It was evident, however, that their experiences, particularly those relevant to the civil war, were strikingly different from my own. In this sense, my Mexican identity did not allow for a way of connecting deeper to their past; rather, it made me realize that by acknowledging their history, I would be paying respect to their realities.

This conversation made clear that their input in producing the video was vital for articulating particular cultural codes, especially because within the time constraints of this project, we would gloss over their cultural complexity. Together we determined which cooperatives to visit, who should be interviewed and what themes should be addressed. The primary components of the video highlighted the quality of their threads, the making of weavings and the just pay provided to women for their work. These elements were discussed within the context of the formation of TRAMA Textiles, and it called the audience to engage and/or purchase the work of the association.

For one of our interviews, Oralia suggested going to Pujujil II, a small community outside the city of Quetzaltenango, where we could meet and interview members of the cooperative. This was Oralia's home. She wanted to introduce us to her family and to the women weavers. In this cooperative lived Juana Cojtín, who had several days earlier visited the weaving school, where, by coincidence, I had the opportunity to meet her. She made an impression on me. Oralia informed her then that the crew was producing a video for the association. Without delay, Juana felt inclined to give her testimony, despite my not having a camera or the crew with me. Since she only spoke Kiché, Oralia translated while Juana narrated. Juana told me about surviving the violence of war that resulted in the loss of her husband and father. Despite not understanding what she was saying, her visceral rendering exposed great emotion, which moved me.

In planning for our trip to Pujujil II, Oralia insisted we visit Juana to record her story on video. Oralia said, 'I think it would be good to visit Juana and her family in Pujujil because, *pobrecita*,[7] she is really needy, *sería bueno*.'[8] To an extent, I was persuaded to do the on-camera interview. Oralia believed that although it was difficult for Juana to tell her story, it could help her heal; and giving her that attention would demonstrate that she was a valuable member of the community. Oralia also felt that Juana's story epitomized the many tragic stories among the women of the various communities; therefore, it would serve as a way to present this part of the past that still afflicts many of the women's lives to this day.

As the crew and I prepared for the trip, I wondered what the implications would be for recording Juana's story. I thought about how she would react in front of the camera, and to a large degree, I felt that interviewing her would capitalize a very personal story. Juana's account was incredibly moving, and in my role as producer, I knew that this story would trigger a strong emotional engagement in viewers. Nonetheless, I felt conflicted. Although, as Oralia insisted, Juana's story echoed the experiences of many other women, I felt deeply accountable for doing the interview. I was concerned about how to visually convey her story, which merited sharing, but doing so in a way that was ethically and morally sensible.

Since visual projects and their creative production processes can raise a number of concerns about the meanings evoked through its representations, it is important to have a degree of flexibility for mediating between different cultural understandings. Moreover, working on projects that are deemed collaborative means that inevitably some tensions and disagreements may arise; nonetheless, one should ultimately be fully accountable for their actions. It has long been argued that the presence of a camera alters the behaviour of participants, usually making them think twice about what they are going to say, how they are going to say it, how they look and so on. In this case, as I learned, the camera affected Juana's attitude. But instead of feeling apprehension about speaking in front of a camera and crew (the reaction I expected from Juana), the camera became an outlet for expression. In other words, the presence of the camera created a space where she revealed herself and shared her grief. She did not shy away from telling her emotional account.

Visual representation is not a harmless activity; an element such as emotional behaviour ultimately impacts everyone involved and the scope of the work (Newton 2001). Moral responsibility and ethical practice also become inevitably entrenched in ethnographic work, and it has been suggested that moral and ethical dilemmas are fluid and that no one solution is the same for all situations (Lassiter 2005). Juana was sharing a very painful part of her past, which to me expressed sorrow. I later realized, however, that what I had considered to be a vulnerable moment was a public recognition of an experience that deeply affected her, particularly since lives lost as a result of the civil war have often been silenced within the nation's discourse. Throughout the interview, it became apparent that Juana wanted to speak, and more importantly, she did so of her own accord. It didn't matter what questions I asked or how I asked them. Juana displayed those same raw emotions I had seen before. I realized that this is who she was. The crew and I were simply fortunate to have been able to share those moments with her.

Second Vignette: The Women of San Martín Sacatepéquez

Media constructions of indigenous people, particularly women, tend to be of 'homogeneous powerless groups often located as implicit victims of particular socioeconomic systems' (Mohanty 1988, 54). However, these outmoded tropes are shifting. In the case of TRAMA Textiles, the women are resisting mainstream representations and are redefining their own identities at the intersection of a traditional past and a clear vision for the future. During a visit to San Martín Sacatepéquez, a small municipality at the outskirts of Quetzaltenango, we encountered many women in the community who wanted to speak and be interviewed. As we proceeded with the on-camera interviews, Amparo clarified the position of the community:

> We want people to see who makes the weavings and how they make them...we want people to know that if they support us, they will be helping all of us...and they [the viewers] can see that the money goes directly to help the women....

It was important to be transparent about the economic dealings of the association and to demonstrate the egalitarian approach to the sustainability of its community. Also, it was important for them that the audience have an opportunity to meet (albeit through video) the individuals who crafted the weavings. They felt it was vital to show the world that 'they existed and worked hard to earn a living'. It was about recognizing their work as weavers.

Approximately 20 to 25 women gathered at Amparo's small home patio, and with an additional production crew of 12, the patio was quite restricted. Interviewing the group in such a limited space became a rather challenging task. The women sat on the floor of the small and narrow patio, filling the space to maximum capacity. I positioned myself next to Amparo, who was seated directly across from the women. Although it was necessary to sit in such manner to accommodate the spatial restrictions of the patio room and production equipment, the seating arrangement made me feel distant, removed from the group of women. In a sense, my position of outsider was drawn more clearly in relation to them because, along with Amparo, I became the focal point in the room and was engaging them from a place that commanded their attention. I quickly became aware that my efforts to erase the different positions of power between us would be difficult; partly because of the space I occupied, but also because of my use of Spanish, rather than Kiché, which in an obvious way made us different. I also noticed that the women saw me as a conduit through which to deliver their message, particularly to the North American audiences that epitomized a new consumer base for them.

Interestingly, part of the unfolding conversation challenged the long-standing discourse of indigenous identity. In other words, notions of indigenous women as powerless victims that so often flood global media landscapes shifted to one that situated the vitality and dedication to their weaving work as part of their present identity. An elderly woman in the group said: 'We aren't asking for charity. We are asking for work. We work hard for our families, and by God's grace, we can continue to work. That is what we want to say to people. ...' It dawned on me that, as crew, we had not been invited to the community to be simple witnesses to the women's living or working conditions; rather, we had been invited into their space in order to understand more deeply the connections between their weavings and community life. As a whole, I noticed similar experiences between the different people and communities we visited throughout our time in Guatemala and wondered whether it would be possible to validate, in a visual form, all of those stories within the constraints of a single project. The short answer, however, was no. Although we hoped the video would aid the economic goals of the association, we also wanted to give a sense of the women's determination for being their own agents of change through the sharing of their experiences and struggles.

Third Vignette: TRAMA's Voice

Video, film and other visual media, such as citizen's media (Rodríguez and El Gazi 2007), can provide an outlet for the communication, defence and cultural strengthening of cultural, national or ethnic identities (Poole 2005). But they also run the risk of erasing the identity of a group because the camera does not present neutral reflections of reality; instead, it presents constructed narratives (Clifford and Marcus 1986). There have also been claims about the potential for empowering participants through visual methods; however, questions about whose 'voice' is actually being represented are still contentious (Buckingham 2009). Giving voice to the women of TRAMA Textiles was not simply a matter of having them speak in front of the camera. Rather, it had to do with the views they engaged in their daily lives that needed to be addressed through the video. And as the crew came to understand, notions of unity, hard work and family welfare were of utmost importance to the members of the association.

Through collaboration and dialogue, we participated in an honest working relationship, even though it entailed 'complicated power plays and difficult negotiations' (Barbash and Taylor 1997, 74). With a student production crew, the nature of collaboration between the crew and instructor, or crew and collaborators, had serious implications for thinking about how we negotiated our authority in relationship to one another. A striking case had to do with how each crew member understood the identity of the indigenous women and how each mediated the overall cultural milieu, all while balancing the logistical needs of the production. Because we immersed ourselves in a new environment, we were learning, adapting, changing and at times struggling to understand that we could not control our social environment. The crew also experienced challenges in striking a balance between collaborative and individual work, which was mostly reflected in issues of control over the narrative, personal egos and creative content. I believe that challenges with the crew arose in the process of getting to know one another more intimately and in negotiating the multiple identities and/or cultural differences within the crew.

I came to understand that my decisions, as well as those of the crew, were culturally conditioned and even justified by the fluid circumstances of the social environment with which we engaged. As it turned out, dialogue with the women of TRAMA Textiles, which often occurred as group sessions, became the natural equalizer to some of the crew's apprehensions about the direction of the video. As the women offered feedback and the more they engaged in exchange of views with students (and vice versa), we grew in tune with one another. The process of active dialogue was particularly important because this project did not fully engage or represent the social and cultural understandings or identity of the indigenous women. In other words, because this video was aimed at an English-speaking American and European target audience, we needed to construct this piece in a way that was relatable to these audiences. Therefore, the practice of mutual dialogue afforded the crew and myself a way of knowing whether the women of the association were satisfied with the work that was being produced.

Conclusions

Throughout this autoethnographic rendering, I hope to have pointed to the ways that relationships of power emerged among collaborators, demonstrating how they challenged individual beliefs or attitudes. I have argued that there are no simple answers to issues of representation and that identity (or identities) can yield multiple reflections that produce a number of perspectives, which are constantly negotiated. The use of autoethnography, first and foremost, attempts to elucidate the positionality of ethnographers in relationship to the environment with which they engage. But it also recognizes that writing is not a solo act; rather it occurs in relationship to other forces – whether social, cultural, political or linguistic.

Within these themes, the cohesive thread here was the examination of the multiple relations of power – whether individual or collective – and their negotiation throughout this experience. Power in this context was most apparent in the construction of the community's image and in the way their stories were framed; and since this is a project that can reach various audiences, there is always the risk of homogenizing the image of the community. To diminish this possibility (although it is a nearly impossible task, since each person makes his or her own interpretations), coming to a consensus on fundamental concepts for the video, such as aim, scope or purpose, alleviated some of the crew's and my own struggles for understanding what notions of 'community', 'weaving work' or even 'sisterhood' meant to the women of TRAMA Textiles.

I have attempted to convey that visual representations, as other forms of representations, are sites of political negotiation. Therefore, in making the video, it was important to recognize ourselves as somehow part of the circumstances of those we were filming: that we had impacted each other as collaborators and that we were not just a means to an end. It was vital to understand that we could not control the environment or resources available to us but that access was also contingent on our collaborators. We had to be aware that our political frames were different from those that the women of the association assumed, and so we needed to find ways to understand these different perspectives. Acknowledging that the audience for this video had an impact on its final construction, such as defining the language or format, it became wholly important to account for the political, cultural or otherwise social views of the women of TRAMA Textiles. Although collaborative work is a complex process, I have found it to be an experience of growth and understanding.

Finally, I want to point both to the significance of recognizing identity as important to the writing of this narrative and also to its role in the process of collaboration. To mediate collective and individual identities is a messy task and often a complicated one to interpret. The collective identity of the group was understood as multiple and fluid, full of contradictions and stemming from a variety of analytical, political and social orientations. Even though the aim of the video was to aid the material well-being of TRAMA Textiles, the visual feature of the project became a way for the women to assert their identity as community. As for myself, writing a self-identifying ethnography has not been a simple task, mostly because I am required to claim specific affiliations that assume particular power, which can often be contradictory, such as 'academic', 'minority', 'writer/author' and 'women of colour'.

The lives of the women of TRAMA Textiles are as intricate and colourful as their weavings, and their history is reflected in their art: their weavings have diverse patterns which represent past struggles, new beginnings and a changing present that, together, articulate a complex past. Their weavings are a sign of an enduring respect to their ancestors, and in myriad ways they represent the long fight of the past and the challenges of the present. It is in the beauty and distinguishable patterns of these women's weavings that, perhaps in a less obvious way, their stories are told.

Notes

1. According to anthropologists, the indigenous cosmovision generally refers to the system of beliefs and values, which includes religion, politics, economy and nature, that articulate the social life of indigenous groups (Lopez Austin, 1990).
2. There are also some men who practice weaving, but today it is mostly a woman's activity.
3. This project is part of a course that is supported by San Francisco State University's Broadcast Electronic and Communication Arts department and taught by Dr Betsy J. Blosser.
4. Through the video-based community service component of this project, students and instructors donated their time, resources and skills to aid the organization.
5. I refer here to Dr Betsy J. Blosser of San Francisco State University, who was also executive co-producer of this project.
6. See www.socresonline.org.uk/6/4/letherby.html#fine1994.
7. *Pobrecita* is translated from Spanish as 'poor little thing'.
8. *Sería bueno* is translated from Spanish as 'it would be good'.

Section 3

From Soap Opera to...

The increase in the number of female-centred television dramas and sitcoms since the 1990s has spawned a number of feminist analyses of television which investigate the feminist credentials and antifeminist sentiments displayed in these texts (see, e.g., Johnson 2007, Pender 2002). As Amanda Lotz (2006) highlights, the discovery of (often white and middle-class) women as a previously neglected consumer group with disposable income by American advertisers in the post-network era meant that a wider variety of images of women were made available. The resulting feminist analyses have, however, continued in the line of earlier feminist criticism in search of role models, research which was carried out by, among others, Betty Friedan's influential NOW group. As Joanne Hollows makes evident, this form of criticism has often implied a vilification of femininity and the 'feminine other woman' (2000, 17), while the larger structures of patriarchy and the problems caused by traditional gender roles (including those of masculinity) have remained neglected. Karen Boyle (2005) makes visible how limiting such an analysis can be for our understanding of texts which are perhaps more radical in their foregrounding of the problematic connection between traditional heterosexual masculinity and violence, as *Buffy: The Vampire Slayer* does, a drama considered in a negative light by the NOW research (Lotz 2006, 16). It also continues to overlook the polysemy the texts offer and which has enabled generations of women to interpret programmes in radical ways and find (feminist) pleasures in them.

Indeed, earlier feminist analyses were often focused on television – even when, as Geraghty's chapter highlights, they came together as a women and *film* group – because scholars recognized the role television and radio played in women's lives (Hobson 1982). Moreover, through their analyses, scholars hoped to validate the broadcast media, which had traditionally been looked down upon as a result of their connection to women, their domestic location and their repetitive structure (Gledhill 2006/1994, Hilmes 2007). Their analyses therefore centred on the potential pleasures the soap opera might offer women, leading to insights into the specifics of television spectatorship (Modleski 1979), identification (Ang 1990), form (Geraghty 1991) and the role television and radio play for audiences (Hobson 1982, Ang 1985, Seiter 1993). In many ways, feminist scholarship helped to establish broadcasting as a medium and soap opera as a genre (see Brunsdon 1995) that needed to be taken seriously. Charlotte Brunsdon continues that the soap opera also allowed feminists to engage with its others and in particular the problematic femininities that Betty Friedan (1963) and Mary Daly (1979) had decried. The work on audiences in particular made evident the complex reading strategies that audiences (and in particular women) deployed in order to engage with television texts. Such readings showed significant awareness of the problematic politics, while also ensuring 'pleasurable negotiations' (Gledhill 2006/1994) that allowed female viewers to identify with and relate to soap characters.

The feminist work on soap opera, then, was fundamental in forging understanding of broadcasting more generally, and insights developed by feminists were used for analyses that gradually moved into other areas of interest. In particular, the specific cultural conditions impacting on production have become of interest to scholars since Julie D'Acci's (1994) influential analysis of *Cagney and Lacey* indicated the negotiation between production personnel and network in the development and continuation of the groundbreaking series. In this collection, Skoog examines the role of female producers in the production of the much-neglected radio soap opera *Mrs Dale's Diary*. Skoog's analysis weaves a complex picture that highlights the interconnectedness of the series' low status, its primary female, part-time staff and its interest in feminist politics, which were replaced by more traditional feminine endeavours in the support of men once a male producer and writer were employed full-time. Skoog emphasizes that these changes are closely linked with deeply gendered discourses of the private and the public. More importantly, in the early years of the serial, the discourses about the private brought to the fore key social and political debates of the time, meaning that *Mrs Dale's Diary*, even in its discussions of the most intimate relationships – such as those of a mother and her child – ultimately always addressed the public as well. Skoog therefore concludes that the serial offers a particularly noteworthy site in which the redefinition of gender roles and the merging of private and public concerns in the experiences of women in the supposedly antifeminist post-war era can be observed.

A similar concern with discourses surrounding content directed at women is evident in Weissmann's chapter. Here, scheduling practices are investigated in relation to their impact of meanings available around the series under discussion. Weissmann examines in particular how the development of a dedicated slot in the afternoon for women's programming meant that some of the more feminist meanings of a range of American sitcoms shown on the British Channel 4 were undermined. In the context of the history of the public service broadcaster, which gained the responsibility to sell its own advertising nearly a decade after its initial inception, the decision to develop such a slot must be understood, Weissmann argues, as part of a move to abandon its original remit to provide content to minority or neglected groups, including ethnic minorities and women. Thus, the scheduling practice must be seen in the wider neoliberal context of deregulating television, which in Britain implies a return to more traditional definitions of gender roles, suggesting that the market, rather than really catering to everyone, as is so often suggested, actually enforces gender hierarchies.

Ball reaches similar conclusions in her discussion of recent British television drama centred on women. Placing her analysis in the context of and as national counterpoint to those about American female-centred dramas, Ball is particularly interested in representations of the working girl and the return to more traditional femininities and, crucially, masculinities in British drama of the early twenty-first century. In particular, the decision to cast younger women, dressed in tailored skirts and wearing long hair and make-up, seems an attempt to undermine their potential power in favour of consumerist 'empowerment' and choice narratives. Thus, these women appear as 'girlies', who are infantilized and follow the lead of older men who often display sexist attitudes. Ball argues that these dramas take part in the establishment of a 'new girl order', which is really an old patriarchal order. Ball hence argues vehemently for the return of feminist methodologies, including the use of the term *sexism*. Ball ends with a rallying cry for the repurposing of second-wave feminist tools to continue the work against a culture which repackages traditional gender roles as consumerist fantasies of empowerment and choice. The section then not only continues but explicitly returns to earlier feminist writing on television in order to expand its scope and impact.

7

'They're "Doped" by that Dale Diary'

Women's Serial Drama, the BBC and British Post-War Change

Kristin Skoog

Mrs Dale's Diary (1948),[1] a seemingly mundane soap opera – today very much forgotten or neglected in broadcasting and other histories – was at one point a radio phenomenon. The serial started on the BBC Light Programme in January 1948 and ended in 1969. It depicted the everyday life of a middle-class family in a North London suburb, the fictional Parkwood Hill. It followed the main character – Mary Dale, a doctor's wife – and her husband, Jim; their children, Bob and Gwen; and their friends and immediate family, including Mrs Dale's sister, Sally, and their mother, Mrs Freeman. The 15-minute broadcast was transmitted Monday to Friday at 4 p.m., and in 1949 a daily repeat was introduced at 11:45 a.m. The serial soon attracted millions of listeners and was particularly popular among women – largely, it seemed, because of its daytime placing in the schedule.[2] Most listeners were aged 30 and upwards; the majority from a working-class background.

This 'phenomenon', however, puzzled commentators within the BBC just as much as those outside. Comments in the press and critique from the BBC Drama management suggest that the serial's focus on the private, intimate, domestic side of life was a little too sordid for the BBC and not enough to differentiate it from its 'American counterparts'.[3] The BBC's Head of Drama, Val Gielgud, early expressed a resistance to soap operas and domestic serials, as documented by Michele Hilmes (2007), who has examined the BBC's first attempts to create a radio 'soap opera', *Front Line Family* (1941). It is clear that this 'resistance' continued well into the post-war period. Gielgud had a clear view on the matter: *Mrs Dale's Diary* was not of an 'aesthetic quality', nor was its audience reasonably intelligent. Instead, the serial was described by him as 'pabulum for the domestic hearth';[4] he was convinced that these kinds of serials were 'dramatically inept and sociologically corrupting'.[5]

Yet the serial had its defenders, too. Although *Mrs Dale's Diary* was fiercely criticized and its listeners seen or described as 'addicts', there were people who recognized its popularity and appeal and particularly the idea of identification: that listeners could recognize themselves or, rather, that popular culture (mass culture) was something that the majority of Light Programme listeners actually liked and were familiar with. The Acting Controller of the Light Programme, Tom Chalmers, strongly defending the serials *Mrs Dale's Diary* and *Dick Barton* (1946), pointed out that the aim of the Light Programme was to entertain a mass audience and that serials like these provided a pleasurable source of escapism.[6] It was also stressed, by the authors of a BBC audience research report on the serial, that the appeal of 'real' people and 'ordinary, homely credible incidents was very much in evidence'.[7] The family in the serial was middle class; most listeners of a working-class background appear not to have been a major problem. Instead, it is possible to argue that the popularity of the serial derived less from a 'class perspective' than from a 'gender perspective'. Women enjoyed the serial because they could identify with family life: relationships, marriage and motherhood. The serial offered a fusion of reality and fiction – rather, a way of bringing dramatic value to the apparently mundane. Thus, for example, on the BBC's own critics' programme, theatre critic M. R. Ridley suggested that 'a lot of ordinary people see the ordinary events of their own lives, as it might be, made into something dramatic, or semi-dramatic'. And the art critic J. M. Richards explained it thus: 'I think that is the appeal of it, that listeners are encouraged to identify themselves all the time with the Dale family, or to relate their own experiences with it, which gives it a kind of vicarious realism which you don't get in any other kind of programme.'[8] The serial thus offered companionship and identification. Each episode would create an end product that talked closely to the listeners; even prompting some listeners to feel as if the characters were for real. 'They are my friends', one listener said; another said, 'I feel as if the family were relations of mine or very close neighbours.'[9] Beneath the obvious plot – focused on family and relationships – one can detect a serial which is in itself dealing with the stresses and strains of post-war Britain and, specifically, with women's changing experiences.

The concept of separate 'public' and 'private' spheres is ambiguous, often problematic and highly contested (see Fraser 1989). This chapter is about distinctions of what 'private' and 'public' meant and how these distinctions were being defined differently by different groups, or different people, in midcentury Britain. *Mrs Dale's Diary* appears to have changed in content as it moved from a female-production-staff-dominated period mainly interested in the 'private' lives of women, to a mixed gender–dominated period interested in more 'public' debates. We can clearly see how the serial in its early years negotiated not just the role of women as mothers and workers but also expected and changing roles within marriage (and a middle-class family). In the transcripts, words and phrases such as a 'modern girl' were often juxtaposed with being 'old-fashioned', and the struggle to be a mother and a worker – the 'double burden' – was being examined dramatically, day after day, on air in front of an audience of millions of women. But the serial's focus on the domestic sphere was problematic for the BBC (and for some critics), whose main argument appears to have been that the serial was detached from public life, thus lacking social responsibility. As will be demonstrated below, once the serial changed its content to greater emphasis on topical and political issues – council housing, local elections, focus on the wider community – it gained recognition and some status within the BBC. Interestingly most of these 'public elements' occurred after the introduction of a permanent male producer and a male scriptwriter, suggesting a more 'masculine' version of the serial was more accepted.

These 'periodical' distinctions, however, are further problematic. Indeed issues that the serial covered even in its early days (domesticity and work, for instance) were widely debated in public discourse as part of a concern about post-war reconstruction. The domestic sphere – and women's responsibilities within this – was therefore acknowledged by contemporaries (and by historians since) as a major public interest. The early years of *Mrs Dale's Diary* is very much about the merging of the public and private realm; it was a public matter, for example – either way – whether women stayed at home or went out to work (just as rationing and austerity measures had implications in both public and private life; food control and consumption were heavily debated in Whitehall but it was experienced and debated by women on a daily basis). As Fraser (1989) highlighted in her feminist critique of the Habermasian public sphere, raising children, for example, is just as much a 'material' as a 'symbolic' reproduction since it has implications in the material world. The example thus demonstrates the importance of the private – and its complex relationship – to the public. These observations will be further untangled below.

Post-War Changes and Women's Lives

At one stage the overall historical perception of the British post-war period was quite simple: a country in the grip of austerity, where women who had been out at work in the war were now returning to domestic life; an era condemned by a generation of feminist writers as oppressive and stifling. Indeed, the image of the 1950s housewife is still one which is constantly reproduced in stereotypical fashion in contemporary discourse; as Melanie Bell has observed, 'this decade is lodged in the popular consciousness as a period of gender conservatism' (2010, 1). More recent studies, however, have complicated this image considerably and particularly highlighted how the home was a key feature at the centre of post-war social policy and thus post-war reconstruction (see Langhamer 2005). Rationing, austerity and affluence, and public health were all issues that were dealt with at a domestic level, but this 'private' level was at the same time interestingly political, public. Psychologists and politicians were all interested in the state of the family, and at the centre of the home was the post-war woman. As the key purchaser of food and clothes, she became a direct participant in the immediate post-war austerity and therefore an important political target. Due to labour shortages women were also needed as workers, and the removal of the marriage bar, together with the increasing availability of part-time work, meant that more married women could take up paid work (see Holloway 2005, Bourke 1994). Historians have therefore shown that women were considered important citizens, crucial for the rebuilding of Britain both as *mothers*, *workers* and *voters*, which ensued in debates about woman's role in society (see Lewis 1990, 1992; Thane 1994, 2003; Zweiniger-Bargielowska 2000; Holloway 2005). Concerns about marriage, motherhood, childcare, domesticity and work all affected the post-war woman and gave her a central role in the rebuilding of Britain.

One achievement of this recent work is to 'unpack' the changing patterns of work and domestic life as experienced by British women. The domestic role presented to women has, for instance, been examined by

Stephanie Spencer (2005), who studied the various roles of adult females that were presented to young girls in the 1950s. By approaching a range of sources, such as social policy documents, employment manuals, career novels and magazines, she shows that the domestic role presented to women was not always looked upon as oppressive at the time; rather, it gave women a high status. Spencer also points out that employment for women in combination with domesticity was presented as something important and that women were seen not just as a 'spare workforce'. Instead, 'career's advice placed emphasis on the process of choosing suitable paid work which could be interrupted, not terminated, by a domestic interlude' (2005, 79). And further, that 'girls and women's participation in the work force was seen as part of their duties of citizenship and social responsibility' (2005, 80). It became more accepted for a married woman to work, and the cycle of combining part-time work with motherhood was for many seen as the 'ideal' solution, as theorized at the time by academics such as Alva Myrdal and Viola Klein (1956).

Spencer is not alone in questioning prevailing assumptions about the post-war period. Judy Giles has argued that 'the fact that domesticity was such a key issue in the late 1940s and early 1950s enabled many middle-class women to speak as housewives and mothers' (2004, 162). She further suggests that 'the home, far from being simply a haven from the demands of modern life or a stifling place from which to escape, became central to the modernity of British life mid-century' (2004, 60). One particularly useful aspect of Giles's analysis is her discussion on suburbia, where she looks more closely at some of the criticisms and fears of 'the masses', as expressed in George Orwell's book *Coming Up for Air*, published in 1939. Orwell and other intellectuals saw suburbia and its association with everyday life, often linked to femininity, as something degrading. Suburbia was lowering and cheapening, in contrast to the modernity of the urban, masculine ideas about the city. But Giles argues that for many, especially for lower middle- and working-class women, suburbia did give a sense of modernity. It represented something better, as illustrated by the example of Joyce Storey, a working-class woman from Bristol who moved into a new council house after the Second World War. Her encounter with the modern was the experience of a bathroom, a luxury she had never had before, and this, Giles explains, symbolizes a distance from Joyce's past. Suburban modernity offered something new, and she argues that it was just as important as the vote in 'enabling people to see themselves as full members of a modern society' (2004, 49). The emerging image, then, of post-war womanhood is therefore more complex, as Bell (2010, 10) has put it: 'the contours of normative femininity were clearly under pressure, being transformed and rendered increasingly ambiguous by the greater economic, social and sexual freedoms that many women experienced'. It is in the field of 'ordinary life' – suburban, family, domestic, 'feminine' – that changes in post-war Britain can vividly be seen and understood. These changes and tensions were apparent in popular culture, and *Mrs Dale's Diary* is a vivid example of this complexity.

It is worth highlighting that most of the scriptwriters of the serial were women: Jonquil Antony, Melissa Wood, Lesley Wilson and Joan Carr-Jones. The Dale 'office' was organized by a Mrs Jean Child, who was in charge of keeping records of storylines, characters, scripts, listener research and so on.[10] At several times it was noted in the press coverage that the scriptwriters often took inspiration from real life. Antony, for example, in 1951 ran a series of articles in the *Daily Graphic*, where she was described as one of the highest-paid women at the BBC – spending her time between her Kensington flat and Hampshire cottage. She made the point that the writers, including her, were all married women with their own homes to run.[11] Antony revealed that quite often it was events in their own lives that provided inspiration and copy for the serial. She said in one article that when Mrs Dale was on a diet this was due to Joan Carr-Jones's experience of dieting, and Sally's dog Bella was based on Antony's own experience taking care of an ill-treated dog.[12]

In the serial's first years many of the storylines revolved around family and relationships, and some revealed a quite intimate style in dialogue and tone; others were distinctly more 'escapist' in nature. One example in 1949 was Mrs Dale's friendship to the foreign Count de Renzy, a relationship echoing that of Laura and Alec in *Brief Encounter* (1945). Another example of an extended examination of human relationships and, in particular, the tension in a post-war marriage can be found when Sally married Stephen, a foreign correspondent. Sally was in many ways the complete opposite to Mrs Dale. She was divorced once and remarried twice, her character clearly more independent.[13] Her lack of domestic skills is referred to at various times in the scripts. In the BBC's editorial policy from 1949, she was portrayed as being 35, more 'gay' than her sister, sometimes selfish and a quite flirtatious person.[14] Although fairly 'boisterous', Sally was quite a sympathetic character and very popular among the listeners. In 1951 the *Daily Express* referred to her as a 'national hero'.[15] Settling into married life was never going to be easy for Sally. In one episode she quibbled with her husband and told him, 'Well, I shall dress how I want to. You can't dictate to me about things like that.' And, she continued, 'You get awfully bossy sometimes, Stephen. You forget that I've been on my own so long – I must be allowed to lead my own life.'[16] Sally emphasized in a later episode that Stephen 'never expected [her] to be domesticated'.[17] In a conversation with Dr Dale, she was asked if she was happy with Stephen. Sally replied, 'I'm divinely happy with him – when he's here. But he never seems to be here, does he?'[18] Sally was also often portrayed as a 'modern' woman. For example, in one episode her mother, Mrs Freeman, was invited to join her and Stephen for dinner. Sally, all excited, had cooked the food in a pressure cooker, something Mrs Freeman was not keen on: 'Well, I like to think I've kept abreast with the times, but I don't like these modern inventions, Stephen.'[19]

There are frequent references to characters as 'old-fashioned', spot-lighting a tension between tradition and change. These tensions, how-ever, are particularly felt through Mrs Dale's daughter, Gwen, who illustrates most persistently generational and gendered experiences of change. In 1949 she was described, by the programme's editorial policy, as being 19 and 'approaching the time when she will decide whether to pursue a professional career, marry and devote herself to domesticity, or attempt to combine a career and married life'. The policy continued: 'From time to time these questions exercise her mind considerably. She is often irked by the restrictions of family life and on those occasions regards independence as a primary objective. Alternately, she finds the idea of leaving home unthinkable.'[20] Gwen represented the new genera-tion of women who had a choice of whether to stay at home or continue to work after marriage. But she also conveyed vividly how difficult this choice was. In the first years of the serial Gwen was keen to pursue a career and started to work as a secretary to a glass and china exporter. Her grandmother Mrs Freeman was especially supportive: 'She can go on with her career after she's married, can't she? That's what all the girls seem to be doing these days. Don't keep harping on marriage, Mary – let the child concentrate on her career.'[21] Gwen who was very happy about the job and the prospects of a career also made the point that her generation was different from her mother's:

> I don't want to marry anyone for ages. I want to go about and meet
> people and learn things [...] well, I'd like to go abroad and see a bit
> of the world before I settle down. I know you're very happy, mummy,
> but you were awfully young when you got married. Not much older
> than I am. And you never had a job or anything.[22]

Gwen had several romances, and over the years the scriptwriters tossed Gwen back and forth between work and domesticity. Once married and after her first child, Gwen decided to stay at home full-time; her

child came first. But her decision did not come easily and was negotiated in the script over nearly a year. For example, in the early stage of
her pregnancy, Gwen wanted to keep working as long as she could. But
it was clear that her husband, David, wanted her to stay at home. In one
episode Gwen told her friend Maud French about the dilemma:

> Maud: Oh, my dear! But you mustn't! It would make such a differ-
> ence to you financially –
> Gwen: Not if we have to pay someone to look after the baby!
> Maud: But you'd find it so dull! [...] Gwen, and you'd be bored to
> tears staying at home all day with a baby – nobody to talk to but the
> milkman! [...] I think you'd be most unwise to tie yourself like that,
> dear! You'd lose all contact with the outside world, and *anyone* will tell
> you that's bound to make you – well, a little dull, maybe. It keeps one
> alive, Gwen dear, to have outside interests. And, whatever you say,
> I'm sure David likes being married to a modern girl with a career!
> Gwen: (*Rather wearily*) Perhaps, Maud – but he'll just have to get
> used to being married to an old-fashioned girl with a baby!

The words 'old-fashioned' and 'modern' are set against each other. The
use of the word 'modern' is here implying a fuller personal life, which
includes the combination of marriage and a career. Gwen, later in the
episode, told her grandmother Mrs Freeman about the issue:

> Mrs Freeman: You don't make enough [fuss]! In my day it wasn't
> heard of for a young woman who was expecting a baby to go out
> to work as well! It's quite wrong, and David shouldn't let you! [...]
> Your child must come first, Gwen, it would be quite wrong for you
> to attempt to stay on as Richard Fulton's secretary. It can't be done –
> one or the other would be neglected, and you'd worry yourself into a
> nervous breakdown![23]

This passage demonstrates the influence of child psychologists in the
post-war period, which stressed the dangers of leaving youngsters, with
the consequences of juvenile delinquency or 'latch-key' children. John
Bowlby's *Child Care and the Growth of Love* (1953) and similar books
became increasingly popular, and these thoughts were picked up by
social workers and guidance counsellors and considered central even
outside the world of psychology (Lewis 1992, 18). The 'state' of the family was of importance to the nation; thus women's domestic role did
have public consequences. A woman's decision either to stay at home
or to work was now of major public interest; it was no longer a 'private',
intimate decision. It was debated and negotiated – even on national

radio – acknowledged by the scriptwriters as a key issue for women's changing experience. Interestingly the serial recognized the need felt by some women to have a job and not to be 'housebound', predating early second-wave feminists, such as Betty Friedan (1963), who criticized the mass media image of a woman who would only be fulfilled by staying in the home. Writing about second-wave feminism, S. Thornham sums it up: '"[S]econd wave" feminism [...] sought both to voice or "name" women's immediate and subjective experience and to formulate a political agenda and vision' (2000, 47). Although *Mrs Dale's Diary* did not formulate 'a political agenda and vision', it clearly raised questions concerning women's subjective experience and placed it within the discourse of a decidedly women-centred post-war reconstruction. The serial thus indicates that the image of the domestic sphere was, at least in Britain, more complicated than previously suggested.

Later, after having baby Billy, Gwen returned to part-time work, and Billy was left with Mrs Dale. But working *and* taking care of the home proved too much for Gwen: 'It would be all right if I had nothing to do when I got back, but, of course, there's all Billy's washing and ironing and the flat and – oh, one thing and another. Still, I expect I'll get used to it.'[24] In March 1953 listeners complained about Gwen leaving Billy too much with her mother; consequently it was decided by the producer and the scriptwriters that Gwen would focus more on her family and her home, and a few months later she left her job altogether.[25] Listeners clearly felt that it was not appropriate for Gwen to work, and they had an impact on the outcome of the storyline. According to a listener research report made in 1952, the majority of listeners were of an older age, above 30, with many 50 years and over.[26] This indicates that listeners' attitudes towards work and domesticity were clearly shaped and influenced by age, suggesting generational change.[27]

Private and Public Worlds?

Although the serial was hugely popular, it was under threat of cancellation by the Drama Department several times. The critique it faced led to several changes, and in 1952 *Mrs Dale's Diary* began to transform. Measures had already been taken inside the BBC in the early 1950s to make the *Diary*, in their view, more topical and outward looking (in a sense, less 'feminine'). This transformation appears to have been prompted by three incidents: first, changes to the editorial policy; second, increasing competition; and third, reorganization in the production, with the appointment of a 'fixed' male producer and a male scriptwriter.

The first change to the serial can be seen in the editorial policy. According to the critics within and outside the BBC, the characters in the serial, overall, lacked an interest in the 'outside' world – for instance, topical events and politics – which to them implied vagueness about their social status: they did not behave as middle-class people. In 1950 an outside commentator was commissioned to produce an independent report on the serial, focusing on the social status of the family. In the finished report was this highlight: 'the fact that they [the characters] make no comment on any events of the day – either sport, theatre, films, music or politics, or anything other than local details – tends to produce a feeling that they are isolated from the normal features which play a part in other people's lives.'[28] It was further clear that the family's geographical location and neighbourhood implied certain status (middle class), but the family's behaviour did not comply with this, since such important details as religion, community relationships, sport, politics – the elements or parts that are defined by a family's social status – were absent. The report also coincided with a plea from the scriptwriters, Lesley Wilson, Jonquil Anthony and Joan Carr-Jones, for a change in policy. The strict editorial policy set out in 1949 had made it clear that characters should remain 'permanent' – not allowed to change, remaining 'mentally, physically and spiritually intact – the same people, in the same stage of development, tied to the same background, inhibited by the same hopes and fears with which they were introduced.'[29] This was not feasible from a creative point of view, as the scriptwriters pointed out: listeners would find it unnatural and not representative of a 'real-life' family to not progress.[30] The report and the plea resulted in small policy changes; for example, references to cinema and books and Mrs Dale's activities on various committees, such as the Women's Voluntary Services, were introduced.[31]

The second influence on the serial was the competition it faced from *The Archers*. In 1952 it was evident that *The Archers* had taken over in popularity, with a listening figure double that of *Mrs Dale's Diary*.[32] *The Archers*, a domestic serial about a farming community, was introduced on the Light Programme in January 1951; it was first broadcast in the morning but later at 6:45 p.m. Significantly *The Archers* had more men listening due to its later airtime; also, a more mixed group of listeners in terms of age.[33] Going through its early archival records it is further apparent that the production team was male dominated (in contrast to that of the *Diary*); the editor was Godfrey Baseley, and the scriptwriters Edward J. Mason and Geoffrey Webb.[34] *The Archers'* writing and production process, with emphasis on longer storylines that developed over time and regular script meetings, was seen by the Light Programme management as a good working model and would thus be applied to *Mrs Dale's Diary*.[35] By October 1952 small changes in the editorial policy began to be noted, and with increasing competition from *The Archers*, the serial began to see a new emphasis on research and topical 'outward-looking' storylines. One of the first focused on Mrs Dale's son, Bob, who would be the victim of dishonest estate agents and consequently be caught up in a 'housing racket'. These changes would start to transform the serial, but it would take a new direction with the third incident: the introduction of a male scriptwriter and the addition of an 'executive producer'.

In 1953, when scriptwriter Lesley Wilson left the serial to have a baby, Basil Dawson was hired. Dawson was an actor and playwright, and the press release that the BBC released on his appointment suggested he would bring '[a] male angle on the Diary'.[36] A few months later another male arrived. Being a domestic serial *Mrs Dale's Diary* was from its very inception categorized (and devalued) as popular, feminized mass culture, mainly written by women for a female audience, and therefore it was not admired among BBC producers. This had resulted in producers' working on a rota or in the engagement of outside producers on an ad hoc basis.[37] This changed with the appointment of Antony Kearey – an actor who had started to work on the serial as Assistant in the Drama Department Script Unit – and in June 1953 he was hired as the main producer for the serial.[38] His appointment would enable greater editorial control and continuity. As main producer he was dedicated and keen to improve the serial. Already in April, he had responded to a plea made by the Chief Assistant to the Light Programme to make the serial more topical by suggesting that a complete break with the current editorial policy was needed and that national events could be mentioned.[39] Before Kearey's appointment it had also been confirmed that the serial was to be allocated not just a producer but also an assistant – Betty Davies, who took over as the main producer when Kearey left in 1955 – and that the budget for the serial would increase from £287.10s to £290 per week (the budget increase was also to enable greater topicality).[40] A few months into his new position, Kearey said that the main priority was to raise the level of scripts by better reflecting the life of a middle-class family in a London suburb: 'greater research by scriptwriters into their material is necessary if the past "vagueness" is to be overcome', he continued. Kearey also emphasized that, 'the diary should reflect current trends of thought and opinion on matters of interest

to Londoners [...] a simple example being the rise in transport fares'.[41]
A consequence of the changes was that the serial steered more towards
content that often involved the community. For example, the building
of a new housing estate which threatened the peace of Parkwood Lodge
would see Mrs Dale together with other residents forming a Resident's
Protest Committee, along the way falling out with her husband, who
was in support of the housing scheme. In 1954 it was also planned that
builders working on a nursing home would go on strike and that family
members would have different views on this.[42]

It was in this context that it was noted by a senior member of the
Light Programme, in a memo to the Head of Drama, that 'there is beginning to be a new "sense of responsibility" in these scripts which, without
destroying the fictional attraction, is making the series slightly more real
and in consequence more attractive.'[43] Focus was increasingly placed on
topicality and research, and according to a report in 1954 the Appreciation
Index for the programme had increased.[44] With the changes it appears
that the serial gained new listeners – and different ones. In 1955, Kearey
noted that he had received many listener requests for an omnibus edition of the programme on Sundays and that many of these came from
men. This, he continued, 'would seem to indicate that the programme
has broadened its sphere of interest and is now reaching a potentially
new public I referred to when I first came to the programme.'[45] In the
view of the BBC Drama management *Mrs Dale's Diary* clearly changed
from being a fairly typical domestic drama with a focus on the feminine,
the personal and the intimate into a more outward-looking serial with
longer storylines and emphasis on topicality.

Conclusions

In the 1930s and 1940s critics were keen to judge soap operas for being
far too obsessed with the home and the personal, as Charlotte Brunsdon
has put it: 'the elevation of the individual over the social, the private over
the public' (2000, 46). This chapter has tried to highlight the changing
definitions or distinctions between the 'private' and the 'public' in the
British post-war period. *Mrs Dale's Diary* aimed to hold a mirror to daily
life, but being early on characterized as too 'feminine', it thus struggled
to be taken seriously. The female scriptwriters clearly believed that
concerns about marriage, domesticity and work were of public interest.
Obviously women's experiences would have varied, depending on age,
class and social and educational background. But as mothers and wives

and as workers, listeners could identify with some of the dilemmas or at least find some recognition. As Giles (2004, 24) has argued, 'life stories, letters, diaries and fiction have [...] traditionally functioned as a space in which women could articulate their sense of the world.' This aspect of the 'everyday' was evident in *Mrs Dale's Diary*, which dealt with the events and happenings, the worries and concerns of modern life. This seemingly mundane soap opera worked particularly well as a site where post-war womanhood could be confirmed, negotiated and challenged and issues of class identity and behaviour further explored. The period may have lacked the fury and noise of second-wave feminism, so notable in the 1960s and 1970s, but there is evidence that there was clearly a consciousness raising about women's changing experience.

Mrs Dale's Diary took part in a redefinition of what 'public' meant; and increasingly that included the 'private'. Debates around marriage and work – the double burden – were clearly questions of public and national interest (as seen in the work by Bowlby and by Myrdahl and Klein, for example). The focus on the feminine, the personal and the intimate side of life was, however, not good enough for the BBC and other critics who loathed the serial. Changes brought by increasing competition, pressure applied from within and without the BBC and, in particular, the introduction of a 'male angle' suggest that the serial's feminine redefinition of the public was too radical; it had to eventually be replaced by a more masculine outlook, one understood to be synonymous with 'social responsibility'.

The early radio soap opera therefore affords a unique opportunity to investigate how at specific times 'the public' became defined. For *Mrs Dale's Diary*, the BBC suggested it encompassed the masculine world of work and politics: questions on housing (the building of council housing), emphasis on the community rather than the family, builders on strike and the like. However, the early years of the serial captured post-war tensions in the redefinition of the public as already encompassing the private, indicating fluctuations between tradition and modernity. This was a time when clearly private and public roles and responsibilities were being changed and redefined, and the example further demonstrates how complex these redefinitions were.

Acknowledgements

Archival citations are from the BBC Written Archives Centre, Caversham Park, Reading (unless otherwise specified). My thanks to

Jacqueline Kavanagh and the staff at the BBC Written Archives Centre. I am also grateful to Elke Weissmann and Helen Thornham for their useful comments and feedback.

Notes

1. *The Star*: 'They're "Doped" by That Dale Diary', by Denis Atherton, 28 November 1950.
2. Popular programmes that attracted audiences were, according to Asa Briggs (1979), seen as 'castle' programmes (using the chess term), meaning they 'draw an audience wherever placed' (56).
3. The editorial policy set out in 1949 states: 'this serial has a simple object: to hold a mirror to the everyday life of a normal, middle-class family. It is not a soap-opera of the kind which abounds in American daytime radio [...] In other words, *Mrs Dale's Diary* should strive to achieve a realism which is specifically withheld from its American counterparts.' BBC Written Archives Centre, Caversham (hereafter BBC WAC), R19/779/1: 'Editorial Policy', 26 May 1949.
4. BBC WAC R19/280/5: Memo from H.D. to Acting Controller, Light Programme, 31 March 1948.
5. BBC WAC R19/280/6: Memo from Head of Drama to CLP, 23 August 1949.
6. BBC WAC R19/280/6: Memo from Controller, Light Programme, to H.D., 31 August 1949.
7. BBC WAC R9/9/16: 'Listener Research Report', LR/52/941, 21 August 1952.
8. BBC WAC Programme as Broadcast Transcript, *The Critics*, 9 November 1952.
9. BBC WAC R9/9/16: 'Listener Research Report', LR/52/941, 21 August 1952.
10. *Daily Graphic*, 'Backroom Girl Turns Diary Pages', by Jonquil Antony, 24 March 1951.
11. *Daily Graphic*, 'Mrs Dale's Secret', by Jonquil Antony, 19 March 1951.
12. *Good Housekeeping*, 'Looking Back on 4 Years with Mrs Dale', by Jonquil Antony, March 1952.
13. For example, Sally worked in a florist shop and eventually became manager. In 1954 she ventured into her own business: a hat shop in the West End. BBC WAC R19/779/3: 'Script conference', 4 March 1954.
14. BBC WAC R19/779/1: 'Editorial Policy', 26 May 1949.
15. *Daily Express*, '"Sally Lane", friend of millions, quits "Mrs Dale's Diary"', by Robert Cannell, 9 November 1951.
16. BBC WAC Programme as Broadcast Transcript, Episode 256, 3 January 1949.
17. BBC WAC Programme as Broadcast Transcript, Episode 394, 19 July 1949.
18. BBC WAC Programme as Broadcast Transcript, Episode 440, 22 September 1949.

19. BBC WAC Programme as Broadcast Transcript, Episode 216, 6 November 1948.

20. BBC WAC R19/779/1: 'Editorial Policy', 26 May 1949.

21. BBC WAC Programme as Broadcast Transcript, Episode 197, 11 October 1948.

22. BBC WAC Programme as Broadcast Transcript, Episode 201, 15 October 1948.

23. BBC WAC Programme as Broadcast Transcript, Episode 1132, 19 June 1952.

24. BBC WAC Programme as Broadcast Transcript, Episode 1304, 19 February 1953.

25. BBC WAC R19/779/3: 'Script conference' no. 106, 12 March 1953; 'Script conference' no. 107, 26 March 1953; Programme as Broadcast Transcript, Episode 1358, 11 May 1953.

26. BBC WAC R9/9/16: 'Listener Research Report', LR/52/941, 21 August 1952.

27. In the BBC's other main women's programme, *Woman's Hour* (1946), it had been noted a few years earlier that the 'mailbag' had received a large number of letters from grandmothers showing strongly worded criticism about 'the lack of pleasures displayed by the young mothers in their children and home duties'; the criticism prompted the suggestion of a discussion between mothers of 1910 against mothers of 1950. BBC WAC R41/243: 'Summary of Woman's Hour Post for Week Ending 3. 3. 50'.

28. BBC WAC R19/779/1: McMillan to Adam, 'A report on the social status of the Dale family', November 1950.

29. BBC WAC R19/779/1: 'Editorial Policy', 26 May 1949.

30. BBC WAC R19/779/1: Letter to Cleland Finn, 30 November 1950.

31. BBC WAC R19/779/2: 'Script Conference' no. 83, 20 March [1952].

32. In January 1952 the figure for *Mrs Dale* was 13 per cent and *The Archers* 19 per cent, and by June 1952 the figure was even lower: *Mrs Dale* 10 per cent and *The Archers* 19 per cent. These daily listening figures were based on an estimated percentage of the adult civilian population of Great Britain; BBC WAC R9/12/7: 'Barometers: Listening: Daily', 15 January and 27 June 1952.

33. BBC WAC R9/9/16: 'Listener Research Report', LR/52/941, 21 August 1952.

34. BBC WAC R19/47/1: Entertainment *The Archers*, 1950–1953.

35. John McMillan, Chief Assistant to LP, suggested that the technique he applied to the *Archers* team should be tested on the *Diary*. BBC WAC R19/779/2: Memo from McMillan to Lefeaux, 1 August 1952.

36. BBC WAC R44/277: 'A male angle on the Diary' [press release], 13 April 1953.

37. BBC WAC R19/779/3: Memo from A.A. Drama to A. R. Bell, 13 January 1953.

38. BBC WAC R19/779/3: Letter, 'Charge to *Mrs Dale's Diary* Budget' [to Kearey with contract enclosed], 11 June, 1953.

39. BBC WAC R19/779/3: Assistant Script Unit Drama (Sound) to AAHD (Sound), 27 April 1953.

40. BBC WAC R19/779/3: Memo from A.A. Drama (Sound) to A.O. (Ent), 29 May. On topicality, see BBC WAC R19/779/3: Memo from Mr. H. Rooney Pelletier to CLP, 10 April 1953.

41. BBC WAC R19/779/3: 'Script Conference' no. 116, 13 August 1953.

42. BBC WAC R19/779/5: Memo from Pelletier to CLP, 23 December 1954.

43. BBC WAC R19/779/4: Memo from Mr. H. Rooney Pelletier to HD (S.), 25 November 1953.

44. The Appreciation Index is a BBC-specific form of audience measurement, indicating not numbers but how much audiences liked or disliked the series. In 1948 the Appreciation Index for the serial drama had been 56, in 1952 the figure was 62, and in 1954 it had an average of 65. BBC WAC R19/779/5: Memo [see attached report] from Mr. A. Kearey to CLP and Mr. H. Rooney Pelletier, 4 October 1954.

45. BBC WAC R19/1788/1: Memo from Mr. Antony Kearey to H. Rooney Pelletier, 18 February 1955.

Scheduling as Feminist Issue

UK's Channel 4 and US Female-Centred Sitcoms

Elke Weissmann

In the early years of the twenty-first century, an increasing number of British journalists again[1] bemoaned the feminization of television and the consequent loss of quality in the programme schedules. The highest-profile complainants were two prominent broadcasters, Jeremy Paxman and Michael Burke, who argued that women were taking over the high-powered positions in television and were consequently filling the schedules with insignificant entertainment (West 2008; Savage 2008). The claims made by the broadcasters regarding women's role in television are easily refuted, despite some successes chronicled in Ball's chapter. Women remain in lower positions than most of their male counterparts, and where they are successful, they are usually greeted with bile and contempt.[2] However, the idea that the schedules have become more feminized needs further investigation, particularly as there are indications that in the late 1990s, there was a move to offer more clearly established slots for women.

One of these slots has attracted the attention of the Midlands Television Research Group (MTVRG; Brunsdon et al. 2001), which focused on the ostensibly 'feminized' 8-to-9 p.m. slot (Brunsdon 2003) on British terrestrial television in the 1990s, a slot which was largely filled with lifestyle and factual entertainment programming. The group highlighted that the move of traditional daytime programming into the slot opened up discourses and spaces, traditionally gendered 'feminine' to men (Moseley 2001, 32), while commentators were still devaluating women-centred programming and characterizing the often female-oriented afternoon schedules with a 'dismissive tone reminiscent of early criticism of women's genres in literature, cinema and television' and often described them as 'undemanding and, by extension, uninteresting' (Moseley 2000, 300; see Ang 1985 for similar arguments about the prime-time soaps).

This chapter continues in this tradition by offering an investigation of how one – apparently progressive – channel was still constructing the afternoon schedule as a slot dedicated to women at a time when women were actually rarely available to watch. As I will point out, such a construction of the afternoon schedules as targeted at women had a significant impact on additional meanings offered around the programmes placed there, causing a devaluation of programmes that engaged quite explicitly with feminist concerns. The chapter will reintroduce a more complex understanding of hermeneutics as theoretical framework to the study of television and will highlight how this theory can allow us to investigate how meaning is *agreed upon* (rather than made) between television makers and audiences in the *continuing* frameworks that television offers. In this light, scheduling, as a means to control the industry's relationship to audiences in ways similar to audience measurement (Ang 1991), can be understood to take part in the essentialization of gender and gendered address, which we see more generally develop in the 1990s (Negra 2009), addressing women as either stay-at-home housewives or singles, eternally connected to the search for Mr Right. Scheduling, then, a much underinvestigated topic in the area of television studies anyway, demands a more sustained feminist analysis in order to counter this essentialization and perhaps also to intervene in the attempts to control our relationship to television.

Philosophical Hermeneutics

Although a basic hermeneutics – that is, the science of interpretation – underlies much scholarship in television (Brunsdon and Spigel 2008, 6), few writers have so far worked through the more complex aspects of a philosophical hermeneutics in order to theorize the reading processes involved in television spectatorship. Tony Wilson's *Watching Television* (1993) is one of the few theoretical engagements with Husserl (1970) and Gadamer (1965) that is utilized for understanding how meaning is created when watching television.

As Wilson highlights, such an understanding means that neither the text nor the viewer is in the foreground. Rather, the central interest of a hermeneutic understanding must be in the reading *processes* involved in making sense of television. These processes include the movement between the different positions that are offered by the text and those already existent in the viewer's a priori knowledge. David Morley (1980) has shown how this process can lead to significantly different understandings of a single text, a fact also emphasized by Newcomb and Hirsch (1983). As a consequence, Newcomb and Hirsch argue, it is less important what solutions television texts offer than that they raise certain questions at all in order to start a discussion which allows television to act 'as a cultural forum' (1983). Such an understanding of television texts and audiences has been embraced by feminists, who similarly point to television texts as offering a beginning for the construction of diverse and sometimes contradictory meanings, depending on the viewers' backgrounds (Ang 1985, 1991; Dow 1996). Thus, meaning is also always dependent on social environment; hence, inherently intersubjective: meaning and knowledge are developed in a constant play between the individual and the social world. Within this context, 'horizons', a key term for both Gadamer and Husserl, 'denote these definitional frameworks: they are emphatically social in origin, existing prior to the particular individual' (Wilson 1993, 15).

If horizons exist in a shared commonality, they also allow us to predict what something is before we see its full extent. As Wilson points out,

> directed at our surroundings and for the most part supporting our anticipations concerning them, our horizons of understanding generate a sense of the already experienced. As they thus constitute the familiarity of a life-world, horizons allow a cultural knowledge to be used and (apparently) confirmed. (1993, 17)

Horizons, therefore, are part of the experience of common ground which, Wilson argues in reference to Habermas (1987), is necessary to facilitate communication.

Wilson discusses how, for example, talk TV develops a common ground by addressing an intended audience with an assumed cultural horizon. But he also points to the inevitable difference between the horizons of an ideal audience, constructed by the text, and a real member of the audience. As he writes, 'the complete closure of the epistemic "gap" between text and "empirical" reader is logically impossible.

Reading is always appropriation of meaning from a position of greater or lesser semiotic difference' (1993, 21).

Wilson's theorization is particularly useful for an understanding that relates to reading processes of particular programmes. By highlighting the 'epistemic gap' between assumed horizon of an intended audience and the horizon of an empirical or 'real' audience in relation to programmes, he can give an explanation to why texts are polysemic (Fiske 1987) and viewers tend to develop negotiated readings of texts rather than dominant or oppositional ones (Morley 1980). But such an understanding requires that horizons already exist and therefore that what television offers is comparable to the life-world and experience of its audiences. Programmes with an indexical relation to the real world offer such an opportunity. But this becomes more problematic with something as ephemeral as scheduling.

Wilson argues that the schedules 'define the passing of time, producing a "regulation of simultaneous experience"' (1993, 24), thus essentially replacing the clock. But as the work of Hill and Calcutt (2000) highlights, something more complex is going on: schedules are filled with meaning beyond that of time, which viewers are aware of and negotiate. Indeed, Hill and Calcutt discuss how British adult fans of *Buffy: The Vampire Slayer* (WB, 1997–2003) and *Angel* (WB, 1999–2004) protested against the scheduling of the programmes in early evening slots on the grounds that these slots addressed a teenage audience, which meant that the programmes had to be cut and modified, hence changing the meaning of the two series. Importantly, part of the fans' objection also stemmed from their being assumed to be predominantly teenage.

These meanings connected to address need to be further unravelled in order to understand the importance of scheduling to the feminist project. The philosophical hermeneutics of Gadamer (1965), with its emphasis on *process*, seems a particularly useful tool to develop this further, as it allows us to unravel how meanings are agreed upon between audiences and schedulers. For audiences, schedules create rituals and repetition. An investigation of their mechanisms continues Newcomb and Hirsch's project to focus on 'process rather than […] product' (1983, 47) by indicating how scheduling contexts develop additional meanings around programmes. Such additional meanings are part of the industry's attempt to categorize and systematize the audience's relationship with television. Much like audience measurements on which it is supposedly based, scheduling assumes that audience groups are relatively homogenous and will watch and understand programming in anticipatable ways (Ang 1991). Thus scheduling constructs an ideal audience;

more importantly, construction of such an ideal audience also affects what we expect a programme to be like.

Such an understanding requires, first, that we focus our attention more strongly again on aspects of *continuance and repetition* in the televisual text (understood here as the web of programmes, trailers, ads and other segments which are broadcast). Secondly, this necessitates that we rethink the definition of horizon as something that is always changing. Horizons, in Wilson's definition, appear as relatively fixed; partially prior to the individual, partially connected to a viewer's life experience; in the moment of reading they are prior to the text and hence fixed in the moment. But as Gadamer highlights, the fusion of horizons, which occurs in the moment of reading/understanding, also means a shifting of them and often the creation of new ones.

For Gadamer, the central condition to all understanding is commonality. However commonality is not pre-given, but partially beginning and partially a result of the hermeneutic process. At the beginning of the hermeneutic process lie legitimate prejudices. These do not involve a wrong judgement but pre-existing judgements which allow us to *decide* what is false and what right: they constitute our knowledge. Pre-existing knowledge or legitimate prejudices are part of the society with which we have engaged and have developed gradually and are connected to tradition. They are thus part of the common experience we share. The person attempting understanding engages in a process of gradual unravelling of meaning – the hermeneutic circle – which leads to the development of understanding and thus new commonalities. Gadamer continues thus:

> The circle is then not of formal nature. It is neither subjective nor objective, but describes the process of understanding as the interplay of the movement of custom and tradition and the movement of the interpreter. The anticipation of sense which guides our understanding of a text is not an action of subjectivity but proceeds from the commonality which connects us to custom and tradition. *This commonality is in a constant process of becoming in our relation to tradition. It is not simply a precondition which always already guides us, but we create it ourselves, if we understand, take part in the process of tradition and thereby determine it further.* (1965, 298–9; my emphasis)[3]

Importantly, this suggests that tradition and its connected meanings are in a constant process of becoming, too, and that they rely essentially on the processes of understanding conducted by individuals. It is in this context that the meanings surrounding scheduling can be unravelled.

Scheduling develops traditions. If scheduling is about the passing of time, it is also about the organization of time and in particular the organization of time for particular audience groups. As a process in the production of television, scheduling is about gaining the largest or most desirable audience groups possible at specific times, and it is in this respect that demographic figures, as provided by BARB in the UK and Nielsen in the USA, play an important part. John Ellis (2000) points out that the BARB figures are studied for who watches what when by schedulers but that the demographics are also interpreted in relation to assumed likes and dislikes of particular audience groups. Thus, underlying the scheduling process is an assumed audience with assumed hermeneutic horizons. Importantly, one key demographic factor is that of gender, particularly in more recent years as advertisers have focused on women as an important target group (see Lotz 2006). Thus, as scheduling develops traditions, it also develops notions of gender and in many ways genders time slots for consumption purposes.

Ellis (2000, 26–7) highlights that schedules work as a grid of relatively arbitrary decisions around perceived typical viewing behaviour of a nation. Thus, although the BARB and Nielsen figures are studied, their lead is not always followed. Moreover, schedulers' decisions, Timothy Havens has shown (2007), are formed on the basis of observing the schedules in other countries rather than in the target nation. Importantly, audiences are aware of how the schedules operate and structure their days around them (Mikos 1994). This is perhaps most notable in relation to the British watershed at 9 p.m., which creates a division between family and adult viewing. Andrea Millwood Hargrave, who conducted audience research into the watershed, notes that the watershed as division is 'accepted and expected' (1995, 75) by viewers (see also Colquhoun 1995). In other words, audiences engage in a process of understanding, in which meaning is defined by target audience and therefore viewers are involved in the process of tradition making. Thus, the schedules are gradually established as a result of a tacit agreement between schedulers and viewers about whom particular slots are for. This is connected to address, genre, aesthetics, content and, perhaps most importantly, meaning.

Cathy Johnson (2005) has shown how specific meanings are gradually established for specific slots by discussing the early evening slot in which *Buffy* was first shown in Britain. She points to a tradition of programming in the slot that began with the teenage magazine programme *DEF II* (BBC, 1988–92) and continued over a series of repeats of cult and sci-fi programming, including *Dr Who* (BBC, 1963–89), *Star Trek* (NBC, 1966–9) and *Blake's 7* (BBC, 1978–81) to first showings of *Star Trek: The*

Next Generation (syndicated, 1987–94), *Star Trek: Deep Space Nine* (syndicated, 1993–9) and *Star Trek: Voyager* (UPN, 1995–2001) to eventually include *Buffy*. Johnson argues, rather than simply understand it as aimed at a teenage audience, the slot had by then become established also as a cult TV slot into which *Buffy*, with its cult theme centred on teenage protagonists, seemed to fit perfectly. In other words, Johnson unravels how specific meanings were agreed upon over time between producers and consumers.

In the following, I examine the development of a similar dedicated slot on Channel 4 in the 1990s. Instead of teenagers, this slot was aimed at women and created meanings around women's lives that were conservative at best. Importantly, it also impacted on the meanings developed around women's programming of a particular kind and suggested the development of a rigid, backward-looking televisual address.

Women-Centred Sitcoms on Channel 4

Channel 4's particular place in British broadcasting is determined by its remit to cater to previously neglected audiences. As Lez Cooke (2007) highlights, this diversity was originally offered primarily in dramas which challenged traditional formats and took into consideration minority interests, including those of women. As the years progressed, home-produced dramas were increasingly replaced by American imports, which often continued to represent minority interests.

In order to understand this development, Channel 4's particular institutional history needs further examination. Unlike most other public service broadcasters, Channel 4 is not paid for by a licence fee or set budget by the government but was originally funded by a levy that it received from the ITV franchises in return for its advertising time. As a consequence, Channel 4 had a secure and relatively large programming budget (particularly when compared with Channel 5; Fanthom 2003) which it could use to provide programming in line with its remit. But from the very beginning, Channel 4 was under pressure to deliver audiences to advertisers, and this pressure increased as it was put in charge of selling its own advertising time in 1993. However, the increased commercial orientation of Channel 4, in which the popular American imports played a significant part, started before 1993: Maggie Brown (2007) traces it back to the time Michael Grade took over as chief executive from Jeremy Isaacs in 1988, but indications for an earlier 'commercial turn' exist (Weissmann 2009). This emphasis increased as the 1990s progressed, when the general outlook of British broadcasting moved away from public service towards a more consumerist approach.

In the early years of Channel 4, American dramas and sitcoms were primarily understood as 'fillers', as a means to cover the holes which were left in the schedules (Brown 2007, 51). Within this climate, repeats of American sitcoms were used to set up a regular slot between 5:30 and 6:30 p.m. which was aimed at the whole family. The sitcoms included *Get Smart* (NBC, CBS, 1965–70), *I Love Lucy* (CBS, 1951–7), *The Munsters* (CBS, 1964–6), *The Dick van Dyke Show* (CBS, 1961–6), *Bewitched* (ABC, 1964–72) and *The Mary Tyler Moore Show* (CBS, 1970–7). Several of these sitcoms, most notably those centred on women, have been lauded for their engagement with women's gender role and their subversive potential, often underlined by the performances of their respective leading actresses (see Rowe 1995, Doherty 2003). Lucy, for example, though kept in the home, is performed in such excessive ways as to emphasize the physical restraints of 'appropriate' feminine behaviour. The more apparently feminist *Mary Tyler Moore Show* presents a woman leaving her home in order to establish herself as a successful working woman whose life is also filled with the friendships (rather than just the dates) she forms in the city. However, as Channel 4 increased its audience share to nearly 10 per cent (it reached 9 per cent in 1988; see BARB 2009), these repeats were gradually replaced by new American sitcoms, including *Family Ties* (NBC, 1982–9), *The Cosby Show* (NBC, 1984–92) and *Roseanne* (ABC, 1988–97); in other words, sitcoms that could be more clearly claimed for a family audience.

As the example above indicates, repeats of American sitcoms were used on Channel 4 to set up a dedicated time slot that could later be filled with first run American sitcoms. From a hermeneutic perspective, the repeats were used to establish a tradition which could gradually be negotiated by viewers as new sitcoms were brought into the schedules. Thus the regular scheduling of repeats created meanings around the slot; meanings such as those of family address, dedication to American sitcoms, humour, but also engagement with more serious issues such as the impact of gender roles. As the slot was increasingly taken over by first-run American sitcoms, these meanings, as a shared agreement between broadcaster and audience based on custom and tradition, already existed and could be further negotiated. First, by placing *Family Ties*, *The Cosby Show* and *Roseanne* into the slot, the family address became more visible as the cast reflected its target audience. Second, the slot continued its serious address by bringing in sitcoms that dealt with key concerns of modern societies, including the divisions created by class (*Roseanne*) and race (*The Cosby Show*). Later, these sitcoms were replaced with some that were increasingly aimed at teenagers, with teenage-centred sitcoms and dramas such as *Blossom* (NBC, 1991–5), *The Wonder Years* (ABC, 1988–93), *A Different World* (NBC, 1987–93) and *Party of Five* (Fox, 1994–2000), indicating another shift towards a more teenage audience. Once this address was established, *Hollyoaks* (C4, 1995–), the Channel 4-commissioned teenage soap, was easily placed into that slot.

As this slot developed towards first-run sitcoms, the women-centred repeats were increasingly moved into the afternoon. In 1993, *I Love Lucy* was first shown at an early afternoon time, between noon and 12:30 p.m. Then other, more mixed repeats, such as *Batman* (ABC, 1966–8) and *Mission Impossible* (CBS, 1966–73) took over. In 1997, repeats of the relatively new sitcom *Cybill* (CBS, 1995–8) were shown between 1 and 1:30 p.m. and repeats of *Caroline in the City* (CBS, 1995–9), another sitcom based around a central female character, was shown between 12:30 and 1 p.m., with double episodes following later (both *Cybill* and *Caroline in the City* were shown in first runs in the prime-time 9-to-9:30 p.m. slot). This afternoon slot was at one point also used for teenage drama, including the critically acclaimed *My So-Called Life* (ABC, 1994–5), shown in August 1997; that is, during the school holidays, between 12:30 and 1:25 p.m., indicating that the 'slot for women' had to be abandoned as soon as a different audience group was available. In the same year, *Bewitched* was repeated at a later time, between 4 and 4:30 p.m., and was also shown in the mornings, between 9 and 9:30 a.m. This earlier slot also saw some new American imports, including *Something So Right* (NBC, ABC, 1996–8), a comedy based on the marriage of a couple who have both been married before, and *The Monroes* (ABC, 1995), a soap opera based around a family involved in national politics. Thus, Channel 4, with its mix of women-centred comedies and feminine-gendered soap operas, signalled that women were also perceived as the main target group in the mornings. However, the slot was scheduled to coincide with the post-breakfast period, when the working population would have left for work, suggesting that Channel 4 imagined that the proportion of the population not working was largely female.

Similar developments occurred in 1998, when *Bewitched* and *I Dream of Jeannie* (NBC, 1965–70) were stripped over weekdays for most of the year, in the early afternoon (12:30 to 1 p.m.) slot, except during the school holidays, when children and potentially their fathers were available and were offered *Mission Impossible*. There are three ways of understanding this strategy: women were perceived as the audience of lowest prestige for advertisers – but this runs counter to contemporaneous developments in American broadcasting where women were increasingly courted as a lucrative audience group (Lotz 2006). This therefore seems unlikely. Alternatively, women were perceived to be busy once the rest of the family was around and hence dropped from the list of available audiences. Or finally, schedulers understood that programming for women still had low cultural status and knew that they could not bring in the rest of the available audience with women-centred programming.

In 1998, however, female-centred sitcoms were still to be found in prime-time schedules: they continued to be shown in the 5:30-to-6:30 p.m. family viewing slot, and they continued to be shown in the more adult-oriented 9-to-9:30 p.m. slot. In this later slot, which was increasingly filled with American 'quality' drama, including *ER* (NBC, 1994–2009) and *Friends* (NBC, 1994–2004), the main women-centred sitcom to survive was *Ellen* (ABC, 1994–8), a sitcom which had gained significant media coverage and as a consequence partially also the quality-related 'Must See' label after Ellen DeGeneres came out as a lesbian in 1997 (McCarthy 2003). Thus, in 1998, the schedules remained, overall, still rather mixed.

In 1999, the scheduling on Channel 4 shifted slightly in prime time. American dramas moved increasingly out of the 9 p.m. slot to be bundled into a 'quality slot' from 10 p.m. onwards. Here, dramas and comedies such as *Frasier* (1993–2004), *Friends*, *Sex and the City*, *NYPD Blue* (ABC, 1993–2005) and *Ally McBeal* (Fox, 1997–2002) were shown. At the same time Channel 4 also more thoroughly developed the afternoon slot as the 'women's slot'. This was gradually extended to cover roughly the period between noon and 2 p.m. with repeats of *Bewitched* and *I Dream of Jeannie* and new episodes of *Suddenly Susan* (NBC, 1996–2000), which had previously been shown in the late night slots (after 10:30 p.m.). In 2000, the slot became even more filled with first-run sitcoms, including *Jesse* (NBC, 1998–2000), and *Suddenly Susan* and repeats of *Cybill* and *Roseanne*, while *Bewitched* and *I Dream of Jeannie* were relegated to the morning schedules.

Such scheduling strategies had several effects. First, in regard to the 10 p.m. slot, it created commonalities between the programmes as American imports and as belonging to a group of dramas and sitcoms that aim to challenge traditional formats on American television and address a very specific (urban, affluent, well-educated and relatively young) audience. In this environment, programmes such as *Sex and the City* and *Ally McBeal* appear as noteworthy, not because of their engagement with women's issues, but because of their relationship to this trend in programming and their address of this audience. Thus, these 'dramedies' are partially ungendered by their scheduling as well as by their content: they incorporate a male perspective by offering women to be looked at but also by offering something different and innovative as other 'American Quality Dramas' (Thompson 1996). This sense of innovation crucially connects to concepts of progress, which is placed in opposition to the feminine-gendered concept of repetition (see Kuhn 1984).

While *Sex and the City* has on occasion been lauded as a feminist statement that encourages women to celebrate their sexuality (Henry 2004; see also Arthurs 2003), several commentators have highlighted that the programme engages with a narrative in which 'choice' and consumerism is central and in which the women are eventually settled in committed relationships, indicating a post-feminist rhetoric which revolves around the return to the private and a move to more conservative values (Negra 2009, 10–12; McRobbie 2004). On top, what *Sex and the City* shares with *Ally McBeal* is the emphasis on the women's relationships to men. All are, significantly, cast as single girls (Akass and McCabe 2004; Lotz 2006, 88–117). Hence, the women's identities are in large part based on their relationship to men and less so in relation to each other. Thus, Charlotte is defined by her romantic ideals of relationships, while Samantha's identity is built around her ability to 'have sex like a man' (see also the description of the programme's premise in Akass and McCabe 2004, 3). Similarly, Ally's key characteristic is that she is still in love with her childhood sweetheart. This suggests that despite their formal innovations (*Ally McBeal*'s quirky moments when Ally's imaginations come to life; *Sex and the City*'s female voice-over and emphasis on talk about sex), the two dramedies are actually quite conservative in how they imagine femininity, a fact that is underlined by the casting of conventionally pretty, slim women who are also presented as taking pleasure from dressing up in expensive and often revealing clothes. Moreover, they return much of their feminist attention to the private realm of relationships, a fact that is underlined by the lack of discussion of the elevated economic and social situation that binds the four women together.

Secondly, in regards to the establishment of a dedicated slot in the afternoon, the scheduling indicates that Channel 4 imagined a significant portion of the female population to be stay-at-home women and thus created a tradition that connected women with the private sphere. It is notable that this slot was gradually established out of a mixed slot that showed repeats of American drama and sitcoms. But from 1999 onwards, the slot became dedicated (with the exception of the school holidays) to sitcoms based around women and often dealing with women's issues. Particularly the newer comedies (*Suddenly Susan*, *Jesse* and *Cybill*) deal with a variety of matters that affect specifically women. *Suddenly Susan* is a work-based comedy in which issues such as the negotiation between work and social life, female friendships, romantic relationships and sexism are addressed. *Jesse* focuses on a single mother (Christina Applegate) who tries to juggle her work as waitress with ambitions of becoming a nurse as well as the strains that come from being a single mother, having a close male-focused family and wanting a romantic relationship. The sitcom also offers a representation of a working-class woman which, after the demise of *Roseanne*, became increasingly rare. Similar to *Suddenly Susan*, *Jesse* presents the life of women as stressful rather than, as in both *Ally McBeal* (with its emphasis on personal problems at work and evenings in the local bar) and *Sex and the City* (with its constant return to lunches with the girls, shopping and parties), as a leisure-focused lifestyle. *Jesse* and *Suddenly Susan* were therefore able to deal with issues of women's work (including as members of families) and responsibility that went beyond the choice rhetoric of *Ally McBeal* and *Sex and the City*. *Cybill*, which seemed largely based on the British comedy *Absolutely Fabulous* (BBC, 1992–2005), engaged somewhat more subversively with issues such as ageing, particularly in the fame-and-youth-obsessed Hollywood, motherhood, divorce and appropriate and inappropriate feminine behaviour. None of the series, however, addressed women as other than white, indicating a continued prejudice that feminism is something primarily for white women.

By placing these sitcoms increasingly in the afternoon, which became established as women's slot, Channel 4 signalled that they did not think that these issues were of interest to a general audience. The sitcoms were thus connected to the meaning of niche or minority audience; but whereas in its early years Channel 4 under its remit felt obliged to place dramas and sitcoms for and about minority audiences (including women) into prime time, they were now relegated to the afternoon. The afternoon has traditionally been connected to family viewing (as children are potentially around to watch), meaning that programmes placed at that time, even if they are placed in an established women's slot, gain meanings that highlight their playfulness and child-friendly content. This is amply demonstrated in comments about afternoon programming from that period, as Moseley highlights (2000, 300;

see above). Thus, the sitcoms are not imbued with a strong sense of seriousness; on the contrary, their placement in the afternoon suggests a slightly condescending attitude towards them. This contrasts to late night (post 11 p.m.) slots, which are often reserved for particularly gruesome material or high art and foreign dramas, all of which demand the sensitivity of an adult and educated audience.

The establishment of a dedicated slot for women in the afternoon also misunderstood women's real lives: 44 per cent of the workforce in 2001 were female, and 72 per cent of women of working age were 'economically active', which compares to 79.3 per cent of all men (Twomey 2002). That meant that only a minority of women were actually available to watch, particularly if we take into account that child and other care arrangements which are not seen as part of economic activities would otherwise keep them engaged. By developing a dedicated slot in the afternoon, Channel 4 indicated that they worked with a rather conservative understanding of women's lives, one which imagined them as that group most likely to spend a significant time during the day in the house.

As women were addressed as at best only partially partaking in the labour market, the sitcoms which engaged more centrally with questions of work – that is, *Suddenly Susan* and *Jesse* – were presented as dealing with issues that were of only minor relevance to their audience. Thus, the sitcoms presented issues to laugh at and about, not to think about. This was particularly true as these programmes were perceived to be of less importance than the ones placed into the post-watershed slots; they addressed an audience that was relegated to the private sphere of the home. That meant that the political potential of the shown programmes, which recognized the connections between the private and the public, was also undermined, as they were offered for consumption to an ideal audience situated only and firmly in the private.

Perhaps most problematically of all, Channel 4 signalled with its establishment of a dedicated afternoon women's slot that only traditional femininities such as those of *Sex and the City* and *Ally McBeal* were of interest to a mainstream audience and that other, perhaps more feminist discussions of women's issues were of no relevance to the public. This is particularly problematic in an environment in which traditional masculinities and issues connected to them represent the norm, indicating a marginal status for women's issues. But this is in line with a broader trend. Research conducted by Lewine Jones and Mitra (2009) highlights that gender roles are deeply ingrained in advertising aimed at children. Importantly, it is more acceptable for girls to transgress the boundaries of their gender role than it is for boys; when adverts are aimed at both sexes, they tend to utilize a more male aesthetic. Thus, children learn that it is normal for women to engage with what is perceived as masculine domains, but it is inappropriate for men to do the same. *Sex and the City* and *Ally McBeal* allow a way out of this dilemma, as they both constantly show that men are at the heart of women's identities and also create the space for a male gaze to be deployed.

By developing such increasingly rigid scheduling structures, Channel 4 developed a tradition that viewers were able to unpack as gendered address. Like the makeover shows in prime time on all terrestrial channels in Britain (Moseley 2000), prime time on Channel 4 more generally presented an ungendered address, where programmes specifically for and about women increasingly incorporated male perspectives. Importantly, ungendering involves an address that explicitly includes men – as there are higher stakes for them in engaging in women's issues than there is for women in men's. As a consequence, however, dramas and sitcoms dealing explicitly with women's issues, particularly if this is more feminist, were again marginalized, signalling to women that these issues were of minority interest only. Moreover, because they were also placed in the afternoon, they were presented as of less serious nature than, for example, the 'quality' programmes placed at 10 p.m. Because schedulers perceived stay-at-home audiences to be women, they also signalled that women who saw these comedies were firmly situated in the private, which meant that the political messages of these comedies could only with great difficulty reach the public space that evening and night time television, addressed to an audience that engages in the public world of work, so naturally occupies.

Conclusions

As the case of the US sitcoms in Channel 4's afternoon slot indicate, scheduling establishes ideal audiences whose demographic construction impacts on the meanings available around programmes. Scheduling as a continuous process develops knowledge about ideal audience groups and their viewing behaviour, likes and dislikes, which through the process of systematization is also shared with real audiences. The process of scheduling therefore is also closely connected to gendered address: the establishment of an afternoon slot focused on women-centred sitcoms through repeats of earlier examples of the genre is connected to the construction of an ideal audience of stay-at-home housewives, who are addressed as such. The more feminist meanings of the work-based sit-coms therefore appear as of little consequence to this audience. While real audiences might have recognized the feminist meanings and ignored the gendered address – as I did when I watched the programmes before I started my shift in a bar – the placing of the series in the afternoon meant that they were not easily accessible for other working women, nor were they presented as relevant to and thus perhaps also overlooked by them. In other words, the scheduling contributed not only to the fixing of gender roles (via the explicit feminine address as connected to the afternoon with its housewives connotations) but also to making invisible the few more varied feminist voices than those presented by the post-feminist, consumerist ones of *Ally McBeal* and *Sex and the City*. Scheduling then contributes to the containment of feminist voices and hence demands further analysis.

Notes

1. As the work of the Midlands Television Research group indicates, a similar wave of criticism struck television in the 1990s.
2. See, e.g., comments made on the *Media Guardian* website on the article 'Michael Grade to Step Down as ITV Executive Chairman' (2009).
3. Author's translation of the original.

Separating the Women from the Girls

Reconfigurations of the Feminine
in Contemporary British Drama

Vicky Ball

In recent years, feminist television studies have grappled with identifying the discursive shifts to fictions addressed to relatively affluent and mobile sections of the female audience in the post-second-wave-feminist context. Given the international distribution, accessibility and popularity of programmes such as *Ally McBeal* (20th Century Fox, 1997–2002), *Sex and the City* (HBO, 1998–2004) and *Desperate Housewives* (ABC and Cherry Productions, 2004–), discussions of feminine-gendered fictions' embodiment of feminism and post-feminism have been heavily focused upon few American texts. By way of contrast with the rich and nuanced accounts of American television drama's engagement with post-feminism, very little sustained feminist analysis has been given to other nationalized systems of broadcasting and, therefore, how their feminine-gendered fictions have negotiated shifts identified as post-feminist.

This chapter offers to supplement feminist television studies' engagement with post-feminist media culture by exploring the relationship between feminism and femininity in contemporary representations of the working girl in British television drama. As in North America, it is predominantly through the figure of the working girl that television

Figure 7 The working girl in *Secret Diary of a Call Girl*

attempts to construct and address women in the wake of the liberalizing movements of the 1960s and women's increasing visibility and participation in the public sphere.[1]

The starting point for thinking through British television's contemporary constructions of the working (post-feminist) girl and narratives of feminine mobility was prompted by the premiere of *Secret Diary of a Call Girl* (*SDCG*) on ITV2 in 2007. Based upon the award-winning blog and novelization of Belle de Jour (see Figure 7),[2] *SDCG* is significant because its representations of the affluent lifestyle of a high-class call girl embody many post-feminist attributes that have made feminist academics anxious (McRobbie 1994; 2009a; Gill 2007a, 2007b; Negra 2009). Representations of the independent working girl have historically involved a commodification of women's sexuality (Radner and Luckett 1999), so much so that there is 'an insistent equation between working women, women's work and some form of sexual(ized) performance' (Tasker 1998, 3). What is of concern regarding *SDCG* is the way in which sex work is foregrounded within the text as representing the epitome of *feminine* success, choice and empowerment in this post-feminist landscape.

It is such representations of feminine empowerment and (upward) mobility within post-feminist working-girl dramas which this chapter explores and problematizes. By contextualizing such representations in relation to discourses of cultural feminization that were circulating during this period, this analysis will investigate how such representations and narratives of feminine 'empowerment' reposition feminine subjectivities in relation to the spaces and discourses attached to twentieth-century femininity.

While *SDCG* forms a central case study, the analysis of the post-feminist girl and how she figures in other British television dramas will also include later series of *Trial and Retribution* (La Plante Productions, 2009–)[3] as well as a new generation of British texts that have emerged in the 2000s, such as *Ashes to Ashes* (Kudos Film and Television, 2008–10) and *Above Suspicion* (La Plante Productions, 2009–).[4]

Cultural 'Feminization'

As McRobbie recounts, in the 1990s the quality and the popular media constructed narratives of female success in a decade in which feminism was perceived to have been 'taken into account' (2004, 255) across the cultural landscape. Similarly, from cultural commentaries to government-sponsored publications (Wilkinson 1994), the 1990s were popularly hailed as 'the decade of women', in which a 'genderquake' took place: a fundamental shift in power from men to women (Wolf 1994, 19).

The gendered shifts to both economic and cultural spheres have been increasingly explored with reference to processes of reflexive modernization (Giddens 1992, Beck and Beck-Gernsheim 1996, Adkins 2002). For cultural commentators, processes of reflexive modernization refer to the 'freeing' of agency from structure (Adkins 2002, 3), whereby the certainties of tradition have been displaced by processes of reflexivity, detraditionalization and individualization in the late modern period. As discourses of the crisis of masculinity that circulated within this period indicate, however, the gendered implications of such processes of reflexive modernization have not been felt equally across the cultural landscape. Rather, discourses of the crisis of masculinity suggest that men and masculinity are 'reflexivity losers', decentred within this detraditionalized and post-industrialized context from the powerful place granted to them as the norm which defines everything else. This is by way of comparison with the revised place and status attached to both women and the feminine, which have ostensibly displaced masculinity as culturally dominant in this period.

As Radner argues, this scenario has created a 'New Girl Order', in which feminine destinies have been redefined in relation to the public sphere as 'fundamental agents', as 'workers and consumers', in the global economic system. In other words, '[t]his new economy depends upon a mobile workforce, including women, with significant discretionary income' to participate in contemporary consumer culture (2011, 14). Such discourses of cultural 'feminization' not only refer to women's mobility in social and economic spheres but to feminine mobility in the cultural sphere. Processes of reflexive modernization create a shift in which the values aligned with the feminine are understood to be the dominant aesthetics and practices of contemporary consumer culture. This includes, as Adkins has argued, 'the predominance of surface, simulation and masquerade; the authority of the consumer; and a dedifferentiation of the social, involving a domestication of the public sphere' (2001, 674).

Television and the New Girl Order

Significantly, such processes of cultural 'feminization' have impacted television from the 1990s. The 'multi-layered feminization' of British television (Brunsdon 2003, 8) is discernible in two broad ways from the mid to late 1990s. First, at the level of representation, the 'feminization' of British television refers to a more central positioning of women both in front of and behind the camera in prime-time television. In light of equal opportunities policies and, as Brunsdon has noted, the need to innovate within the increasingly commercial, competitive market of broadcasting, women have made substantial inroads into media production (2000b, 169). The momentum gained by women such as Eileen Gallagher and Jane Root in acquiring significant posts in broadcasting in the late 1990s, for instance, has not been lost in the 2000s with an increasing number of women gaining substantial responsibility of television channels and services.[5] In the area of British television drama, this includes positions in traditionally male domains of production. Kate Harwood, for instance, is currently Head of Serials and Series at the BBC; Channel 5's Acquisition team is headed by Katie Keenan; Polly Hill is commissioning editor of drama; Lynda La Plante and Kay Mellor own their own companies; and younger female writers such as Abi Morgan and Lucy Prebble are carving a career for themselves in television drama. Simultaneously, broadcasters' recognition of women as a relatively affluent target demographic has contributed to the greater visibility and more central positioning of female subjectivities and fictions in prime-time television drama (Brunsdon 2000b, 168–9).

Secondly, there has also been a 'feminization' of prime-time television schedules, with the discourses associated with feminine genres of daytime television displacing masculine-identified programmes such as documentary and current affairs (Brunsdon 2003, 7). From drama to lifestyle programming, it is the values of aestheticization, performativity and consumerism that have come to dominate prime-time television. Rather than attempt to address women exclusively, however, established 'feminine' formats and tropes are deemed a successful way to address consumer citizens of television, given the more general 'lifestyling' of late-twentieth-century British culture (Brunsdon 2003, 8).

This chapter offers another perspective of cultural 'feminization' by reviewing how such processes have impacted the relationship between women, the feminine and feminism in British television drama. Through the analysis of shifts to the working-girl drama and attendant narratives of mobility in relation to television within this 'feminized' context of broadcasting, this chapter engages with two central themes of feminist analysis of post-feminist media culture.

First, it suggests that while processes of cultural 'feminization' signify the way in which feminine values have become culturally dominant, such processes should not be equated with feminist progress. Rather, this analysis will suggest that narratives of feminine (upward) mobility that structure contemporary post-feminist drama depoliticize representations of feminine subjectivities. As with other accounts of post-feminist media culture (McRobbie 2004, 2009a; Gill 2007a, 2007b; Negra 2009), this analysis will explore the way in which such depoliticized representations of women assume and ignore feminist ideas (Brunsdon and Spigel 2008, 1).

Secondly and most centrally, it problematizes the proposal that in this detraditionalized and post-feminist context, women now occupy more reflexive positions in relation to the discourses and spaces attached to twentieth-century femininity. In other words, it is concerned to address and exemplify the limits of gender reflexivity in the current climate. This is a significant issue to investigate given the performative turn in feminist media studies[6] in light of discourses of detraditionalization and post-feminism that circulate within this cultural and critical climate and that suggest the freeing of women from traditional gender and sexual norms.

At issue here is not only how post-feminist media culture suggests that feminist values have become common sense across the cultural landscape (McRobbie 2004, 256) but how it suggests that women have achieved equality and choice, including the option to engage with cultural practices associated with 'the feminine', such as marriage, pornography and prostitution, since their empowerment has distanced them historically from these oppressive positions and practices. Such discourses suggests a non-contradictory unification of feminism and femininity in this post-traditional, post-feminist context and privilege neoliberal discourses of choice and individualism that make invisible deep and pernicious gender inequalities which continue to affect women in differently situated positions such as those of class, age and ethnicity (McRobbie 2004, 261; see also Negra 2009; Gill 2007a, 2007b; Radner 2011).

Through the analysis of recent shifts to representations of the British working girl, this chapter refutes the celebration of the non-contradictory unification of feminism and (traditional) femininity by British television drama. That is to say, while the analysis acknowledges that levels of feminine reflexivity regarding second-wave feminism do exist, this does not, as Adkins (2004, 433) has argued, mark an erasure of the distinction between the two categories. Rather, I argue that representations of the non-contradictory unification of feminism and femininity in British television drama are sold to audiences as post-feminist freedoms, depoliticizing the cultural sphere and rendering feminism redundant.

In making such claims, this chapter is not attempting to artificially reinstate an outdated distinction between feminism and femininity, given the cultural shifts that have taken place in recent years. On the contrary, it makes these arguments from a position of feminist reflexivity regarding the shifting configuration between these two identities in the current climate, not despite them. While I agree with feminist theorists, such as Hilary Radner, who argue that feminist media studies need to engage with the ways in which post-feminist girly culture is attractive to women 'as the sign of a new and revitalized feminine identity' (2011, 196), this is not to suggest that feminist criticism of such girly texts and practices should uncritically celebrate them or be afraid of critiquing them in case we should be castigated as outdated feminists in need of a makeover. To do so is to collude with the neoliberal discourses that are arguably embodied in the texts themselves (Curran 2006, 143) and to shift the object of feminist analysis away from patriarchal representations of femininity to feminism itself (Brunsdon 2006, 45).

Drawing on Adkins' earlier research as a framework to analyse contemporary representations of the working girl in this 'feminized', post-feminist context, this chapter illustrates how processes of reflexivity do not lead to a linear process of dissolution of gender but how 'they are ... central to new articulations of gender and sexuality' (2002, 5). Indeed, this point is exemplified by the way in which shifts that make up the degendering of culture are *re*gendered at the point of interpretation; that is, articulated during this cultural period as processes of *feminization*.

Through the analysis of British working-girl dramas this chapter explores how representations and narratives of feminine and post-feminist mobility reconfigure women in relation to the discourses and spaces of traditional femininity. Rather than see the traditional gendered ideologies and practices that inform these texts as a 'static hangover of the past' (Adkins 1999, 124) which is in the process of being destroyed, they will be understood as being constantly remade and re-enforced. This analysis will therefore allow us to consider the ways in which gendered hierarchies are reinstated through new subtle forms of resurgent patriarchal power in the current, detraditionalized and post-feminist context (McRobbie 2009a, 47).

Retrogressive Narratives of Feminine Mobility

The reconfiguration of the working woman in relation to femininity is symbolized by the way in which the white, middle-class working woman in 1980s and early 1990s dramas has been displaced in recent texts by white, middle-class girls.[7] This regression from working woman to girl, a figure who is identified in relation to discourses of femininity and consumerism, is, I want to suggest, a contemporary incarnation of the figure of the Single Girl made popular by Helen Gurley Brown in the 1960s. Just as the Single Girl emerged amidst the opening up of lifestyle choices available to women, the post-feminist girly is a popular cultural figure across television[8] (as well as film, magazines and advertising) that would be unthinkable without women's role being redefined in relation to spheres of production as well as consumption in the post-war period.

And just as the emergence of the Single Girl as a feminine template emerged as the paragon of an expanding consumer culture in the 1960s, the reincarnation of this figure in the late 1990s and 2000s suggests the intensification of these same consumerist discourses and the increasing commodification of feminine mobility in the twenty-first century. And just as TV's earlier representation of the Single Girl in such a British text as *The Liver Birds* (BBC1, 1969–78; 1996) emphasized the expression of the self through the female characters' independent living space and clothing, in these post-feminist texts the intensified consumer address is evident in their embodiment of 'flexi-ad aesthetics' that echo advertisements and pop videos in deploying signifiers for their intrinsic 'values and lifestyle' appeal (Nelson 1997, 25). This emphasis on lifestyle and the shifting conceptions of identity formed through consumerism are also registered in these texts at the level of narrative which shifted from pivoting around a 'rational/moral axis' in the 1980s and 1990s 'to be profoundly informed by ideas of performance, style and desire' (Brunsdon 1997, 85).

The similarities between the figure of the Single Girl and her contemporary counterpart, the post-feminist girl, suggest a lineage of feminine representations of women and the consumerist strategies of broadcasting which have addressed them. However, I want to suggest this lineage of such feminine representations is retrogressive because of the way in which it marks a retreat from the more feminist-inflected cycle of working women dramas that overtly engaged with issues of gender and sexual politics in and through their role-reversal narratives in the 1980s and earlier 1990s. Thus the working woman has been represented as a police inspector in *Juliet Bravo* (BBC, 1980–85) and *Trial and Retribution* (Isle of Man Productions for ITV 1997–2009); as a detective in *The Gentle Touch* (LWT for ITV, 1980–4), *C.A.T.S Eyes* (TVS Television for ITV, 1985–7) and *Prime Suspect* (Granada for ITV, 1991–2006); as well as an armed robber in *Widows* (LWT for ITV, 1983), as a warden in a male prison in *The Governor* (La Plante Productions for ITV, 1995–6), as a pathologist in *Silent Witness* (BBC, 1996), and as a manager of a professional male football team in *The Manageress* (Witzend Productions for Channel 4, 1989–90).

Such role-reversal narratives mark the mainstreaming of concerns aligned with the feminist movement on British prime-time television during the 1980s and early 1990s. As such they can be framed in relation to the more general take-up of liberal feminist discourses via equal opportunities discourses and policies in British culture during this period. Engaging with discourses of feminine mobility and equal opportunities in masculine institutions of law and order made good commercial sense, given that the crime genre has often boasted a privileged relationship to reality (Hurd 1981) and given the way 'equal opportunities has been shown to have very particular inflections in the context of the police force and the justice system in the 1980s' (Brunsdon 1998, 226).

Broadcast at the same time and even being informed by the very public cases of sexual discrimination and misogyny of the police and justice system from the 1980s and 1990s,[9] these role-reversal narratives gained symbolic significance, not only 'accord[ing] a degree of legitimate

Figure 8 Role reversal with the working woman in *Prime Suspect*

status to women's demands for equal rights' (Baehr 1980, 31) but, as in the instance of La Plante's *Prime Suspect*, highlighting the masculine hegemony and institutional misogyny of public institutions and services (see Figure 8). As Brunsdon has suggested, the impact of discourses of 'equal opportunities' has been so far-reaching on television that it has become inscribed as a discourse within the generic conventions of the police series in the 1980s and 1990s, when 'even grumpy old Morse has to learn to be civil to female pathologists' (1998, 227).

As these textual shifts suggest, the return of the working girl is retrogressive in terms of displacing a feminist with a post-feminist discourse, one which aligns progress with traditional femininity and consumer-aligned ambitions. In turn, as Radner has argued in relation to the recent cycle of US post-feminist girly films, such a 'neofeminist' discourse is only 'tangentially a consequence of feminism' (2011, 2). Although this discourse is quick to incorporate phrases such as 'empowerment' and 'self-fulfilment', it is formed in relation to the needs and designs of media conglomerates, rather than feminism, in an ever-expanding consumer culture (ibid.).

The embodiment of a neofeminist, or perhaps more aptly, *neoliberal feminine* discourse through the figure of the post-feminist girl depoliticizes representations of the feminine subject in the way in which it simultaneously recalls and repudiates feminism. The post-feminist turn in representations of the working girl is aptly captured by Kelly Reilly, who plays the young female detective, DC Anna Travis, in Lynda La Plante's latest drama *Above Suspicion*. When interviewed on whether or not she was the new Jane Tennison, the heroine of *Prime Suspect*, Reilly replied,

> No, my character, DC Anna Travis, is just at the beginning of her police career; Jane Tennison had reached the upper echelons and was one of a generation of women who needed to prove that they were as good as any man. Anna resides in a more contemporary era, where it isn't about sexual politics anymore. She is strong, intuitive and overtly female. (quoted in Lockyer 2008)

Reilly's comments are telling because they suggest that, in contrast to the embattled heroines fighting institutional misogyny and sexual discrimination in the previous decade, the fight for equality has been achieved, as evidenced by an increasing participation of younger women in such employment structures and the subsequent decline in such texts' focus upon sexual politics.

A similar discourse is discernible in *Ashes to Ashes*, wherein Detective Inspector Alex Drake is sent back in time to confront the institutional misogyny of 1981. In placing the modern heroine in relation to 1980s television and its representations of law and order, the jokey and ironic post-feminist discourse seems to say 'look how far we have come' in both social and representational terms. The focus upon a crime narrative takes a back seat in *Ashes to Ashes*, and as Brunsdon and Spigel have argued in relation to other texts produced within this post-feminist context, the gendered politics that structured texts in the 1980s and 1990s are put in 'quotes'. In this instance, *Ashes to Ashes* is a parody of earlier role-reversal texts and their equal opportunities politics (2008, 4). Moreover, notions of narrative or plot are eschewed in *Ashes to Ashes* in favour of the performance of 1980s gender roles, as evidenced by the popular and critical acclaim that actor Philip Glenister has received for his portrayal of the iconic 1980s misogynist boss Detective Chief Inspector Gene Hunt.[10] In so doing, *Ashes to Ashes* successfully evades dealing with the gendered and sexual politics that continue to structure or have been reconfigured in the contemporary period and deflects from contemporary television's retrosexist discourses regarding the gains women have made in the public sphere.

The affluent and successful females whose lifestyles and narratives embody ideas of (consumerist) choice and empowerment are the poster girls for post-feminism on British television; a utopia in which female identities are structured not only by equality but by empowerment and individualism (McRobbie 2004, 2009a; Gill 2007b; Negra 2009). In such texts, feminine mobility is misrepresented as feminist success, which reinforces myths of progress circulating within this post-feminist context in which the goals of liberal feminism – particularly, equality in the workplace – have been achieved. Such representations of the post-feminist girly are pernicious not only for overstating the successes of liberal feminism but for rendering feminism obsolete (McRobbie 2004).

Moreover, rather than explore the fallacy of sexual equality in the workplace, the feminized workspaces in these texts are represented as evidence of progress for women. To recall Reilly's quote, she suggests that having achieved sexual equality, women are now allowed to be themselves: 'overtly female'. Reilly's use of the adjective 'female' rather than 'feminine' suggests a feminist backlash in her resurgence and celebration of discourses of natural biological difference that are pervasive across the wider post-feminist culture (Gill 2007b, Negra 2009).

The celebration of natural sexual difference is signified in these texts through the girly appearance of their central female characters. In contrast to the working women of the earlier dramas, whose professionalism was frequently represented by their attempts to blend into the masculine institutions they inhabited, the appearance of these younger heroines celebrates youthful femininity: ponytails and 'come-to-bed' hair, false tans, pink satin shirts, fluffy cardigans and high-heels. While the former strategy of assimilation is problematic given the way in which binary oppositions which structure constructions of gender are left intact, it also suggests models of female success are based upon their ability to fit in with male structures. However, the overtly girly characterization of the female protagonists is equally problematic; it not only is reactionary to feminism but infantilizes and repositions women into sexualized roles. This infantilization and sexualization is most worrying in the instance of *SDCG* and the childlike representation of Belle as prostitute, which contradicts the current moral panic regarding the trafficking of young women. Nevertheless, in each of these contemporary dramas the infantilization of the female protagonist suggests her apparent empowerment, and access to public domains remains within the parameters of patriarchal control. The infantilization of working women thereby diffuses any potential threat they pose to male patriarchal power in the public sphere (Radner 1999, 10).

Discourses of sexual difference and sexual politics within these texts are made comical (Travis smirks as she bats away come-ons from her male colleagues) or, more conservatively, 'serve to re-eroticize power relations between men and women' (Gill 2007b, 159). The entrance of sexualized post-feminist girly DCI Roisin Connor to replace the more feminist inspired 'new woman', Pat North, in *Trial and Retribution* in 2003 is indicative of the latter as it is played through in terms of sexual tension between herself and old foe DCI Mike Walker. Similar themes are also evident in *Ashes to Ashes* and *Above Suspicion*, where the sexual tension between Travis and Langton, in the latter text, has provided the ongoing storyline across its three series. At the end of series 3 ('Deadly Intent'), this sexualized storyline threatens to eclipse future investigatory narratives as Travis falls in love with her 'powerful and controlling' boss,[11] a development that appears to reinforce essentialist myths regarding women's inability to resist powerful men. In these crime texts, the narrative emphasis is increasingly placed upon the 'will they or won't they' rather than the 'whodunnit'. Consequently such 'feminized' post-feminist texts not only depoliticize representations of the working girl by evading gender and sexual politics but, simultaneously, reconfigure female subjectivities in relation to romance narratives akin to 'traditional' feminine-gendered fictions.

The Reprivatization of Women's Work

The 'depoliticizing and retraditionalizing' rhetoric of these texts extends to the way in which women's narratives within these texts are reprivatized. In contrast to La Plante's earlier dramas *Widows* and *Prime Suspect*, which utilized a central female heroine to provide a critique of the male hegemony of policing, the narrative of her latest heroine Anna Travis's ability to move up the career ladder in *Above Suspicion* is recast in personal terms. In some ways, this focus upon the individual successes of single working women can be perceived as following on from the 1980s and early 1990s cycle of professional woman dramas and their embodiment of liberal feminism. As Nunn and Biressi argue in relation to Tennison in *Prime Suspect*, although she introduces new, conventionally 'feminine' strategies to the workplace, she makes little sustained attempt throughout the series to improve its culture for other women or indeed for other subordinated groups (2003, 194). Such dramas may therefore have achieved a critique of the male hegemony of policing but only because the text (as with *The Manageress* and *The Governor*) is able to accommodate the story of career development without hindering the familiar pleasures of the genre (Brunsdon 2000b, 208) and thus, by extension, the masculine institutions of policing that it critiques.

If these earlier textual examples illustrate the way in which the 'grammar of individualism' (Gill 2007b) has dominated popular television historically, they also exemplify the way in which these liberal feminist discourses blur with neoliberal ones in contemporary representations. The latter embody the rhetoric of neoliberalism, in which girlies are represented in utopian employment scenarios, enjoying the material benefits based upon individual capability, merit and self-interest. In turn, such narratives tally with Radner's reading of the depoliticization of contemporary post-feminist films, in which narratives of consumption are divorced from fiscal responsibility, resulting in 'unabashed self-gratification in which fantasy prevails over notions of professionalism and work' (2011, 25). These narratives, then, do not only depoliticize feminine-gendered fiction but serve to 'reprivatize' issues of gender and sexual politics that have only recently been made public (Gill 2007, 153).

The same individualizing, self-serving discourses depoliticize *SDCG*'s representation of sex work. As Belle states near the beginning of the text,

> There are as many different types of working girl as there are kinds of people, so you can't generalize. [...] But, I can tell you about me. I should say up front that I wasn't abused by a relative, I've got no children to support and I've never been addicted to anything. Except for maybe the fourth season of *The West Wing*, but, you know. So why do I do it? Well, I love sex and I love money. And I know you don't believe I enjoy sex, but I do. Plus, I'm fundamentally lazy. What I really like is being my own boss. (series 1, episode 1)

Debuting in September 2007, only nine months after the murder of five prostitutes in the English town of Ipswich, *SDCG* not only is insensitive to the ongoing politics of street prostitution but manages to avoid telling usable stories about the politics that underpin the high-class working girl's life.[12] This is particularly so given that Belle (Billie Piper) represents the growing market of middle-class sex work and the dedifferentiation of the roles women perform across private and public roles, as embodied in the growing market of 'the girlfriend experience' (Attwood 2010).

The first three series of *SDCG* try to visualize the problems Belle experiences in attempting to keep her personal and professional lives separate given the dedifferentiation of these roles. In fact, the text appears ambivalent in terms of its own point of view of prostitution and the psychological costs of sex work on its participants. During the more contemplative moments we share with Belle as she lies on her bed (series 1, episode 1) or takes a shower (series 1, episode 3), it is difficult to distinguish whether we are being offered further opportunities to objectify the youthful, girly body of Billie Piper or whether these scenes subjectify her and grant viewers 'private moments' (Dyer 1980, 95) of reflective intimacy with Belle regarding her double life and the emotional and psychological costs of her chosen profession/lifestyle. Knowing how to read these scenes is made problematic by the lack of characterization of our hollow, emotionless 'heroine' – a problem, I think, which can be attributed to eschewing melodrama for postmodern irony as the dominant aesthetic through which to tell Belle's story. This example illustrates the problem with viewing the post-feminist consumer text and its emphasis on lifestyle over emotion or plot: it is all (life)style and no substance. While the text does draw attention to the vacuous character of contemporary consumer culture via a speech by Belle's best friend, Ben (series 1, episode 8), the text goes on to celebrate and exploit these consumerist values in an attempt to appeal to audiences for another three series.

Given the contemporary post-feminist texts' tendency to reconcile women with marriage and domesticity (Probyn 1997, 128), Belle's decision to choose her career over marriage to Ben could be perceived to undermine this heteronormative discourse. However, this more optimistic reading is problematized given Belle's chosen career. Her choice of an independent single life is paradoxically one that repositions her in sexually subservient roles to men. Viewed from this perspective, Belle's choice does not look so liberating or empowering, undermining as it does the shifts in terms of the heterosexual contact that underpins the working girl's identity. As Radner has argued, revisions to the heterosexual contract from the 1960s may have contributed to sexual prowess replacing chastity as the working girl's predominant form of cultural capital. However, prostitution challenges the working girl's right to sexual pleasure in this revised system based upon mutual erotic need and fulfilment. In other words, it is precisely the working girl's working status – which affords her a 'package of rights', including the erotic possibilities of free sex – which prostitution undermines. Such a narrative returns Belle to positions occupied by women prior to the transformation of the heterosexual contract based upon its 'inequitable distribution of financial capital and sexual pleasure' (Radner 1999, 17).

Paralleling post-feminist fictions that reinstate marriage as the life choice for women, *SDCG* repackages normative notions of femininity (Gill 2007, 162) – in this instance, forms of sexual exploitation – as post-feminist freedoms. The prevalence of the sex worker figure in post-feminist culture, however, suggests *SDCG* is not alone in its conservative representations of women (Radner 1999, 2011; Negra 2009). As Radner argues, the prostitute represents the mode for all human behaviour in a neoliberal culture in which getting the best deal that can be capitalized upon by aggressive individualism is celebrated (2011, 33). In this context, 'men constitute neither allies nor enemies, but a series of opportunities and obstacles that a woman encounters in her attempts to achieve economic stability' (Radner 2011, 19). Belle represents the neoliberal subject par excellence, who testifies to the way in which anything is up for sale if it guarantees a good financial return. In a similar vein, *SDCG* represents the neoliberal *text* par excellence, having no qualms in resexualizing and refeminizing women's narratives of mobility for a share of the broadcasting market.

The New Girl Order as Old Patriarchal Order

While these textual shifts symbolically represent how women have not straightforwardly benefited from an intensified process of cultural 'feminization', their characterization as girls responds to the way in which discourses and processes of feminine mobility would appear to be threatening to male patriarchal power (Radner 1999, 10). This would explain, for instance, the way in which there is a tendency in the later series of the established crime dramas *Silent Witness* and *Trial and Retribution*, as well as *Above Suspicion* and *Ashes to Ashes*, for the patriarchal figure to be reinstated as the head of investigation and for women to return to occupy more subordinate and 'rookie' roles and spaces within the rank and file of pathology and the Metropolitan police. In *Ashes to Ashes*, there may be an investigation into the corrupt, misogynistic patriarchal figure of DCI Gene Hunt, but he is recuperated with god-like status in the finale as the paternal good shepherd who guides his team safely to heaven(!).

In *SDCG*, women being reinstated in subservient roles to men translates to being reinstated as patriarchal fantasies of sexual subservience. In so doing, *SDCG* can be seen to retraditionalize women in relation to sex work but also to definitions of 'potent and attractive female sexuality' associated with pornography (Boyle 2009, 99). While Belle, talking directly to the camera, suggests how she enjoys sex with her clients, her discourse is rendered incredible as we witness her 'riding' a rather frumpy and inhibited middle-aged man with a horse saddle and riding crop (series 1, episode 1). This miscalculated attempt to represent sex work as empowering for women in *SDCG* foregrounds the repositioning of women in servicing roles to male sexuality in post-feminist culture. In turn, this example also illustrates how the sexualization of culture and the mainstreaming of porn translates into confusion between empowerment and role restriction (Negra 2009, 100). Despite Belle's claims that she does the job for her own sexual fulfilment, actually, as Karen Boyle argues, 'Belle's job is to please men and her own physical pleasure is incidental and often faked':

> That the show can present these contradictory claims – that she prostitutes because she loves sex, and that the sex of prostitution is a performance that has nothing to do with their own sexual pleasure – without recognizing or thematizing the contradiction speaks volumes. (2010, 114)

The gendered politics that underpin constructions of new femininities in these more mobile feminine times and the critical tools needed to deconstruct them are evocative of the terms of debates that structured the early years of feminist television studies. In such a context it would seem fitting, as Rosalind Gill argues, to resuscitate older critical tools of analysis, such as sexism, in order to understand the contemporary gendered politics that structure social, economic and cultural life. As she argues, while this term has also been mocked as old-fashioned, along with the feminists who use it (2011, 61), we need to consider how sexism, like gender, has not disappeared or dissolved in the contemporary detraditionalized context but how it continues to inform culture in its more 'agile, dynamic and diverse set of malleable representations and practices of power' (2011, 62). The resurrection of such critical concepts is needed in order to prevent the depoliticization of feminist television studies in the post-feminist context. As Gill declares, it's time to get angry again.

Notes

1. For a discussion of the relationship between television's representations of the working woman and feminism, see Baehr (1980), Baehr and Dyer (1987), Radner (1999, 2011), Brunsdon (1982, 1997), D'Acci (1994), Dow (1996), and Brunsdon, D'Acci and Spigel (1997).

2. Belle de Jour (2005), *The Intimate Adventures of a London Call Girl* (London: Weidenfeld and Nicolson).

3. See also *Silent Witness*, in which the established pathologist, Professor Sam Ryan (Amanda Burton), is succeeded by Dr Nikki Alexander (Emilia Fox) in series 8 (2004).

4. The lack of writing regarding post-feminist British drama is by way of contrast to the rich body of research that has accumulated around British lifestyle television texts, given the successful exportation of formats and texts, including *Wife Swap* and *Extreme Makeover*.

5. This is not to suggest that women's achievements in media production have been perceived as socially progressive. Rather, women's increased participation in broadcasting production has been frequently blamed for the reported 'dumbing down' of television within this cultural period (see Ball 2012).

6. For a discussion of the performative turn in Feminist Television Studies, see Brunsdon and Spigel (2008).

7. Radner argues that even when the female characters are older, they still bear the signs of 'girlyness' (2011, 5).

8. As I have argued elsewhere, there has been a discernible attempt by British broadcasters to replicate the consumer-led style of American texts generally and *Sex and the City* specifically through the girlification and sexualization of British feminine-gendered fiction (Ball 2012). For a discussion of the ways in which *SDCG* borrows from *Sex and the City*, see Boyle (2010).

9. *Prime Suspect* has received considerable critical attention for the way in which its critique of the institutionalized misogyny of the police via DCI Jane Tennison juxtaposed with the real-life sexual discrimination case of Assistant Chief Constable Alison Halford in 1990 (Brunsdon 1998).

10. Gene Hunt has been hailed as a 'national hero' by David Usborne in *The Independent* (18 May 2008) and took 25 per cent of the votes to be crowned favourite television hero in a TV poll in the *Guardian* (Media Monkey, 4 July 2008).

11. This was Langton's description of himself in the third series of *Above Suspicion*: *Deadly Intent* (part 2).

12. *SDCG*'s ineffectuality at communicating something meaningful about a high-class call girl's lifestyle would appear somewhat ironic given that it was based upon the blog and subsequent novel (2005), *The Intimate Adventures of a London Call Girl*, of real-life call girl Belle de Jour, who was revealed as Dr Brooke Magnanti in 2009.

Section 4

Futuristic Feminisms

Since the technological turn of the early 1990s, new media has been constructed as an ideal platform where such traditional signifiers as gender, race, age and sexuality can be, and are, radically disrupted. Sherry Turkle's early work, for example, argued that cyberspace 'gives people the chance to express multiple and often unexplored aspects of the self, to play with their identity and try out new ones' (1995, 12). For Turkle the possibility of interacting in a way that was not fundamentally tied to a corporeal understanding of identity was both profound and incredibly positive. Not only did it facilitate a space for the construction of new identity signifiers *per se*; it also shifted power to the users, who could construct and represent themselves online in any guise, whether near to or removed from their 'real' identity offline. These are powerful arguments, and they have reoccurred sporadically since the 1990s. More recently, they can be seen in relation to social networking sites, where theorists have drawn on Goffman's (1959) concept of impression management to argue that certain social networking sites, including Facebook, MySpace, and Bebo, provide a new terrain for the construction of a carefully negotiated visible identity performance (see Mendelson and Papacharissi 2011, Davis 2010). Although these arguments focus on notions of visibility, display and power rather than interaction *per se*, the basic premise remains the same: that users can re-present themselves in a variety of ways and through a variety of media. Further, this re-presentation can be consciously different or can emphasize key attractive aspects of a personality (whether this relates to image or relationships, for example). Seen in this light, social media today are used to explicitly or implicitly construct a visible representation of Self. This representation is the product of a dialogue between the fantasized, desired and imagined sense of Self and a lived and performed one.

When we assess the arguments around new media, a number of issues emerge. It seems at first glance that Sherry Turkle's prophecies have been realized: the Internet continues to radically disrupt traditional signifiers insofar as users can amend, play with, or inhabit a range of identities online. When we look more closely, however, we see two diverging shifts. One is a shift towards users, who have the power to mould an increasingly malleable space to their desire. The second is in relation to use, where the technology becomes a site to play out already existing power relations in potentially generative or deeply ambivalent ways. In relation to the first shift, it is the agency and assumed expertise of the user who can direct navigation through the Web, which becomes important.

For Andi Zeisler, the first contributor to this section, the agency of the user and the malleability of representation online become key contributory factors to the feminist political presence online. For Zeisler, it is the ability to author one's own blogs, zines, or networks combined with the various levels of visible commitment which make the Internet such a powerful feminist tool. As she suggests, users may blog in one forum and browse in another, while their identity can remain completely or partially obscured. Utilizing the available spaces provided by the technology becomes a conscious, activist and visible feminist-authored intervention. This makes the authoring of, not just content, but representational strategies even more important as a political statement and as a claim over and into more mainstream spaces. Her own online magazine, *Bitch Media*, is an example of this, and she draws on the statistics related to the site's visitors to argue that feminist political blogs, feminist online magazines, feminist memes and zines, not only exist; they are widely used and read by a range of people – not just feminists.

As many feminist new media theorists have noted, however,[12] the emphasis not just on the user *per se* but on the agency that user has (to author, to direct navigation, to present and construct online personas or avatars) is inherently gendered, not least because it re-evokes a Cartesian logic whereby the corporeal elements of identity are negated in the reconstruction of new online identities. The irony of this shift is that the Cartesian logic embedded in such individual and neoliberal fantasies was critiqued in the early 2000s in feminist new media studies, as well as in long-standing and seminal feminist work that argues for a lived and corporeal understanding of identity (Butler 1990, Doane 2000, Sobchack 1995). The fact that the Cartesian logic re-emerges again in recent writings around social networking sites, where identity is 'managed' rather than lived, could be seen as evidence of the power of the neoliberal and individual politics so characteristic of late modernity or even (more sceptically) as an indication of the lack of impact feminist writings have had on this particular canon.

For Zeisler, however, agency and expertise have to be located with the user, whose political feminist leanings are always already in existence.

Zeisler details how the Internet is a space of identity management, but it is one that has a wider political and social purpose. Her focus on the representational spaces available for and used by feminists produces a more cautiously optimistic account of new media. As she argues, at the very least the Internet facilitates a public space in which and through which feminism as political activism can be voiced. It allows a (re)turn to community or grass-roots politics insofar as it facilitates multiple, sometimes contradictory, voices and opinions to be collectively viewed. While her conception of the user seems to embrace the neoliberal and individual agenda characteristic of wider new media and/or politics and critiqued by some feminists, it does so for a political purpose of its own: to claim the Internet as a political space.

If the first shift has been towards the user, the second shift we can identify is towards use *per se*, and this, in turn, has a number of repercussions. The first repercussion is that the 'real' identity of the user continues to remain undertheorized. New media spaces become spaces of performance, and the implicit assumption (online at least) is that control and agency over that performance is located elsewhere – away or apart from that particular performance. This not only strengthens the Cartesian emphasis discussed above, it also works to construct the technology as a tool, to be used and appropriated by a user (an expert). For feminist media theorists and ethnographers, this has been a starting point for much research investigating the lived experiences of technological use.[3] The overall aim for this body of research has been to intervene in the oversimplified account of technology as a simple 'tool', as well as to investigate the relations users have with technology in a more empirical way. Indeed, when we consider the accounts of the Internet above alongside research into a wider range of new technology, such as television (Ang 1992; Silverstone, Morley and Hirsch 1992), the videocassette recorder (Gray 1992) and videogames (Walkerdine 2007, H. Thornham 2011), it becomes clear that each technology, in turn, is (and has been) appropriated in different and complex ways to support gendered (and sexed, raced, classed) identities. This work, which investigates the material and social relations with technology, starts from a very different premise and assumes that the technology, insofar as it is made and imagined within social relations, continues to be used within them.

H. Thornham and McFarlane, in the second chapter in this section, also start from this point. Their concern is to investigate the articulations of technology by adult women and teenage girls and the ways certain technologies are disparaged or enjoyed by these demographics.

They argue that the way the technology is imagined and articulated impacts actual use, so that even when users do have knowledge, space and access to use that technology, they do not necessarily have the inclination. Rather than open up potential avenues of technological exploration and use, such avenues (such potentials) are closed down, and teenagers and adult women resort to more familiar and highly gendered claims.

The social and material approach to new media espoused by H. Thornham and McFarlane is very different from Zeisler's more mediacentric approach, and this is also a crucial point for feminist new media theorists. Taken together, these two chapters represent the two halves of a now familiar cycle of critical engagement with new media. In relation to their starting positions, Zeisler (who starts from the point of the technology) and H. Thornham and McFarlane (who start from the social and material) encapsulate a long-standing and inherently gendered process of engaging with new media. This cycle, which sees technological potentiality followed closely (and belatedly) by a consideration of actual use, is gendered not only because the turn to technological use over possibilities is usually a domestic or social turn; it is also gendered because, as Bassett has argued elsewhere, the domestic or social turn is synonymous with a devaluing of the technological aspects of that technology.

> The case for the autonomy of technology is very often explicitly made or implicitly adopted in the analyses of new technologies, while the case for the social shaping of technology, which reorganizes this relationship, tends to re-emerge as technologies lose the patina of the new, as they become 'old'. (Bassett 2007, 52)

While the first two chapters of this section could be said to represent this cycle, insofar as Zeisler's chapter focuses on the cautionary potentials of technology for feminism and H. Thornham and McFarlane's chapter assesses social use and understandings of new media technologies; the third chapter of this section consciously intervenes into it.

Bassett's account of new media technology is made with full consideration of previous interventions in mind. From the material constructions of technology of the 1980s, to the cyberfeminism of the 90s, to software studies of today, she argues that at every stage in the 'technological turn' of the past decades, the technology has been both celebrated for its possibilities and critiqued when these possibilities failed to emerge. This highlights that the gendered cycle of technology (from the technology itself to the social and back again) is an oversimplification and a misrepresentation both of what is actually negotiated and of critical accounts of technology. In response to this cycle, Bassett calls for a 'retooling' of feminism, not only so that this cycle can be intervened in but also in order to celebrate the potentiality of new media technologies in ways which call into question the Cartesian assumptions or oversimplified understanding of identity, agency or use. A retooled feminism facilitates a critical interpretation of new media technology made with the full spectrum of previous feminist interventions in mind.

If the first two chapters both require and actively call for a feminist intervention, Bassett's chapter is a reminder that neither these calls nor the tools with which these calls are made are necessarily new. The forgetfulness that seems a characteristic of feminism and new media technology throughout the technological turn is part and parcel of Zeisler's and H. Thornham and McFarlane's chapters. On the one hand, this further emphasizes the continuing need for a feminist 'retooling'. On the other, it highlights that there continues to be an inadequate discursive framework with which to approach new media technology. Indeed, the very act of establishing a discursive framework – as both Zeisler and H. Thornham and McFarlane do – is an act of locating and re-membering the disappeared voices of a feminist agenda.

Taken together, then, the three chapters of this section look both forward and back, tangibly enacting and commenting on the nuances and contradictions of feminism, particularly in relation to new media technologies. In this section, feminism is re-constructed variously as an activist movement, a lived and embodied discourse and a theoretical and critical lens with which to approach new media technologies. These heterogeneous understandings and/or applications of feminism further detail the personal and political resonances feminism has for researchers of gender issues. Feminism is not seen to simply or uniquely impact the terrain of new media technology. It is always already there, in the promises of and anxieties about the technology itself, in the ways technology is constructed by those who use it and in the various histories called upon in order to 'tool up' for the critical enquiries of technology, which are detailed in this section.

Notes

1. See, e.g., Grosz 2001; S.Thornham 2007, H. Thornham 2011; Braidotti 2002.
2. See, e.g., Gray, 1992, Walkerdine 2007, H. Thornham 2011, Kerr 2003b, Hobson 1980.

New Media, New Feminism

Evolving Feminist Analysis and Activism in Print, on the Web and Beyond

Andi Zeisler

As we at *Bitch Media* (http://bitchmagazine.org) know all too well, the print industry has been in a prolonged free fall for the past few years.[1] Magazines and newspapers have rarely been profitable businesses, but right now they are endangered ones, and it's impossible to imagine a future where they will recapture the relevance they once had. In the USA, the site Newspaper Death Watch (http://newspaperdeathwatch. com) lists the US metropolitan dailies closed since 2007, along with those papers adopting a more hybrid (print and online) format. In 2009, News Corp announced a 97 per cent drop in global newspaper profits,[2] while the BBC in the UK regularly runs stories about declining newspaper print sales since 2008.[3]

For feminist media, this isn't necessarily a bad thing. Mainstream print outlets – large city papers, glossy general-interest magazines, women's magazines and small respected political and cultural journals – have contributed a lot to the media landscape, but they have also been, historically, spaces showcasing a limited range of opinions and voices. While feminist print media publications, such as *Spare Rib* (1972–93), should also be noted here, such print outputs have tended to operate on the periphery for a range of financial, geographic and sociocultural reasons and have had limited impact on the mainstream print media landscape.

The advent of the Internet, however, has upended many of media's traditional notions of expertise, authorship, ideological leadership and cultural relevance. For feminist media, this is crucial, as it poses an alternative – in fact countless alternatives – to the idea of a monolithic feminism that is the backbone of mainstream dialogue and assumption about women's rights. This is not to say that such alternatives never existed before, only that because of the varied conduits by which Internet content is shared today, there is much more of a chance that these alternatives will actually have a chance to speak as loudly as the dominant media simply by virtue of being readily accessible like the alternatives (I'm referring here mainly to newspapers, network and cable news and the most widely read websites, blogs and aggregators). For those of us who have incorporated new media into our work for several years, the fact that the larger world has seemed to only recently 'discover' the alternatives offered through new media is worrisome, as there is always the risk that in trying to demystify this confusing new world for the average Joe and Jane, the mainstream media will use it to replicate the past hierarchies and erasures of old media. In a similar vein to Bassett's chapter in this collection, we can already see reiterations and replications of past hierarchies, most notably in the realm of political blogging, which I return to below.

Despite these notes of caution, I argue that the crucial word in talking about the evolution of new media is just that word: evolution. Everything stands to change. Three years ago, Facebook was still used mainly by college students, few people had heard of Twitter, and iPhones were only for the most hard-core (and wealthiest) of geeks. It seems impossible to wrap one's head around the potential of new media as a whole, but what we can do is look at the ways feminists of all kinds can shape it and use it in the service of a movement that is, itself, always evolving.

The contemporary feminism that is centred in new media, particularly blogs but also videoblogging, podcasting and social-media applications,[4] can be linked to past iterations of feminism, particularly the well-known second wave of feminism, in one crucial way. Much of what occurs on feminist blogs is consciousness raising, which was the bedrock of second-wave feminism and in many ways its most indelible legacy. The mindful connection of individual problems to societal ones is crucial and must happen continuously to counteract narratives put forth in mainstream, non-feminist media.

The other way new-media feminism connects to past iterations of feminism is in the community-mindedness that it foregrounds in practice. With a few exceptions, there is a sense of wanting to enhance dialogue by including as many voices as possible, deferring to those with demonstrable expertise on a subject and using word of mouth to let readers and participants know where they might learn more. There is also an admirable reluctance to consider fellow blogs and organizations as 'competitors', and in many cases a great deal of crossover via guest blogs, cross-posting, trackbacks and shout-outs. All of this increases the connective and activist potential of online communities, adding both strength in numbers to intersectional movements and exponentially increasing visibility of issues and initiatives.

But the feminism enacted via new media is in many ways wholly different from that at any other time in history simply because of the potential of the media itself. Connections across both geographical and theoretical divides are in theory limitless. There is community to be found online for marginalized populations, like the popular group blog 'Feminists with Disabilities for a Way Forward', which closed in 2011 (http://disabledfeminists.com/), and for niche interests, like writers of feminist speculative fiction (e.g. http://femspec.org/ and http://femspec.blogspot.com/).

Because of the visibility of and accessibility to these communities, there is a spreading awareness that analytical frameworks (both online and off) also need to be expanded to encompass different kinds of feminism, to include historically marginalized or inconvenient groups (people of colour, transgendered women and men, religiously devout women who identify as feminist). New media have introduced memes that percolate in blogs and then spread beyond them, seeping into mainstream discourse. One example might be the concept of 'slut shaming', which was a term first coined on feminist blogs a few years back and which one can now hear referenced in real-world conversations. According to the *Finally Feminism* blog, slut shaming can be described as 'the idea of shaming and/or attacking a woman or a girl for being sexual, having one or more sexual partners, acknowledging sexual feelings and/or acting on sexual feelings'.[5] Another example of memes seeping into mainstream media would be the concept of 'fat positivity' and Health at Every Size, which has forged online communities in the realms of analysis and activism, as well as more quotidian arenas like fashion blogging.

Much of new-media feminism foregrounds, or at least attempts to foreground, the importance of an intersectional approach to feminist theory and activism. And activism itself has changed with the advent of new media. Many people who would not turn out for a march or sit-in or political rally are using tools like Twitter and Facebook in activist ways and, furthermore, in ways that themselves point out the way new technologies often sideline non-white-male voices. I'm thinking here of things like the women journalist website (http://ladyjournos.tumblr. com/), an initiative that came about when journalist and author Sarah Posner noticed a report stating that people followed the tweets of male journalists three times more than those of female journalists. A seemingly minor action can quickly pick up momentum and attention in ways that more traditional activism cannot.

This is not to suggest that the feminism enacted within sites of new media is better than past iterations, nor is it saying that the Internet and social media are utopias for feminist activism and identity. Though the legacy of consciousness raising holds strong in new-media-based feminism, particularly in the feminist blogosphere, there is simultaneously a strong tendency towards individualism and a resistance to the urge to universalize and speak for others. This means that, although feminism can in many ways be seen to be more intersectional and wide-ranging than ever before, in many ways it can also be seen as more fragmented.

Further, because the media does not demand an immediate or sustained investment of identity and because the Internet offers its users so much anonymity in terms of presentation, audiences are both more engaged and, again, more potentially fragmented. As the statistics to my own website at *Bitch Media* details, plenty of people who have little background in feminism or who are not ideologically invested in it nevertheless spend time on feminist blogs or 'gateway' general-interest blogs that include feminist voices. Challenges here involve accommodating what can often be strikingly different levels of competence and understanding.

Finally, we also need to avoid the tendency to romanticize the democratic potential of new media – blogs in particular – without interrogating the way that potential is stunted by a collection of diverse but equally crucial factors. First, there is the existence of the digital divide, which in the United States is a reality for a huge number of people who either do not have Internet access, full stop, or whose access is limited because they go online from libraries or other public institutions that have numerous filters and blocks. Access and, perhaps more importantly, encouragement to embrace new technology is crucial if women, who may also be women of colour and low-income women, are to influence the development and direction of future technologies and the public policy that dictates how they are used. If the long-professed hope of technology is to make life better for everyone, the barriers to access to that technology have to be considered a central issue within the larger realm of both understanding and policy, not considered a side or special-interest concern.

It must also be acknowledged that the limitations of new media for feminism in particular are circumscribed by still-existing mainstream media. Many of us, for instance, can probably recall reading something in a newsweekly or newspaper op-ed asking 'Where are all the women bloggers?' or receiving a press release for a panel discussion titled Politics and the Blogosphere where all the panellists were white men from establishment organizations, journals and progressive outlets. Though women have been involved in new media since its inception, the public perception of the online world is one that is heavily white, heavily young and invariably male. The now famous paper published by the Hansard Society found that 85 per cent of the top political blogs were authored by men and that while those bloggers linked to one another, they overwhelmingly failed to link to female-authored political blogs.[6] In turn, those blogs became the default and the go-to for mainstream media looking to research what was occurring in and around political blogs. This then led certain media outlets to assume that women simply do not blog about politics rather than recognize that a lack of visibility and/or knowledge about women political bloggers and blogging sites was an issue of exposure and legitimacy rather than actual absence.

Similarly, because the mainstream media have a tendency to do something I call the misamplifying of feminist concerns – for instance, turning a nuanced study of women and happiness into a dozen headlines about how feminism makes women unhappy – feminist media has to do an incredible amount of justifying its very existence. My experience highlights how too much energy is spent every week trying to legitimize long-standing and incredibly basic concerns to disbelieving mainstream outlets – for instance, that the wage gap still exists. This results in an excess of exposure for the same issues over and over, while a myriad of equally important issues are shunted to the sidelines indefinitely.

Finally, there is the related subject of the development of a feminist new-media canon. A surf through some of the prominent feminist outlets online reveals that certain names, certain references and certain memes repeat, and one can see that there is already a canon of new-media feminist content taking shape. This includes frequently referenced or linked texts, real-world events, jargon and even guidelines for how to interact as a new blog commenter or an ideological ally. As with any canon, there's the risk that as new-media feminism evolves, it will replicate the erasures and underrepresentation of past canons. In addition to this is the concern that the spokespeople for new-media feminism will look exactly like the figureheads of past iterations of feminism. Issues of race, class and ability are constant dividers in spaces where division is not the intent. Issues of privilege, of safe spaces, of silencing and of authorship all come into play when discussing how some sites of new media come to speak for entire groups and populations. The question of whether there should *be* a canon is beside the point. The structure of new media makes its creation almost organic. But the effort to make sure this creation is inclusive constantly changes because of the medium. It's worth noting that perhaps the best-known feminist blog, Feministing (http://feministing.com), recently instituted a policy wherein members of the collective each have a chance to be the general editor and public face of the blog.

So what does it mean to be a part of an evolving feminist media? If you are new to feminism overall, it may mean that you will simply come to feminist theory in a completely different way than women before you. Your first feminist action may be to participate in email bombing a corporation whose advertising insults women rather than, say, a Take Back the Night Rally. It may mean your feminist icon is a blogger or podcaster rather than a politically or historically recognized activist. Someone who identifies chronologically as a second- or third-wave feminist may be working to reconcile a background in heavy-duty theory with the dynamic, fast-moving, slangy, meme-saturated environment of new media.

It also means that there are many, many opportunities to get active in spaces of both new and old media. Many women who do not have the option of speaking up in their daily lives, whether because of their age, or their job or their religion, nevertheless enact their feminism online. And that is important. It is also important, however, to understand that online anonymity does not necessarily equal real-world progress. There must be real efforts to correct the record. This means that when you hear someone say 'I do not read women bloggers' or 'women aren't software engineers', you need to find out what they are really saying and why. Finally, we have to take seriously the phenomena of harassment, racism and sexual objectification, which are very real hindrances to full participation in online spaces by women, people of colour, those who identify as transgendered and many more.

Many of us are passionate about the social-change possibilities spurred by the constant development of new media and new modes of communication. But what we all know by now is that no matter how much activism it inspires among non-activists and no matter how many revelations of privilege or identity or understanding it brings about, new media alone *do not* and *cannot* constitute a feminist utopia. Feminism itself must evolve both within and with regard to new media. Feminism is also still fighting the same battles, both internal and external, that it has struggled with for decades. Technology has long promised a wealth of virtual possibilities, but it simultaneously threatens a continuation of divisions unless everyone is given a chance to participate. My ultimate call, then, has to be for widening participation, in order to ensure that the past hierarchies and canons are finally, and once and for all, disturbed.

Notes

1. See, e.g., www.oecd.org/dataoecd/30/24/45559596.pdf for the 2010 report on the decline of global newspaper sales by the Working Party on the Information Economy.
2. See, e.g., www.pressgazette.co.uk/story.asp?storycode=43590 (accessed 17 August 2011).
3. See, e.g., http://news.bbc.co.uk/1/hi/business/7739103.stm (2008), http://news.bbc.co.uk/today/hi/listen_again/newsid_7591000/7591404.stm(2008), www.bbc.co.uk/news/business-14501920 (2011).
4. See, e.g., http://bitchmagazine.org/blogs/audio, http://bitchmagazine.org/blogs , http://feministing.com, www.takebackthenight.org/.
5. http://finallyfeminism101.wordpress.com/2010/04/04/what-is-slut-shaming/ (accessed 17 August 2011).
6. www.hansardsociety.org.uk/blogs/press_releases/archive/2011/07/07/why-are-political-blogs-dominated-by-men.aspx (accessed 17 August 2011).

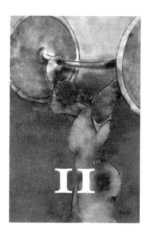

Articulating Technology
and Imagining the User

Generating Gendered Divides across Media

Helen Thornham and Angela McFarlane

Celebrated for their post-gender possibilities and the ability to create new media identities away from the gendered dichotomies of a lived body, new media have, at their most utopian, been conceptualized as a means to radically move beyond the gendered stereotypes of our culture (see S. Thornham 2007, Grosz 2001, Hayles 1999). In the discourses of the cyborg (and early cyberfeminists), in the promises of virtual reality and in the celebration of a ubiquitous mobile modernist subject, new media hold out the promise of new subjectivities and identities beyond a traditional gendered dichotomy. Such celebratory accounts of new media, however, are often the preserve of a technologically determined or mediacentric approach. This, in turn, tends to focus on what is offered to the user, constructing that user primarily as *done to* by the technology, while the experiences and activities of the user are located elsewhere – in the matrix of the new media being explored (see, e.g., H. Thornham and McFarlane 2011, Newman 2004, 2008).

Drawing on two complimentary research projects, this chapter offers a very different approach. Rather than start from the site of new media, we focus on how new media are *articulated* by potential and actual users. Consequently we argue, in keeping with much feminist ethnographic work investigating gender and media, that new media are always already inherently and materially gendered. Further, they are gendered well beyond the specificities of any one medium: they are gendered through the articulations of new media by female users, in the material and discursive constructions of new media and in the motivational reasons offered for engagement. This gendering is wider, deeper and far more profound than any one media form and calls into question the more celebratory accounts of new media detailed above. Such gendering occurs across generations, across research projects, and despite the *supposed* inroads, not just of feminism, but also of cyberfeminism, to the extent that, in keeping with Bassett's suggestion (Chapter 12), we need a 'tooled-up' return which remembers the critical interventions feminism has made and has been making in relation to new media and technology (Bassett in this volume).

In this chapter, then, we explore the discourse of expertise as a material social relation (McNeil 1987, again, Bassett, in this volume) where gender emerges as a complex enabler of carefully constructed media engagements and as a distancing device facilitating a claim of and towards disinterest. Material understandings of technology are further nuanced through the normative practices and behaviours that also emerge in relation to initial claims of exclusion and through a discourse of choice. Our argument is that the women and teenagers cited here selectively *evoked* certain aspects of their understandings of a wider popular discourse of post-feminism and femininity to stake their claims. In turn, this created a discourse that constructed normative femininity as, first, premised on a post-feminist agenda and, second, as naturally excluded from the ideal user demographic of the new media they discuss. Such claims may *appear* to celebrate individual agency and autonomy, but they work to re-emphasize traditional conceptions of gender, such as sociability, care for others and technological disinterest. It is a more critical concept of post-feminism we evoke, then, in keeping with feminist scholars who see it variously as a move towards the individual (*consumer* is implicit here) (Gill 2007, McNay 2000, S. Thornham, 2007), in relation to the notion of *lifestyle choice* (McRobbie 2004, McNay 2000) and in terms of a claim towards an (insistently depolitical) *authorship* (S. Thornham 2007, Arthurs 2003). In these conceptions, post-feminism is recognized as being collapsed somewhat with a concept of a neoliberal subject who claims authorship through an individual pleasure and agency. This agency, however, is often based on a construction of themselves as female consumers and subjects who may identify with, even claim, some notions of feminism (equality, mobility) but refigure these very insistently back into a personal (rather than public or political) discourse. We can see feminism 'taken into account' (McRobbie 2009, 1) here.

In conceptualizing post-feminism as an articulation and celebration of certain qualities, our argument is that the discourse of post-feminism facilitates certain claims and engagements, particularly around new technology. Seen in this light, the discourse of 'choice' is one of the normative practices and behaviours becoming ritualized over time and through continual articulation. However, this discourse also shapes and restricts engagements with new media, so that mediations with technology are only feasible as long as more traditional qualities of femininity are *also* prioritized. Far from being claims of independence or agency, then, such articulations continue to emphasize what Valerie Walkerdine has termed the 'habitual "feminine" position of incompetence' (2006, 526). Ultimately, then, these claims and articulations raise pertinent questions about a new and troubling discourse of femininity. They also raise questions around the post-gender possibilities of new media, particularly if normative practices of engagement are being constructed as exclusionary for women and teenagers. Finally, if we consider these claims alongside the cautionary and critical interventions always already located at key moments in the technological turn (McNeil 1987, Sobchack 1995, Grosz 2001), we have to think about the tangible, lived impact of feminism on these women and girls, as well as the clear need for a new (continuing) feminist intervention.

What Teenagers and Women?

The women and teenagers represented here are from two distinct research projects looking at 'new' digital media. Our argument is that despite the differences in the research projects, the articulations around new media prevail across generations, geographies and research projects, and this is what makes the findings so profound. The first project was a four-year ethnographic investigation into mediations with gaming technology in domestic contexts in adult-shared households. Here, H. Thornham interviewed 11 gaming households (households with videogame consoles) and recorded them gaming. The households included a mix of all male and female, mixed gender, sexuality, class and ethnicity within the UK. Participants were between the ages of 21 and 35. The data presented below come from a selection of these households chosen because they exemplify common themes or assertions. Although a more representative geographic spread was initiated (Brighton, Leeds, Belfast and London), clusters grew in certain areas, such as Leeds and Brighton. These households can hardly, then, be considered representative geographically, but the length and duration of communication (visits would last between 2 and 5 days over 3 to 4 years) offer more intensive and personal insights, which a thinner and greater spread of households would not have facilitated. The final issue to note here is that these households incorporated frequent (over 20 hours a week) and skilled gamers.

The second project draws on ethnographic research investigating teenage use and perceptions of user-generated content through the BBC initiative Blast (2002–10). Overall, the research project addressed constructions of the teenage 'digital native' and the corresponding considerations of the teenagers themselves regarding technological interest and competency. The interviews represented here are from demographics visiting the Blast workshops. Between April and October, the BBC Blast initiative offered local workshops aimed at 13- to 19-year-olds. The workshops ran over a two- to four-day period, and teenagers were invited to participate through the website, schools, parents, youth centres and other local initiatives. The aim of the workshops was to offer 'disenfranchised' teenagers the chance to explore and experiment with new technology in creative and innovative ways. Workshops included DJ-ing and VJ-ing (mixing sound and video), games design, stop-animation, radio, film and music production, fashion, drama and dance. Like the research into adult gaming, what became increasingly interesting are the accounts and constructions of technology and gender by teenage girls.

There are three evident similarities between the projects. The first relates to the initial position of exclusion claimed on the grounds they were girls or women. Indeed, *both* groups (despite differences in age, geography, technological competence, class and ethnicity) constructed themselves as gendered and as (therefore) excluded. The second similarity relates to the subsequent construction of the users of the technology. Both groups constructed the normative user of new media as gendered male. Finally, both demographics ultimately found themselves in positions where admissions of interest in or knowledge of the new media they discuss became untenable and where actual technological and *social* agency became problematic. The implications of these stories of engagement with technology therefore go far beyond future mediations with technology. In positioning themselves as subjected to the more active agencies of co-gamers or co-users, their social agency was undermined, and more traditional gendered power dynamics re-emerged.

Positions of Exclusion

As suggested above, what was notable across the two research demographics was the immediate and initial claimed position of exclusion based on recourse to an essential gendered position. Statements that positioned the users as 'naturally' or essentially excluded were not only common; they were ubiquitous. While the adult women initiated discussions of gaming with comments like 'it's for the boys', 'it's a boy thing', 'it's more blokey' (see also H. Thornham 2008, 132), the teenagers also made such proclamations. Indeed, the comments they offered on their choice of workshop demonstrated a similar rhetoric of exclusion based on the fact that they're girls. Along with the usual claims of disinterest – 'VJ-ing is more for the boys', 'it's more for the boys [game workshop] that though' – which seem to map almost exactly onto the comments of the adult women gamers, teenagers seemed to go one step further and explicitly connect technological inability or incompetence with gender. Many explanations of exclusion included the phrase 'I'm such a *girl*', which was clearly meant as a disparaging comment on technological abilities. One girl who had attended a radio production workshop told me she didn't find it *that* enjoyable because, as she suggested, 'I can't work the dials! I'm rubbish at it. He [her friend] was like, "you're rubbish!" I'm *such* a girl!' Here her own incompetency, articulated through the phrase 'I'm *such* a girl', was noted by her (male) friend and acquiesced to. While we are not suggesting that gender and technological competency are in any way related, what was notable with the teenagers was the easy slippage from genre exclusion to technological incompetency – or to rephrase, lack of expertise – and the fact that both claims were overtly premised on the fact they were 'girls'.

Indeed, in some senses this finding maps much earlier ethnographic work investigating gender and domestic technology, where women expressed similar inadequacies or self-deprecations when it came to technological knowledge and ability. Ann Gray, for example, researching the use of videocassette recorders in the home, found that women, consciously or unconsciously, remained ignorant of the 'workings of the VCR' (1992, 169) and that this had consequent repercussions for them later (Gray 1992, 164–80). Considering these similarities in terms of the proclaimed position of exclusion – and wider ethnographic research investigating gender and technology – such parallels could be read not only as a 'stylized repetition of acts' (Butler 1990, 179) across generations but also, perhaps more worryingly, in relation to the sustainability or sedimentation of some 'acts' which work, over time, to produce normative hegemonic behaviour (ibid., 171–80).

However, as with earlier ethnographic work and the research on adult gamers discussed here (see also H. Thornham 2008, 2009, 2011), when we explore the explanations the teenagers offered in more detail – particularly in relation to their explanations of workshops they *did* attend – we see that the proclaimed positions of incompetence ('I'm *such* a girl') were actually very carefully negotiated. This suggests that in many ways the notion of them being 'just a girl' (like the adult women gamers claimed position of exclusion) was also masking potential negotiated positionalities and engagements which may actually be pleasurable. Indeed, as we see below, technological knowledge may be derided when it comes to games programming, but it is celebrated when it comes to deconstructing clothes. This suggests that there is a careful negotiation around what *kinds* of technological competence or experience are admissible. The careful distinction offered below is not only gendered in the distinction between the games workshop (nerdy, male) and the fashion workshop (useful, female); it is also gendered in terms of what aspects the fashion workshop supports (individuality, ethical issues, recycling). It is here, arguably, that the post-feminist subject emerged.

> G1. It's not that I'm not into games just not the nerdy side. Like I've got a DS, but I'm not going to the programming [workshop] no way.
>
> Interviewer. So which workshop did you go to then?
>
> G1. The fashion one.
>
> Interviewer. Okay. Can you describe what you've been doing?
>
> G2. We've been deconstructing clothes, and then we've been putting them back together and customizing them. But everyone here, we all done raw textiles and textile projects.
>
> G4. We made clothes and stuff.
>
> G3. It's been good coz like we can't really afford to buy new stuff, but this way we've learning [*sic*] how to customize our own things and reuse clothes not just thrown them away.
>
> G1. It's like ethical fashion as well, you reuse stuff.
>
> G4. I'd never really thought about redesigning clothes either, like you buy something and it doesn't fit, it doesn't fit. But this way, you change it. It makes the clothes more individual. (London workshop, 15-year-olds)

In the extract above, we see knowledge and interest claimed in the fashion and textile workshop instead of the games workshop. According to the teenagers cited above, fashion encourages self-expression, individuality and practicality. These are concepts pitted against the games workshop, where the more universal and ambiguous term 'nerd' demonstrated the precise opposite to the concept of the 'individual'. The post-feminist discourses of consumerism, individuality and choice were emphasized here (see McRobbie 2009, 1) and given a practical and everyday lens. Fashion offered the means to express yourself *and* gain control over your finances. The post-feminist qualities of 'cultural and economic freedom' (Tasker and Negra 2007, 12) seem refashioned quite literally here in relation to individual appearance. Such qualities, as McRobbie argues, are 'converted into a much more individualistic discourse, and ... are deployed in this guise' (McRobbie 2009, 1).

If the teenagers seemed to articulate a relatively transparent post-feminist discourse of individuality, consumerism and choice as motivational reasons for engagement in the workshops, the adults offer a more nuanced discourse. It seems that in a similar vein to the teenagers, where certain technologies were derided and others celebrated, the women gamers also offered a critique of gaming but only within certain parameters – as consumers in the first instance and in a way which did not relate to practice. Indeed, in keeping with Aphra Kerr's research (2003a), the women argued that although they may find the avatars, genres or technology offensive, it would impede minimally onto gameplay. One gamer, for example, told me that while she considered Lara Croft a 'male fantasy figure', the construction of the avatars was not 'hugely important' to her. Hannah went further when she suggested that her negative reaction to the character wouldn't prevent her gaming:

> Hannah. I actually find the female characters quite offensive. Like, I'd not say it to Simon who has got all the games, but the Final Fantasy women and Lara Croft – you know what I mean? All these games with skinny, tiny kick-ass women, they're supposed to be liberating. They just annoy me.
> Interviewer. Would it stop you playing the game?
> Hannah. I'd probably play – just to keep Simon happy. I wouldn't buy it though.

For us, this seemed to suggest careful negotiations with post-feminist discourses. It is not that such criticisms can't be offered, only that they were carefully framed in ways that limited or restricted their (political or material) impact. As Negra argues, post-feminist discourses can be celebratory in the prioritization of agency, individuality, individual desire – but only as long as traditional discourses of femininity are also upheld. Problems only arise when the latter become untenable (2009, 36–45). Consequently, we could argue that such accounts of new media are articulations of the tensions between post-feminism and more traditional values of femininity. For Negra, post-feminism is not a new, celebratory concept, then, but a well-disguised rearticulation of traditional gender stereotypes. Indeed, we could argue that the criticisms offered above are only tenable from the position of a consumer, where, in keeping with the post-feminist tradition, economic choice and freedom can be exercised. However, ultimately, although criticism is offered, both gamers emphasized the limited impact such opinions would have on gameplay, suggesting perhaps that, in the end, as McRobbie argues,

> [t]he new female subject is, despite her freedom, called upon to be silent, to withhold critique, to count as a modern sophisticated girl, or indeed this withholding of her critique is a condition of her freedom. (2004, 260)

Finally, then, we could read these comments in relation to McRobbie's concept of feminism taken into account. This is perhaps the most sceptical reading, where a more 'feminist' critique is offered by the gamers but then subsequently dismissed in the articulation of more traditional feminine qualities. Talking from the position of a consumer allowed the women to offer a critique of the female avatars, genre and technology. However, such criticisms were carefully bracketed with proclamations about normative gaming practices to suggest that, although the images were problematic, they wouldn't necessarily prevent gameplay. In turn this worked to undermine any connection to a feminist politics, because it frames such statements as individual and personal reflections with limited power to alter actual gaming dynamics. The criticism of the constructed and unrepresentative images of women in the media does, on the one hand, reiterate one of successes of feminism. Indeed, as Rosalind Gill suggests, one of the initial aims of feminism was to criticize the 'idealized, perfect images of unattainable femininity' (2007, 74). On the other hand, we can also see the discourse of post-feminism at work here, in the simultaneous acknowledgement and (political) dismissal of such critiques.

Social Experiences and Performances

What was noticeable about all the responses, across the research demographics and across generations, was the reference to the *social*. If the first recourse was towards an initial position of exclusion based on (essential, simplified) gender, then the second recourse was a positioning which places the women and teenagers primarily in social relationships. In a similar vein to the teenagers cited above (and below), these articulations prioritized friends, peers and social scenarios, variously constructing the women and teenagers as appeasing and socially concerned individuals, which, as Beverley Skeggs argues, is an important facet of 'feminine cultural capital' (1997, 72). Indeed, the adult women gamers frequently referred to, evoked and situated themselves in relation to other housemates in their description of the games they were playing, emphasizing housemates' presence and importance to the gameplay. Lorna, for example, talked about Joe's instruction, saying that he would tell her what to do if she did play Pro Evolution (see H. Thornham 2008, 131), and Sara went even further when she suggested that the *very reason* for her gaming is actually to integrate herself socially with her housemates.

> They're always telling me what to do. But that's boys isn't it? They have to instruct you ... it's how I *choose* to bond with my housemates, but it doesn't change how I interact with them. I'm still 'the Girl' to them and don't know what I'm doing. (Sara, 27)

In the accounts from the female gamers, then, the competitive aims of the game were downplayed in favour of a gaming scenario, which allowed them to continue to emphasize the social elements of gaming. In some senses, this facilitated claims of preference, not least because they were constructing a particular kind of gaming scenario that accommodated and supported more traditional feminine qualities of care for others and sensitivity. Indeed, in the accounts by female gamers, the emphasis was continually on interaction with housemates.

The teenage girls also consistently prioritized the importance and influence of their friends in deciding what to do and which workshops to go to. It was far more important for them to demonstrate a shared interest with their friends than go to a workshop they were interested in, which could get them labelled a 'nerd' or, worse, a social 'widow' (complete with connotations of abandonment and powerlessness). Indeed, many of the teenagers did suggest they would have liked to attend a different workshop but in the end made a decision based on the desire of the group.

> G1. I was just following these two. I wanted to do VJ-ing but then I saw all those boys and thought 'No way!'

G3. I wanted to do Street Dance but I didn't want to be a widow.

Interviewer. So why did you go to this workshop then?

G1. Coz our friend wanted to go.

G2. I like radio and the music best so we're gonna come back and do the radio one tomorrow, listen to some tunes.

For *both* the teenage girls and adult women, then, it was housemates or friends that were consistently prioritized in motivational accounts of engagement. Friends not only initiated engagement; they also decided what to engage with and framed subsequent engagement. Further, as Valerie Walkerdine has suggested (2006), the characteristics, concerns and traits they consistently outline as inherently important to their mediations with technology are those traditionally associated with the feminine. Furthermore, it is a femininity that, in a similar vein to the findings of Walkerdine's research (2006, 2007) and in keeping with wider ethnographic research into new technology in the home (e.g. Gray 1992, Skeggs 1997), emphasized their role as the carer and the appeaser. Both the adult women and teenagers positioned themselves as socially concerned individuals. Here, they suggested that it was more important to appease friends and housemates than direct their own pleasure. Our argument is that this ultimately reproduces a dichotomy which sees femininity on one side (with ascription of such qualities as sociality, cooperation and care) and technology on the other (with ascription of competitiveness, aggression, violence and nerdy or geek interest). A second way to look at this would be to argue that technological expertise was replaced with a social expertise. In both age groups, this dichotomy worked (along with their own assertions) to distance the women and teenage girls from the technology, from the logics and rationale of the game (winning, competitiveness) or workshop (becoming adept and technologically knowledgeable).

Prioritization of the social and friends was notable during the workshops as well. In the account below, a security guard challenges the group for taking photos of the surrounding areas and buildings. The confrontation is recounted moments later by the group. Here, the technological ineptitude of the teenage girl was refigured into the social encounter with the security guard and ultimately produced the female photographer as the saviour of the group. Her lack of technological ability got them out of a potentially sticky situation when she discovered she had fortuitously failed to save any of her images on the digital camera.

G1. We was [*sic*] in the multistorey car park and right at the top and we was [*sic*] supposed to be taking photos of, like, the surroundings and um, we were starting going down the stairs and like taking photos of the images down the stairs and of the stairs coz they were cool and, um, we sort of got told … to … leave.

G2. Yeah.

[*laughter*]

G3. But then when they saw that we were like, well then they said we can stay but just 'don't take any photos of residential areas'. But I tried to show her what I done just the area. But then it was *blank*!

[*laughter*]

G3. I'm such a *girl* when it comes to technology! But it totally worked coz there was nothing to show! (Scunthorpe workshop, 14-year-olds)

The realization that she failed to save any of her photographed images (and has therefore wasted her time *and* is technologically inept) comes hand in hand with the realization that she has successfully avoided any confrontation with the security guard and her technological incompetency has actually benefited the group. It is an account that constructs her as the accidental saviour in a social confrontation because of her technological ineptitude. Her comment 'I'm such a girl' is less a criticism of herself and more a statement, which allowed her to claim credit for the scenario working in the groups' favour ('it totally worked'). Further, if we return briefly to the adult women gamers, the practice of gaming does not resolve issues around social appeasement; it brings them to the fore, particularly around notions of performance.

Sara. I've made a complete arse of this! Oh it is excruciating!

[*laughter*]

Sara. I thought it was a bike and it was a man!

[*laughter*]

Ian. Oh dear. I don't like that. Come on! You're going to die!! Quick! Quick!

Sara. This is the least amount of fun I've ever had.

[*gunfire*]

Clare. Got a gun now. Got a gun! Stop! Stop at the traffic lights! [*shouting, leans forward*] Oh. [*leans back*] Now where's, where do I have to go now? [*angry shouting*] Why the hell are you shooting at me? [*half out of chair*] I didn't know the police could shoot at me! Where's the? I didn't know they would just shoot me? [*sits back in seat*] It's all gone to the dogs. What the hell? [*raising arms in the air, console loosely held in right hand*]

Chloe. Sweet's nearly dead. Ohh. You'll be arrested!

Clare. Ohh nooo!

In a similar vein to the teenage account of meeting the security guard, the recordings of gameplay are performances of gaming incompetency or inexperience. More importantly perhaps, both performances maintained and prioritized interaction with other housemates rather than competitiveness, by keeping everyone in the living room involved in it. In both cases, technological competency seems less favourable than social appeasement.

Conclusions

Finally, then, the examples cited here raise some pertinent questions in relation to discourses of gender and new media. First, in relation to discourses of gender and femininity, all of the quotes from the adult women gamers and teenagers suggested in one way or another (and these are just snapshots over a five-year period) that both generations talk from an excluded position of femininity, which allowed them to claim a certain kind of knowledge, albeit one where technology seemed to have little place. They each articulated what Walkerdine has termed the 'habitual "feminine" position of [technological?] incompetence' (2006, 526) as a particular kind of gendered, normal femininity. Further, such claims to and towards femininity, worked to produce and shape wider ideologies of femininity, reconfigured here around the post-feminist and neoliberal discourse of *choice*, as well as continuing the traditionally feminine aspects of 'care, co-operation, concern, and sensitivity to others' (see Walkerdine 2006, 520).

Our argument is that the evocation of certain aspects of post-feminism and femininity allowed them to negotiate social power relations in order to speak about the technology and potentially *at least* engage with it on some level. While this would be a far more positive conclusion, when we actually investigate the kinds of engagements experienced, we see self-deprecating performances of inability. Consequently, we are far less inclined to interpret these performances in this way for a number of reasons. In part, our reluctance comes from the problematic alignment of a post-feminist discourse of choice and consumerism, which continued to frame potential pleasures and engagements in more traditionally gendered ways. It is also because such performances and articulations are not new; they have been noted in much (feminist) ethnographic research investigating (new) media consumption (e.g. Gray 1992, Walkerdine 1997, Silverstone, Morley and Hirsch 1992), along with more contemporary research into new media (Cassell and Jenkins 1998, Carr et al. 2006, Walkerdine 2007).

Finally, our reluctance to interpret these articulations in a more positive light also relates to the continual gendering of new media. Indeed, in constructing the normative user and technology as gendered male through the positions of exclusion, new media is still initially being conceptualized along gendered lines. Indeed, we could argue that a two-tier approach to new media is emerging at an individual level, one that may recognize the possibilities of new media but explicitly claims such possibilities as only feasible for certain (male) subjectivities. In many senses, then, these approaches map the criticisms already levelled at new media by (particularly) feminist new media theorists, who argue that a focus on what new media offer constructs the ideal and normative user as male (see S. Thornham 2007, 135). Indeed, as many theorists have noted (Grosz 2001, Braidotti 2002), the ideal user is not only being constructed as male; he is also being constructed along colonial and Cartesian lines, reproducing Enlightenment and modernist discourses of the whole, unified subject who explores, dominates and penetrates the world of new media.

Further, as feminist new media theorists have noted (Braidotti 2002, Grosz 2001, S. Thornham 2007), the gendered binaries evoked often construct the feminine as the corporeal, the terrain or the matrix through which the male subject travels. Such binaries reproduce the dichotomies of feminine object as passive and masculine subject as active. This reaffirms and produces technology and mediations with it as gendered and ultimately reinforces their excluded position. Seen in this light, the articulations by women and teenagers resonate the more macro discourses of new media, and this, in turn, is disturbing for what it suggests not only about the pervasiveness of these approaches but also about their ready translation into individual discourses of choice. The fact that these claims, practices and articulations occur across geography and, perhaps more importantly, across generations is indicative of how pervasive and problematic such articulations and performances have come to be. Although these seem premised on post-feminist and neoliberal discourses of choice, what ultimately re-emerge are more traditional concepts of 'care, co-operation, concern, and sensitivity to others' (Walkerdine 2006, 520). Further, not only do these concepts re-evoke traditional notions of femininity; they seem to actively exclude, not only technology itself, but also any expressions of technological interest.

Rather than celebrate a particular kind of post-feminist agency or experience, then, we would like to call for a (re)investigation of technological use which considers new media through a feminist lens. Rather than start from the site of the technology or medium, however, new media need to be approached in a way that remembers the material construction of technology as always already gendered and remembers the key feminist interventions already made in relation to new technology. Considered through these lenses, the necessity for a feminist intervention becomes blatant, not least because such an approach highlights the way that expertise, technological competency and the ideal user continue to be – indeed have always been – constructed as profoundly and problematically gendered. If we are to consider future directions of feminism and new media, then we need to investigate such relations with the full legacy of feminism in mind.

Feminism, Expertise and the Computational Turn

Caroline Bassett

In matters of technological change, women are more impacted upon than impacting. (Cockburn 1992, 38)

Friedrich Kittler, media archaeologist and medium theorist, was the subject and star of a conference at Tate Modern[1] a few years back. Given that Kittler's recent philhellenic work on ancient Greece (see Winthrop-Young and Gane 2011) lauds a 'mythical masculinity' that, as Breger notes (2006, 131), also has implications for gendered identity in more recent times, this might have been occasion for gender critique – and a brief intervention was made.[2] In response the audience duly (dutifully) applauded and set the matter of gender aside, returning to the real work of the conference: a (now gender-bracketed) exploration of the analysis of the insights and legacy of Kittler's incisive elaboration of a discourse network and medium theory.

It troubles me that participants of this critically engaged event, myself included, passed so quickly over an issue that would have resonated more strongly in different contexts. It occurred, perhaps, because of the mediumcentric nature of the work being explored; to focus tightly on the operations of capture, storage and dissemination that constitute a media system and ask how they organize or determine 'us' might imply that dimensions such as gender *can* be bracketed off – that a series of relations (those of gender, class, race, generation) integral to various (other) forms of cultural theory, media theory, techno-cultural theory is (apparently at least) either not relevant to the *operations* of medium forms under consideration or not amenable to investigation via *methodologies* that might be opened up by medium-theoretic approaches.

Kittler's work, spanning decades, has recently found new influence, as ways are sought to inquire more effectively into the materiality of information networks, to understand the implications of the 'mediatization' of culture through code and to develop new tools to grapple with information systems that are in many ways increasingly invisible to their users (in relation to what we see and can feel and also in relation to what we know is 'there'). This shift has provoked a series of theoretical interventions and developments, variously described as the computational turn (see Berry 2011), software studies, or code studies. It also engages with the burgeoning arena of the digital humanities, all of which are, as Kittler's work is, mediumcentric.

My question then, takes up an aspect of how mediumcentric developments deal with, or can deal with, or can deal critically with, or even invite dealing with questions of gender and technology – and the gender politics of technology; questions of power.

Alan Liu has recently remarked that in one of these areas – digital humanities – 'cultural criticism – in both its interpretive and advocacy modes – has been noticeably absent by comparison with the mainstream humanities or, even more strikingly, with "new media studies"' (Liu 2011). Liu goes on to argue that this is a problem of incommensurate 'scale', suggesting that it is not clear, for instance, how 'thinking critically about metadata…scales into thinking critically about…power, finance, and other governance protocols of the world' (Liu 2011).

I suggest Liu's point has more general purchase in two respects. First, although there are strands of medium-theoretic thinking that do seek to engage with the intersection between technology and social power – and consonant with Liu's argument, scale, as problem and as problematized, is often integral to this work – there *is* a deficit: medium theory is not good at exploring questions of social 'rather than' technological power. Second, this deficit arises as a consequence, not of intentional neglect, but of how technology is framed. Liu's reference to metadata appears descriptive, but what does it mean to 'think critically about metadata', how might that be done, what is being thought critically *about*? In other words, if medium-theoretic approaches in general have problems with engaging in critical cultural or social analysis, this has to do in part with how the object of study – code, software, hardware, 'metadata' – is constructed; what this rules in and what it rules out. In the 'Out' box is gender, the question of the gender technology relation and its implications for a gendered politics of code. What happened in one London auditorium – the setting aside of gender politics and of (or in relation to) medium theory – *is* symptomatic of a tendency in contemporary medium-theoretic analysis in general.

There is some unfinished business here concerning medium theory and the politics of gender. And to take that business up, both in order to think about feminism and (or in its response to) technology and to inquire into what might be a gender politics of code, it is useful to return to earlier encounters, to explore the gender-technology relation and its dynamics in different contexts – and perhaps to recollect previous feminist interventions around it.

This is possible because, if the gender politics of the computational turn are newly minted, we have also been here before. Cynthia Cockburn asked, '[W]hy do gender relations survive so little changed through successive waves of technological innovation[?]' (1992, 44). A different way to put this might be to ask, why do gender relations *wave* with waves of technological innovation? If feminism tends periodically to be 'set aside' as irrelevant to questions of technology, how does this relate to the rise and fall of mediacentric modes of inquiry?

Integral to this is also the question of feminism's response to technological innovation. Valerie Traub (2007), writing of female desire, asks why certain recurring tropes become salient and why they fade. This is a question that might also be asked in relation to feminism and its occasional but recurring love of technology, a love that is usually followed by disillusion – about what technology may deliver and about how it may be appropriated in the interests of feminism's projects.

Tracing some of these moments of feminist technophilia across the decades, a characteristic that emerges is discontinuity and forgetfulness. In relation to technology, in which it at once invests and which it suspects, feminism is *bad* at continuity. It revises, forgets, forces itself back through hoops it has traversed before, is surprised by (even susceptible to) the promise of the new in technology and surprised again when technology fails to deliver what was hoped for. Partly as a result of this dynamic, much that has been written by feminism on media technology is *itself* set aside – as too material or too utopian or quite simply because it is, from the perspective illuminated by the dazzle of the new, talking about the old and irrelevant.

The wager of this piece is that earlier forms of technofeminism, notably those adopting a computational analysis and/or critiquing the assumptions underpinning expertise, can contribute incisively to assessing the business of the technology-gender relation that is pressing today. Notably, it can contribute to questions around the gender-technology relationship that are re-emerging in relation to contemporary computational writing and the injunction to look closely at – to understand in expert ways – the medium itself.

The first stop is to revisit the 1990s moment of cyberfeminism – a visit made with questions of (feminism and) ambition in mind. The second move is towards software studies and the claim that contemporary media investigators require a two-way intelligence – technical skills and analytic critical perspectives – to be effective (Fuller 2008). Third, taking up the gender implications of what I understand as a demand for technical expertise made in the above, I return to McNeil's *Radical Science* collection (1987) in which McNeil herself, Cynthia Cockburn, Pamela Linn, Donna Haraway and others explore expertise, not as a simple question of competency, but as a 'gender relation' (McNeil 1987, 5).

Renewing this take on expertise and its gendering – which of course has implications not only for expertise but for the relation between gender and the technological object itself – enables a tooled-up return to be made to medium theory and its gender blindness. In this fourth turn, the intention is not only to argue that technology is essential to understanding contemporary gender relations. More radically perhaps, the intention is to reinstate, renew, or perhaps *refresh* our memory of Cynthia Cockburn's assertion that 'technology *itself* cannot be fully understood without reference to gender' (Cockburn 1992, 33).

Continuity, Technology and Cyberfeminism

When computers arrived in large numbers in the world of work (in the UK and USA at least) in the 1980s and early 1990s, they were seized upon by some feminists as likely to radically reorganize the gendered relationships within and between humans and their technologies (Cockburn 1992). Investing hope in computational technology was not new even then, of course (see, e.g., Firestone [1979] on automation in the late 1960s), and the vision of computers as able to effect change had more than usual purchase. This was not only because, as theorists such as Cockburn noted, they seemed so very different (even essentially different) from the infernal machinery and oily rags, the dead labour and the living 'hands', of the technologies of industrial revolution, heavily 'coded masculine' (see, e.g., Wajcman, cited in Suchman 2006, 322).[3]

It was also because their reprogrammability and their ability to simulate multiple functions and processes implied an openness to cultural reprogramming of many kinds; perhaps, it was felt, technology could be recoded feminine.

This wave of optimism about informatics didn't last. By the mid 1990s, Cockburn, writing of women in the 'integrated circuit', notes that

> [t]here was a hope (or was it a fear?) that the age of electronics or informatics would weaken the masculine identification of and with technology. Recent studies have shown that IT, mediated by different symbols, has in its turn been appropriated for masculinity. (Cockburn 1992, 41)

The gender coding of computer technology was thus reconfirmed, or to put this another way around, IT was confirmed as a 'technological activity'. However, there have been other, later, moments when developments in computing and the extension of the grounds of computation have once again suggested this identification could be unpicked – and at these moments technofeminisms of various kinds have been active.

General Optimism

> ...A period characterized by general optimism regarding the potential of the internet to provide increased opportunities for traditionally subordinate groups. (Herring 2000)

The best known of these interventions came with cyberfeminism, emerging alongside the first decade of the Internet as a public system in the 1990s (1993 and the World Wide Web is a useful index)[4] and now appearing very remote both from second-wave feminist engagements with technology and modes of post-feminist analysis aligned with the affirmative consumer politics of Web 2.0; cyberfeminism has essentially been dismissed as a resource for contemporary technofeminism. It did, however, mark a moment in which feminism itself became mediumcentric and might therefore be returned to.

The early years of the Web, in that moment of 'general optimism' in which Libertarian and Left hopes both seemed to be held in the network – not without conflict, but nonetheless coexisting (Free Beer and Freedom crossed, as the Net gag famously had it) – was also the era in which cyberfeminism flowered briefly; it was over by the early years of the twenty-first century, squeezed by the dot-com bust and the compression of 'indie' activism that followed 9/11.

As Susanna Paasonen notes, cyberfeminism emerged in the USA, Europe and Australia more or less simultaneously and largely involved avant-garde, activist and art circles and the academy (Paasonen 2011). It also had more populist aspects and connections; for instance, geek girls were figures with certain analogues to girl power in the UK, and there were certainly connecting filaments in and out of the academy via crossover publications and organizations such as *Mondo2000*, *Mute* and others. Cyberfeminism always had its 'in-house' critics; more or less supportive but critical readers (see, e.g., Fernandez and Wilding 1998, Bassett 2009). Moreover, somewhat separate from cyberfeminism (often more sure of feminism and less attached to cybernity)[5] came other (often materialist) forms of more or less technophile feminist intervention (see, e.g., Dale Spender). Finally there were feminist writers critical of technology, critical of the boosterism they rightly discerned in Net hype and fiercely critical also of cyberfeminism itself – which they identified as *itself* only hype (see notably Squires 2000).

Today the most strongly essentialist and speculative versions of cyberfeminism have come to stand in pretty much entirely for the much more varied mix outlined above (see, e.g., Kennedy 2008). Moreover, these writings themselves are much reinterpreted; notably, interventions intended as provocations, speculations or artistic interventions are judged as if they were claiming to be policy documents or social science. Cyberfeminism's addiction to proclamatory styles of writing, its engagement with biotechnological speculation – which it wove, cavalierly enough, into reportage on existing technologies – its tendency to clothe speculation in the rhetoric of declamation, its refusal to distinguish art from real life or hype, didn't help here. However, many of these texts were always intended to be somewhat self-mocking, somewhat performative, and they were certainly not always intended to be read 'straight'.

Moreover, they were written in an era in which 'virtual space', as a new arena, produced certain imaginative possibilities – and produced grounds that demanded exploration. It is through an odd inversion that cyberfeminism, obsessed with (flesh and virtual) bodies and their engagement with the materiality of machines (this was integral to its sense of 'the virtual'), has been rendered into what it reacted against: the gnostic tendencies of a (dominant) masculine version of the virtual sublime.

Cyberfeminism now tends to be reduced in scope and dismissed as idealistic or hopelessly utopian (in the popular sense, where it implies simply the unrealistic). What is lost in this assessment, an example of feminism's continuity problem perhaps, is the degree to which cyberfeminism, setting about a new work of appropriation, had, despite its idealism and abstraction, both hope and ambition.

For some, this ambition produced the beginnings of a feminist hacker culture, a gender politics based on expertise (see, e.g., Sollfrank 1999). For others, at issue was rather recovering a fundamental affinity, an instinctive expertise (a reversal of the more usual declarations of the 'natural' affinity of men with undifferentiated 'technology') which might begin to suggest the general foolishness of the latter assertion. This latter certainly produced a problem for feminism as a politics (if technology is destiny, why organize?) but nonetheless indicated a confidentially expected – and demanded – process of cultural transformation through technology, into which feminism could intervene, which women as well as men might lead.

Exploring the technological scene of the time, it is the reach and scope of feminisms' demands, whichever ways were sought to make another world possible,[6] that are striking, as is the location of these demands; made not primarily in relation to representation (a change in the regime of the visual, as a politics of representation), but in relation to 'life' – virtual or not – and its increasingly technologized practice.

The early cyberfeminist activists argued that digital technologies might build a new world – and that in this environment women might impact technology rather than being impacted by it. What was built was the Internet, which grew later into the extended ecology of locative and pervasive networks and platforms that make up its current configuration and that splice it into the environment so finely that the – real and virtual – division around which so much pivoted in the 1990s (why it was the object of feminist engagements which produced the very idea of life on the screen; see Turkle 1995) seems curiously archaic. Similarly archaic, for many at least, appears a gender politics, or even a gendered analysis of the prospects for women in a networked society, based on technological expertise or even in a sense on 'technology': the new imperative, endlessly repeated in Web 2.0 mantras of the past few years, is on participation in *social* media productions of all kinds. The loss of the sense of these activities as technical is not coincidental.

Software Studies

Kittler realized that he 'had grown up between two fathers and that somehow everything depended on uniting the two'. (Kittler and Banz 1996, 47; cited in Winthrop-Young and Gane 2006, 6)

Software studies is one of a number of medium-theoretic approaches that have emerged in response to this turn or that respond to it. It is notable that, at least in intent, software studies is a project markedly different from some of those adumbrated by Liu (2011; see above) that lack cultural critique. It might therefore seem to open up fruitful avenues for refreshing feminisms' engagement with medium-theoretic approaches in contemporary contexts.

Its starting points are, first, that computational developments are increasingly important in shaping our world – this relates to increased use, increasingly pervasive use and increased mediation of all things. Secondly, it argues that the important objects to understand in contemporary conditions are the processes and materials of computing; following the popular turn away from technological ascription (see Linn 1987, below) and focusing on the social aspects of social media is not an option as a methodology. Rather new tools and approaches are required.

Thus Matt Fuller, introducing a software studies *Lexicon* (2008), makes a cogent case for new forms of inquiry, focusing on the need for sustained attention to be paid to the operations of new media – not a question of language or appearance (see, in contrast, Manovich's writing on the language of new media) but a question of software and its operations, code, hardware, questions of protocols, relations, languages. The imperative is to describe operations rather than explore surface appearance, to understand processes of interaction rather than the mechanics of the gaze and to consider new data patterns rather than traditional modes of storytelling.

The explicit contrast is with traditional media studies, cultural studies or film studies, characterized as work seeking to understand new media in terms of representation. This is common in various medium-theoretic approaches. In the place of chasing shadows, as one theorist has put it, are thus various bids to develop new forms of empirical description (no point in exchanging shadows for speculation) based, for instance, on difficulty accessing experience of change (see, e.g., Mackenzie 2008) or the materiality of informatics (see, e.g., Hayles 1992). To some extent what emerges in the *Lexicon* are often modes of formal analysis. But relatively unusually here, this is an approach that seeks, often *through* formal medium-theoretic analysis, to point to ways in which digital technologies can be prised away from the market alignments with which they are identified and to indicate ways in which new technologies can be understood, ways that do not collapse technologies' potentials with the network of Web 2.0 products and services that operate as an actually existing instantiation.

It is this twin approach that leads to an interesting definition of *who* is capable of undertaking these projects to develop and prosecute new forms of inquiry. Notably, Fuller, arguing that software 'makes more sense understood transversally', suggests that for this reason it demands of critical inquirers a 'two-way intelligence' (2008, 10). This is defined as something that might be produced through an engagement with code-based production. This might provide the necessary skills to engage with the technicity of software through the 'tools of realist description' and might also build skills in forms of engagement with technology operating at some distance from computer science and the contained project of realized instrumentality it prioritizes (see Fuller 2008, 9). Fuller thus demands a certain technical expertise of those who are to critically investigate new and pervasive techno-cultural forms – to investigate the media code that increasingly 'determines us', as one of the contributors (Kittler 2008) put it.

Gender does not come into this calculation, but nor do women come into the *Lexicon* – at any rate, very few of them do. The vast majority of contributors in Fuller's book – but also of those writing in medium-theoretic terms in parallel studies – are male. The point here is not whether women did not wish to enter this field or whether they might have been more actively recruited. I am more interested in asking what this says about expertise – not only its social but in a sense also its technical construction. What is posited as a certain technical skill or familiarity (a matter of simple competence), an expertise demanded and defined by code and defined as something necessary to explore properly those relations and intersections between the language of humans and the language of machines, turns out to also invoke a mode of competency that is highly gendered.

Moreover, the gendering here, I want to suggest, comes into play not only in relation to largely pre-existing gendered (female) computational reticence – most women, it would appear, lack the specific two-way intelligence, a certain technical aptitude twinned with an arty soul – demanded here. It also comes into play in relation to how aptitude is being defined now, in relation to the emerging new media formations that are the subject of inquiry here. That is, at issue is the (gendered) technical object (the object that demands aptitude to be comprehended) that a certain rendering of the computational constructs. Or in other words, an issue here might be 'the "realist description" of what?'

'Software' might be less 'objective' as a construction than might be suggested by the idea of a simple return to honest empirical description construed against the traditionally tricky (is it cheap to add traditionally feminist?)[7] study of representation that it promotes and dismisses. Of the few women writing in the *Lexicon*, it is interesting to note that one of them, Wendy Chun, is elsewhere impelled to warn 'sympathetically', not of the absence of gender debate *per se*, but at least against the fetishization of code (Chun 2008). The fetish of code or software (both beguilingly implying a return to essential building blocks, to things unfreighted by ideology) becomes an abstraction. As such, it stands in for more instantiated media systems that carry the weight of their long-term instantiation within complex networks of social relationships, that contain delegated intellectual, social and material legacies – including those that produce and sustain relations of gender and gendered expertise. Software studies, it might be said, also sets aside gender.

Code love is largely – historically – a fetish that women do not adopt, but the real point here is that the nature of *expertise* demanded by software studies, the kind of skills declared necessary for the defined project of descriptive work, is also related to the fetish object (to 'code' and 'codes' interactions with 'language') which defines it. Thus a rather different set of possibilities and engagements might emerge if the question of 'expertise' in relation to software studies could be readdressed outside these relations. It is here that another return to an earlier engagement by feminism with questions of expertise, technology and social power is informative – in this case a return to a moment preceding the Internet explosion and cyberfeminism.

Expertise as a Feminist Issue

Jobs are skilled because men do them. (Philips and Taylor, cited in Linn 1987, 134)

In 1987 McNeil's *Radical Science* collection on expertise interrogated the degree to which (gendered) operating assumptions about 'what constitutes technology' (Linn, cited in McNeil 1987, 6) help forge expertise as 'gender relation' (McNeil 1987, 5). McNeil's general approach, conditioning the tenor of other contributions, has in common with the latter-day medium theorists a desire to avoid idealism and espouses instead a form of critical inquiry based on exploring material formations. For McNeil technology is material culture and expertise a material social relation which is, by virtue of this social embedding, also a gender relation.

The context of this collection is industrial production and automation. In particular, in the mid to late 1980s questions of computer expertise, gender and social power were central in confrontations between largely male print workers organized in craft-based unions, such as the NGA, and UK press owners – notably Rupert Murdoch and (slightly earlier) Eddie Shah – who, in the context of Thatcherism and an assault on unions, sought to end hot-metal compositing and introduce electronic page make-up. A central element in the conflict, which was painful and bitter and which the unions lost, was expertise. On the one hand, the press conglomerates sought deskilling as a mode of control (and if the shibboleth was freedom of the press, as *Sun* headlines at the time proclaimed, the naked industrial relations–antiunionism here was too blatant for that to really gain purchase); on the other, the unions defended the jobs of the print workers – the only people with right of access to computerized keyboards – through the defence of a craft system which also excluded women and other outsiders.

In contrast to the situation in the print industries in the early to mid-1980s, elsewhere women were already heavily represented in keyboarding positions, taking on roles transformed (see, e.g., Gardey, cited in Suchman 2006, 323) or newly produced through processes of office computerization.[8] In many of these areas other unions (e.g. ASTMS) were seeking to develop new rights for workers. In this context, however, campaigns for VDU workers, input clerks, new clerical positions – all overwhelmingly women's jobs (a valuation based on ascription and headcount) – tended to focus, not on defending computational expertise, but on improving health and safety.[9] One reason this is significant is that, like typesetting, much of this kind of data input also required accuracy, skill and speed at a keyboard. So why were these newly developed or newly feminized forms of work not understood as technical, and why was technical expertise here – in contrast to print – not defended as such?

Feminism actively explored these issues. Winkling out ways in which class antagonism was cross-cut (or intersected) by gender issues in these industrial zones, Cockburn, generally sympathetic to the Left but refusing to pass over the gender politics of the unions, exposed the mutable social meanings of expertise and its deployment not only as a weapon in a bitter class conflict but also as a gender-technology relation (see e.g. *Brothers*, 1983). For Cockburn, technology itself could be defined as a highly gendered medium of power found in owning tools but also found in 'special knowledge' (Cockburn 1985); in other words, a political economy of expertise was distributed across both bodies and machines. This, however, was not a static distribution – and the 'expertise collection' might be said to represent a feminist project precisely interested in exploring expertise and its migration and ascription – and also the potential for a feminist politics of redistribution.

Cockburn argued that technical expertise persists partly through its rapid migration into continuously reforged subdivisions or 'new niches in the division of labour' (Cockburn 1985, cited in McNeil 191–3). One place such special knowledge migrated to, in the case of the keyboard operators named above, was the offices and bodies of computer programmers (for a US-centric account of the rise of this group, see the suggestively titled 'Computer Boys Take Over', Ensmenger 2010).

Grappling with the dynamics of these kinds of shifts and redivisions, Pamela Linn noted the arbitrary way in which, as she puts it, some 'forms of dead labour' are designated technical – and others not – so that the 'ascription technology is full of paradox' (1987, 134). These ascriptions, despite their arbitrary nature, organize what comes to pass for (or be accepted as) technical 'expertise' and are differentially valued as such – '[j]obs are skilled because men do them' (Philips and Taylor, cited in Linn 1987, 134).

Among the benefits of such a line of argument is that it eschews a simple politics of 'catch-up', as McNeil notes (1987). That is, if expertise or skill with technology is a matter of (technologically neutral) ascription, if it is forged and reforged as a social relation, then any strategy based on capturing a specific set of attributes can only result in an endlessly futile chase.

It also indicates the force of what is, being arbitrary (not attached to the intrinsic quality of a set of knowledge or materials), nonetheless an operational distinction: expertise is productive. Moreover it is productive both in relation to material organization and in producing cultural understandings of the gendering of expertise. Linn's analysis thus descrambles something important about the relationship between representations of technology and technological operation, two cultural forms that in her writing are less inimical than the software theorists tend to believe them to be. 'What things get called is not the heart of the matter' (Linn 1987, 135) – but ascription is nonetheless one of those processes that construct expertise and also construct technology, a dynamic social process, a component part in what Haraway defines as 'specific social relations of technology and science' [that] emerge in 'specific historical moments' (1987, 75).[10]

The distance is marked between this conception of expertise and an approach that seeks to, in a sense, follow the *given* ascription (code is technology, expertise in technology demands expertise in code) – even if having accepted it, the intention is then to drill incisively into what it names. Jaron Lanier's complaint (2008) is that code studies in general cannot easily make the distinction between embedded software systems, with their legacies of human and technological inertia, their histories (held in machines and gendered bodies, as expertise, backwards compatibility or earlier constraint) and aesthetic dealings in virgin code,[11] which may be in and of themselves powerful but which do not function well as synecdoches for the specificity of other networks.

For McNeil and her contributors, technologies are emphatically marked by their histories, which is to say that a series of processes carry – in bodies and in code, in hardware and in software, in machine archives and social memory – various kinds of legacies and are conditioned by them (ascription labels but does not determine what it calls expert). It is the distinction between this formulation and the more abstract concept of code – a distinction that is wide despite the fact that both produce a certain work of empirical description rather than a question of a representation versus technology – that divides this feminist approach from the software studies approach. This is also one reason why Cockburn's sense that 'technology *itself* cannot be fully understood without reference to gender' (Cockburn 1992, 33) has purchase in relation to contemporary attempts to grapple with new media forms.

Participation, Expertise, Ambition

Finally I want to argue that feminism, in its turn, needs mediumcentric approaches, not least in order to retain or refresh a certain sense of ambition. At issue here is whether the 'Web 2.0 style' emphasis on participatory content production and social interaction in new media systems, the reascription of the technical perhaps, to layers further down the stack that might seem increasingly irrelevant, might imply, first, that the question of expertise, as an optic to consider gender and new media systems, is less important than in previous times and, second, that feminism itself might moderate or retarget its goals or its definition of what constitutes a problem?

In support of this kind of a reading – which I do not want to make – is the fact that, for more or less the first time, women's access to and use of many computational technologies, at least in the West, parallels that of men. Women identify with and are heavy users of computer technologies of many kinds (see, e.g., Microsoft's recent report on mobile phone use). They are among the computationally involved. Moreover, it could be argued that old barriers to participation – specifically, questions of skill and gendered access to skill – have fallen. If active participation is key and women are active and if participation is enabled through software tools that do not demand high levels of technical skill (tools that tend indeed increasingly to obscure the technical basis of their own operations), then why do questions of gendered use or the gendering of technological expertise matter?

To misquote an old advertisement for male programmers, does it *matter* (any longer) if women are not 'man enough' to 'Command Electric Giants'?[12] Is the very idea that it is a legitimate techno-feminist goal that women might impact rather than be impacted by digital technologies outdated, part of the unrealistic cyberfeminism legacy or the grim materialism of McNeil and her co-authors speaking from a pre-post-feminist era? Should the ambitions of feminism change?

My sense is that this is a route that has been taken up – at least in the sense that feminists writing and operating in digital networks today are largely not operating with that conscious sense of 'doing technology' that marked cyberfeminism or with the sense of 'dealing with technology' that was the project of many in McNeil's collection. While not confined to representation (in fact neglected in games studies), such works largely explore questions of identity and interaction arising in relation to networks as social formations. Questions of technological power and its distribution – an issue at the heart of McNeil and her contributors' questions about expertise and its material constitution – are neglected.

It is uncomfortable (or perhaps ironic) to recognize how neatly this realignment maps onto developments in computing: it is a computational development. Computing design has long followed a path designed to lead to increasing technological 'invisibility' in use – most recently, for instance, miniaturization slices and splices increasingly finely mediated experiences into the world. 'Everybody' sees less 'technology' than they used to, and 'everybody' needs fewer technical skills to use 'skilfully', even while 'everybody' is less aware of what is going on underneath the surface of the application or the platform. Expertise might be said to have been reprivatized on the one hand even as it has been democratized on the other. Of what is left visible of computing, 'anyone can do it'; as for the rest, it is increasingly hidden in the cloud. Perhaps, indeed, we might say expertise itself has been given notice to quit. At least, the putative inheritors of the system, the digital natives (often introduced as a group undifferentiated by race, class or sex) who, we may note, did not build their world, are meant to know instinctively how to use digital systems. Expertise, it appears will be replaced by (a problematic and quasi-evolutionary) form of affinity.

It is in these contexts that it can be useful to demand the development of critical software expertise, a response to a system that makes of computation and its operations something increasingly difficult to see or feel, a system that continually says 'don't look down'. A virtue of software studies is that it is less inclined, perhaps, than some modes of cultural studies to let the twin shibboleths of interactivity and connection obscure the real distinctions between various forms of engagement with new media of all kinds – and the various forms of control such engagement provides or denies. What I am indicating here – since I am not of the opinion that simple participation *is* all that matters – is that a critical feminism needs medium-theoretic approaches (a refreshed techno-feminism rather than post-feminism) to grapple with social media formations at more than a (literally) superficial level.

It seems to me that the desire of software studies to get at the heart of a certain form of production and, in doing so, to refuse the tech-free compensations of invisible technology is where feminism and code studies usefully converge – where a computational feminism might be refreshed. Meanwhile, a gendered critique of expertise might function to connect questions concerning computational power to questions of social dominance in more nuanced ways – developing a reforged material political economy of the new mediums. This is one reason why feminism, as it has so often done in the past, can contribute to shaping a critical response to *new* new media.

Notes

1. Media Matters: Friedrich Kittler and Technoculture. Public and Academic Symposium/Conference/Art Works Tate Modern, 27–28 June 2008 (Collaboration: London Consortium Birkbeck, Goethe-Institut and iRes).
2. Political theorist John Durham Peters, a speaker at the conference, noted the gender implications of various aspects of Kittler's later work.
3. Judy Wajcman notes the process through which 'in the late 19th Century technology came to be equated with engineering, and engineering with (new forms of) masculinity' (Suchman 2006, 322).
4. See, e.g., writers in the *Next Cyberfeminist International*, Cornelia Sollfrank and OBN, Rotterdam, 8–11 March 1999.
5. See Paasonen (2011) for a useful discussion of the two terms of cyberfeminism.
6. Giroux's definition of hope, made with reference to Bloch (Giroux 2007).
7. Representation is clearly not the only way to look at gender and women and in relation to media or medium theory or media and everyday life, as work by many have explained to us over the years. But it is one of the obvious

ways that feminists have engaged with media studies over the years, not least because that wave of feminism first working through difference and spectacle in popular culture and cinema found it central.

8. A parallel process can be seen within the history of computer programming – and computer programmers. Ensmenger's *The Computer Boys* considers how the reskilling of programming and the professionalization of the work involved the regendering of the activity – from female clerks (deriving from switchboard 'girls'), to geeky 'boys" (Ensmenger 2011, 52).

9. Elsewhere computerization of office work was continuing, and other unions, notably ASTMS in the UK, were part of international efforts to reduce eye strain and RSI, many of which took their cue from Australia and go-slower rates (not a work 'go slow' but keystrokes per hour).

10. Haraway adds – and this may be germane – that in games of taxonomy (not necessarily unaligned to lexicography), which in her view are best to be avoided in feminist scholarship, 'the father always wins' (Haraway 1987, 73).

11 There is another way, too, in which Lanier's work intersects with feminism's critique. In arguing for the distinction between various forms of code and, above all, various instantiations of code in use, Lanier is seeking to historicize not only the social contexts of use but the development of software systems themselves. Codeworks – double-edged poems that operate in natural language and computer language – are beautiful objects and might speak for 'code' itself, as an abstracted principle or an idealized relation, and given that the Codework uniquely speaks two ways well enough to become operational, it might be said that Codeworks embody in a different way the two-way intelligence Fuller wants to see in human operators.

12. IBM advertisement; cited in Ensmenger (2000, 52).

Renewing Feminism in the 2000s

Conclusions and Outlook

Anita Biressi and Heather Nunn

Feminist academic Catharine Lumby (2011, 95) recently recalled that, when attending an intergenerational debate entitled 'Is Feminism Dead?' the audience willingly self-identified as feminists. She went on to observe with some bemusement that she had been asked to speak on the same topic no less than fourteen times during the past decade. As her anecdote implies, this repetitious scenario signals both the endurance and the redundancy of the question 'Is Feminism Dead?' It also implies that there are, perhaps, more useful positions from which to begin a discussion of the relevance and route forward for feminism as theory and practice today. So, instead, we would like to take the opportunity in this chapter to enquire more productively about feminism's current status inside and beyond the academy. Which feminist practices and certainties are firmly in place, and which are endangered or under erasure? Which are newly emergent, and how do they or how might they engage with social change (see also Walby 2011, 1–2)? Clearly the answers to these questions are dependent on context. But it's apparent to all involved in feminist scholarship that time spent debating the *existence* of feminism (at least within the academy and political activism) is time lost on its necessary practice, whether in terms of research, debate or action in the field. And for those of us working in cultural or media studies, the need for feminist interventions has never been more pressing, with plentiful evidence of the persistence of sexism in old and new guises (see Gill 2011).

In this chapter we draw upon the work in *Renewing Feminisms* as a spur to map what we regard as some of the distinctive thematics of feminist media studies and feminism more widely and particularly since the 2000s. We have organized these into three broad but overlapping areas addressing narrative and history, experience and social difference, politics and the private and public spheres. In doing so, we highlight some of the key ways in which feminist theory and research are configured and personalized; for example, through narrative, history and anecdote. We also draw attention to the prominence of current scholarship on post-feminism, neoliberalism and consumerism and the continuing relevance of theorizations of the public and private spheres and of how these are articulated in media culture. And finally we argue the continuing and future importance of feminist media studies as a necessary intervention in the practices and discourses of the public realm. Overall, we want to stress feminism's (and feminist media studies') ongoing relevance as a political project and underline our conviction that politics remains the proper domain of feminist practice.

As Lumby (2011, 99) has noted, the 'issues we confront in the field of feminist media studies are central to the broader feminist project'. This project is essentially *political*; that is, a project taking place on public ground which seeks equality and justice across both the public and private spheres. Hence feminists frequently evaluate contemporary media culture with recourse to wider political markers around citizenship, the good society, mutual respect and visibility in and access to the public sphere. Often this project operates as counterpoint and critique of feminism as it is presented and frequently 'misamplified' by mainstream media as strident, outmoded or in other ways misconceived (see Zeisler in this volume; also Ashley and Olson 1998; Hinds and Stacey 2001; Hollows and Moseley 2006; Taylor 2008; Dow 1996, 2004; Mendes 2011). Also integral to contemporary feminist work is a sharp-eyed critique specifically of post-feminism, media and consumer culture (e.g. Lotz 2001, McRobbie 2009, Negra 2009, S. Thornham 2007, Gill and Scharff 2011, and H. Thornham in this volume). Naturally the ground of these encounters is always shifting as we respond to social change and new social pressures on women, men and families. So, as Weissmann and H. Thornham contend in their introduction, in language which is appropriate and also perhaps appropriating, inevitably we need to *retool* feminism so that its critical engagement with media and power remains pointed and its political project stays focused. This volume makes a significant contribution towards mapping the coordinates of the political grounds upon which such projects might rest.

Lumby's article, published in 2011, appeared in the 10th-anniversary issue of the landmark British journal *Feminist Media Studies*, which, like this collection, proves the resilience and the functionality of feminist scholarship, its fitness for purpose and its future longevity. The year 2011 also saw the 10th-anniversary celebrations of the Women's Media Studies Network (WMSN), a grouping supported by the British-based Media, Communication and Cultural Studies Association and whose purpose is to bring together women media scholars, teachers and practitioners for the exchange of knowledge, the promotion of feminist research and the provision of mutual support.[1] The WMSN's inaugural meeting took place on 12 September 2001 in the shadow of the shocking news of the attacks on the Twin Towers in New York. Aptly its 10th-anniversary meeting on 12 September 2011 returned to issues around women, news reporting, war and terrorism. Across the years WMSN symposia and meetings have addressed diverse matters, including female celebrity, gender and the public intellectual, Thatcherism and politics, motherhood and film, representation in television of nearly every genre and gender, feminism and the academy. The WMSN symposia are exemplary of the ways in which feminist scholarship, in its collective forms, regularly refreshes itself, so to speak, in order to engage with and cut through changing political, social and economic discourses about women in the polity. Events and interventions such as these (with many cited in this volume), together with recent scholarly collections (e.g. Brunsdon and Spigel 2008, Johnson 2007, Marciniak et al. 2007, Tasker and Negra 2007, Sarikakis and Shade 2008, Holmes and Negra 2011, Thynne and Al-Ali 2011), are evidence of the appetite for and commitment to a feminist media studies which is frequently topical and, crucially, always politicized. And such gatherings have in a modest way attracted the support of women across the generations, offering conversation, debate and sometimes consolation about the ongoing challenges, frustrations and triumphs of adopting a feminist standpoint within the academy.

History, Experience, Storytelling

The discovery that our individual experiences are sometimes shared (and sometimes not) and that there is a longer narrative of like feminist engagements, disappointments and successes is part of the pleasure of placing oneself in a history of political practice. Looking beyond one's individual experience, discipline or special interest is invaluable. Fortunately, the work of historians, cultural critics and sociologists has provided a reservoir of knowledge from which to draw, offering historical recollections and records of 'becoming a woman' and building the impetus to improving everyday life for women who may inhabit radically different social backgrounds and identities from their own (see Alexander 1994, Rowbotham 2010). Such histories contribute to the shared radical inheritance of women who have insisted on challenging the understatus of women in periods of stability or accelerated change, of social turmoil or political crisis. When faced with the pressures and oppressions of modern life, it is encouraging to recall the women who earlier battled for imagined better futures in response to their political or social marginalization and the iniquitous conditions of work or home or public life. *Renewing Feminisms*, with its attendance to history, identity and experience as the substratum of politics and theory, maintains the importance of retaining the historical and the grounded underpinning of feminism and feminist scholarship. As such, it is usefully part of a wider articulation and mobilization of past and present politics (e.g. Hollows 2000, Juhasz 2001, DiCenzo 2010, DiCenzo et al. 2011) in the service of future critical engagement with culture and its production, circulation and consumption. Essays in this collection attend to the ways in which feminism and its histories have been 'relayed' within the academy (see Aune) and in popular media (see S. Thornham) as well as across new technologies (see Zeisler and Bassett). They also point to the rich exchange of ideas between cultural producers and feminist academic criticism and the ways in which both parties reap the benefits. In reviewing what she describes as the 'push and pull' of activism and media research historically and then specifically since the late 1990s, Margaret Gallagher contends,

> If the early years were marked by the push of activism that contributed to a narrow empirical research approach, the subsequent coming of age of critical feminist scholarship has helped to pull activism away from simple criticisms towards more subtle and persuasive arguments. For me, it is this reciprocity between action and research that defines feminist media studies and that contributes to its intellectual and political force. (2001, 14)

Arguably the mutual exchange of ideas, experience and expertise charted by Gallagher, among others, has contributed towards feminism's current confidence, its variegation, its adaptability and future prospects. Stories abound about how bridges have been built between women in the academy, cultural producers and political activists and the rocky terrain that needed to be negotiated. These stories also offer historical insights into how women work through new feminist methodologies and thereby contribute to feminist thought. One valued dimension of this story mode for feminism is the presentation of personal experience as both document and the basis of theory and productive speculation. For example, Geraghty's opening piece in this volume recalls her involvement in the 1970s with the Women and Film Study Group (WFSG) and its engagement with film and then popular television as a central concern of feminist research. Their work demonstrated that popular culture can be a fruitful object of scrutiny, importantly underwriting the broader conviction that how people are represented in the media matters politically. Interventions and publications such as those produced by WFSG members helped set the benchmarks for subsequent inquiries. For example, Geraghty's own landmark book *Women and Soap Opera* (1991) attended to women's pleasures and the aesthetics of popular drama. Importantly, from our perspective, it also situated them in the context of social change and new delineations of the personal sphere and took leisure women's time seriously. Geraghty's account of the WFSG is equally significant, however, as a recollection of the working through of feminist practice and the group's encounters with numerous misconceptions, misunderstandings and anxieties, both their own and others'. Indeed, both Lumby's anecdote and Geraghty's historical narrative sit within a larger feminist tradition of linking the personal to the political through recollection, autobiography and memoir. Sometimes it is the introduction of a particular incident in one's own life which illuminates a more general condition.

We might, with reference to the work of Jane Gallop (2002), refer to the summoning of particular incidents as 'anecdotal moments', offering as they do personal snapshots which open out to broader political questions. For another example let's briefly turn to Rosalind Gill's (2009) relaying of an ostensibly unremarkable but actually highly illustrative telephone conversation she had with a colleague. Her transcript of their chat, which was reproduced in the edited collection *Secrecy and Silence in the Research Process*, included the kinds of conversations that many of us have had about mutual exhaustion, the emotional cost of academic work and the sense of inadequacy which women can feel when working within institutional structures. She goes on to comment that while some may find her inclusion of this personal conversation rather odd,

...for many more it will appear familiar and may strike deep chords of recognition. It speaks of many things: exhaustion, stress, overload, insomnia, anxiety, shame, aggression, hurt, guilt and feelings of out-of-placeness, fraudulence and fear of exposure within the contemporary academy. These feelings, these affective embodied experiences, occupy a strange position in relation to questions of secrecy and silence. They are at once ordinary and everyday, yet at the same time remain largely secret and silenced in the public spaces of the academy.[2]

Gill kindly shared this account and her reflections on the WMSN mailing list in response to a network symposium called, somewhat wryly, 'My Brilliant Career?' and her email prompted members to respond with recognition and appreciation. It reminded us that such short accounts of singular events or incidents – whether banal, amusing, provocative or confusing – can provide 'access to the real' (Gallop 2002, 9) and thereby allow theorizing to arise from lived experience.

Storytelling, Disclosure and Social Difference

We could regard these accounts as strategic manoeuvres in which personal experiences and anecdotal moments, often unremarkable in themselves, are drawn on somewhat reflexively to revaluate the past as well as to inform current debate, theorizing or practice (see Gregg 2004). For example, to return to Gill's transcribed conversation, it served not only as a point of mutual recognition and comfort but also as a launching pad for a scholarly exploration of how, even though feminist research is generally characterized by a history of breaking silences, there are still omissions and secrets waiting to be aired and their implications unpacked. Contributions to *Renewing Feminisms* also demonstrate a commitment to women's voices, uncovering their presence in archives, championing alternative ways of telling stories and validating cultures and heritages which have been sidelined or disparaged (see Kempadoo and De La Cruz in this volume). And as McNeil's piece on autobiography in this volume also makes clear, the recourse to autobiography, memoir, anecdote and personal experience in feminist scholarship is often contingent and always productively experimental. Her account of key feminists' deployment of autobiography clearly illustrates how these experiments work in counterpoint to the hegemonic discourses of gender, class or sexuality, discourses which they seek to unravel.

There is an honourable tradition in feminist scholarship of marshalling the personal as a prompt for the political with examples far too numerous to cite here. Nonetheless we would like to take a few moments to underline their past and future value as instruments that *renew* feminism, refresh its agendas and, in doing so, serve to ward off any complacency. It is generally accepted that even within feminist scholarship and for a variety of reasons, some women and some women's lives have been less visible than others; that some voices have been less often heard within the academy. For this reason contributions arising from personal experience are especially important, as they can make effective incursions into established cultures, including feminist cultures. For example, in Joan Scanlon's collection *Surviving the Blues*, Iraq-born Nora Al-Ani (1990a, 1990b) recalled her life during the Thatcher years as an immigrant and as a cleaner. She recounted her experience of racism at school, which was rooted in total ignorance of her culture and perceptions of her formed by *Carry On* films and adverts for Fry's Turkish Delight chocolate. She also described her time as a cleaner in a women's resources centre, where she felt invisible, replaceable and undervalued, setting out the disparity between the feminist ideals of the centre and her experience on the ground. She learned that while cleaning is important, the people who do it aren't. Al-Ani (1990a, 15) defiantly concludes: 'So there you have it: what happened, what didn't happen, what I got, but most of all what I want....'

Such moments of personal disclosure and critical reflection continue to be an effective tactic, forcing incursions into established hierarchies and helping to form new programmes of work. A more recent essay by Katarzyna Marciniak (2008) in *Feminist Media Studies* is exemplary. She begins with three anecdotes concerning her job presentation for an academic post, her time as a hotel housekeeper and conversations in which she has been positioned as the 'good immigrant'. Marciniak makes it clear that highlighting her past experience as a cleaner is made at some personal cost in terms of managing the perceptions of others. But the deployment of these experiences also offers her points of entry into scholarship which explicitly and politically connects the public, private and cultural spheres. Here Marciniak demonstrates with aplomb how anecdote and personal revelation work effectively to highlight lives which are hidden in plain sight and pave the way for her scholarly analysis of filmic depictions of foreign women in domestic service. Her recourse to anecdote and experience helps establish why a critical engagement with film fictions, for instance, matters politically.

Mediating Women: Private, Public and Social Realms

What's striking in many of the works which we have cited so far is the ongoing relevance of the public-private axis as a reference point for these critical engagements and a common suspicion of the ways in which women are expected to conduct themselves in the private, social and public realms. We would suggest, for example, that the private sphere and, specifically, the home and the domestic realm remain essentially a denigrated space, and women's association with homemaking and the family as a site of consumption continues to be problematic (and accordingly that cleaning and care work continue to be undervalued). From the outset, second-wave feminist commentary has contested normative and belittling images of women in the home and their reiteration across media texts. In this context, questions of representation, address and ideology, signalled as early as 1963 by magazine journalist Betty Friedan in her exposure of advertising and journalism's 'sexual sell', remain a central plank of feminist media analysis and gender studies.[3] Friedan herself charted the ways in which post-war women were aggressively repositioned within the private sphere of the home and homemaking and pressured to rank their family, its consumer practices and their own appearance (sexual attraction, the fight against aging, etc.) above action in the fields of work, politics and public culture.

Cultural critics have since tracked the tensions between the domestic realm (the home) and the public realm for women and families (Spigel 1992, 2001) and how these have been articulated in television in particular but also in film, advertising and lifestyle journalism. The current failure of financial systems, with its attendant impact on income generation, home ownership, social aspiration and consumerist lifestyles, has arguably renewed the pressure on women to inhabit the domestic realm productively and without complaint.[4] The impact of austerity measures can be seen in women's lives and also in the ways that austerity and thrift become rearticulated through representations of lifestyle choice. One strand of lifestyle programming in particular, which has been referred to as 'retreat TV' (Nunn 2011), has shifted emphasis away from home as financial investment and onto home as site of subsistence, sanctuary and emotional investment. Here, frugality and homemaking arguably run alongside a modified and often modest post-recession lifestyle, with women especially nostalgically figuring as homemakers, crafters and carers. Worryingly, women's expertise in the private sphere is heavily promoted and sanctioned via the redeployment and modification of earlier burdensome models of ideal femininity.

The home and its limits still mark the critical juncture between the public and private spheres while significantly underwriting the fact that the lines between the two are continually under review. Contributions in this volume point to the complex crossing of boundaries between private and public spheres that is enacted by broadcasting in particular. Skoog's research on post-war radio drama unpacks the assumptions and prejudices of producers about their female listeners to female-oriented soap opera. Weissmann signals the relationship between scheduling, context and meaning in the female-centred sitcoms of the 1990s, and Ball's essay explores the relationship between femininity and feminism in TV drama's depiction of working women. Between them, these pieces address all points of the cultural circuit from a feminist perspective and, in doing so, revisit, from new perspectives, key debates about the 'feminization' of media culture and how these impact iterations of private and public culture and women's inhabitation within and across the two.

The rhetorical positioning of women in certain spheres and the narrativization of their conduct within them impacts the way we understand ourselves as citizens, social actors and political subjects. But the media vehicles which convey them are breathtakingly varied and difficult to track. As Jane Arthurs (2004, 1) notes in her book on television and sexuality, the changes in the economic and cultural context within which programmes are produced and distributed have resulted in a 'marked diversity of representations'. Arthurs also makes the larger case that

> ... there is a legitimate 'public interest' in the forms of sexual representation made available; it isn't something that can be left to the market but neither is it simply 'trash' to be got rid of. Television has a significant role to play in sexual citizenship and should be a forum and stimulus for political debate and education, as well as a source of personal meaning.... (2004, 13)

This is a claim to the public importance of feminist media scholarship which all scholars can adopt with confidence. Taking the wider view, it can be said that television plays a significant role in all dimensions of citizenship; its framing, promotion, refashioning or negation, its possible forms and futures (see, e.g., Miller 2007, Ouellette and Hay 2008, Sanli 2012, Weber 2009).

While Arthurs focuses on issues of taste, regulation and sexuality, we would suggest that the diversity of representation she refers to is evident across the board in terms of the depiction of women's lives. For example, our own research interests lie in British factual television's accounts of women's lives in the public sphere: about work, entrepreneurship, social aspiration, political activism, public justice and so on; arguably these topics have increasingly found places in the schedules. Examples from our own content analysis over the last few years indicate both the diversity and the complexity of the images available of women as citizens, workers and political actors. Various activisms and community action are explored in recent documentaries such as *Women's Institute* (2011), *Carry Greenham Home* (2010), *Timeshift: Greenham Common* (2010) and *Women of Burberry* (2011) and series such as *Call Yourself a Feminist* (2009) and *Women* (2010). Similarly, current affairs confront, albeit often quite fearfully, sexual difference and the changing roles of women in series such as *Genderquake* (2011), *The British at Work* (2011), *Why Men Don't Iron* (2011), *Panorama: The Future Is Female* (2011) and *The Trouble with Working Women* (2009). There is also a spate of history programmes, such as *Not Forgotten* (2010), *Spitfire Women* (2010) and *Time to Remember: A Woman's World* (2010), which approvingly recall women's lives during the Second World War and its aftermath. Yet others consider the relationship between women and the media (*How TV Changed Britain: Women*, 2009), sport (*Women at Play*, 2011) or leisure (*True Stories: Guilty Pleasures*, 2011). Meanwhile popular programming such as *Working Girls* (2011) and *Soldier Girls* (2009) champion the ability of women to contribute to public life (albeit as juveniles – 'girls' – rather than women). Others, however, suggest that negotiating women's expectations is still a problem for men and that the battle of the sexes is still being waged; for example, *How to Live with Women* (2011), *When Women Rule the World* (2008) and *Tool Academy* (2009).[5]

Less visible or else depicted as hapless victims of circumstances (often rooted in ethnic or class origins) are women who do not or cannot conform to Western neoliberal models of successful femininity and who consequently struggle to attain recognition as good citizens, vigorous consumers or autonomous actors. Frequently they are depicted as failures within or across private, public and social spheres. When respected documentary series – *Unreported World* (2010), for example – focus on women, the topics tend to be negative, addressing human trafficking, the imposition of the veil, sexual mutilation, honour killings and so on. Closer to home there are programmes which address the lives of girls and women living in difficult circumstances: *Black Britain: Women Behind Bars* (2011), *Walk on the Wild Side: Possil Girls* (2011), *Prison, Mum and Me* (2011) and *Rich Kid, Poor Kid* (2008). While often revealing and frequently respectful of their subjects, taken together they offer a bleak picture of poorer women's lives, subjectivity and autonomy. Even though these depictions may be truthful and informative, taken in aggregate the women depicted in them are implicitly and unfavourably compared with the approved mainstream of white middle-class behaviours more commonly found in the lifestyle programmes which populate our screens. Encouraging stories of poorer or marginalized women who nonetheless insist on their autonomy, independence and effectiveness as citizens are far from common.[6]

Marciniak's essay on women cleaners in film, cited above, is one of a growing number of works which attend to the complex and often dubious media treatment of poorer immigrant or working-class people in both factual and fictional formats (see, e.g., Shugart 2006, Skeggs and Wood 2008, Morley 2009, Skeggs 2010). Recent work has examined the ways in which individuals have been condemned for poor parenting (Biressi and Nunn 2008, Ferguson 2010) and for damaging lifestyles and low aspirations (Biressi and Nunn 2010, Biressi 2011). Attention is being paid to the ways in which women have been negatively styled as single parents, as sexually promiscuous and as non-productive citizens. Arguably we are witnessing what Anna McCarthy (2007) has described as the 'responsibilization' of underperforming citizens who are held to account in political rhetoric and in the media for their own 'failure' to contribute 'positively' to the social realm (see also Palmer 2003, Ouellette and Hay 2008). Imogen Tyler (2008, 18), whose own work on 'chav mums' has been influential in the return to cultural analyses of classed representations, has suggested that the intense fascination and repulsion directed at these figures may be symptomatic of 'heightened class antagonism that marks a new episode in the dirty ontology of class struggle in Britain'. We would argue that with present financial pressure triggering an increased competition for resources (welfare, jobs, housing, education), feminism's engagement with class and race politics will have to become increasingly robust (see Battacharyya 2011).

The diverse examples of women on screen also speak to what Ros Gill (2007, 1) has described as the 'extraordinary contradictoriness of constructions of gender in today's media', adding that 'everywhere it seems that feminist ideas have become a kind of common sense, yet feminism has never been more bitterly repudiated'. As she sees it, arguably supported by some of our examples above, feminism's project of equality is treated as sensible, progressive and fairly successful, and yet 'boring and predictable patterns of sexism persist' (Gill, 2), including the invisibility of older and poorer women, the marginalization of black women and the reductive, depressing and rather scanty representation of women in news and foreign affairs.

Conclusion: Everyone's Citizenship

Where what might be called 'subaltern' women do find a voice in news media, their rarity renders them conspicuous, vulnerable and the object of unlimited fascination. We have recently seen this with regard to the coverage since May 2011 of the accusations made by the hotel maid Nafissatou Diallo against former International Monetary Fund chief Dominique Strauss-Kahn and, more specifically, about Diallo herself. For example, it was reported that the French press extensively appraised her 'attractiveness' as a potential object of assault and her status as a single mother and an immigrant alongside the veracity of her testimony. Diallo's media treatment, whatever her legal claims, can be read as yet another telling case of the 'material limits to dignity and citizenship' experienced by some women in the public sphere (Berlant 1997, 222).

Subsequently we have seen Diallo herself participate in the public realm via a TV interview and the taking out of a civil action.[7] In Lauren Berlant's (1997, 222–3) terms, we might choose to read Diallo's decision to speak in public and directly tell the story from her own perspective optimistically; to view her as a practitioner of 'diva citizenship' and as one of small number of women who publicly testify to their 'imperilled citizenship' through 'acts of risky dramatic persuasion'. Berlant, in her extensive discussion of African American women's citizenship and media events such as the state testimony of Anita Hill against Clarence Thomas's sexual misconduct (1991), argues that a genealogy of sexual power which looked at the nation rather than the individual via cases such as these might establish an archival history that 'claimed the most intimate stories of subordinated people as information about everyone's citizenship' (Bertlant 1997, 221).

Berlant's strategy here is to step back from the particular to the general in order to better understand the wider structural supports which bolster the powerful and reinforce their successes. In this way she addresses the limits of individual testimony and the proscriptive conditions under which women's voices seek to make themselves heard. Ultimately, she argues, these women challenge citizens to take up 'politically what the strongest divas were unable, individually, to achieve' (Berlant, 246). This is an argument insisting that we are collectively responsible for a woman's individual injury and that, in turn, individual injury results in collective damage (everyone's citizenship). Consequently, Berlant's call returns us to where we began this piece: to feminism as a political project and to politics as the proper domain of feminist practice.

The rich responses in this collection all – explicitly or implicitly – converse with feminist predecessors while covering new ground or pointing to refreshed strategies for the twenty-first century. They suggest that feminism continues to be a resource, discourse and force to be drawn upon in the ongoing engagement with the inequities that structure and often undermine women's lives. Feminism is part project, part narrative and part imaginative exercise in its creative engagements with current and future social conditions and cultural scripts. It comes in many forms and is occasionally despairing, frustrated, distressed or indeed properly angry. However, its proponents can also be astute, funny, self-reflexive, technologically savvy, theoretically agile and dogged. Feminists across generations and social and political differences share a wilful refusal to give in to the long struggle to attain a better, more equitable life for all. If we started by engaging with the question 'is feminism dead?' then, as this volume indicates, the heartening rejoinder is that feminism is very much alive. As a political project it refuses conclusion, is incorrigibly plural and is ultimately still well equipped to challenge, to support and to renew social and political aspirations across diverse individuals, groups and institutions.

Notes

1. It seems that the new century also proved a stimulus to feminist communication in other settings. *The F Word* online magazine also celebrates its tenth anniversary in 2011; see www.thefword.org.uk/index.
2. While this appears in *Flood and Gill* (2010), we have reproduced this from the WMSN, where it first came to our attention. To access it and the subsequent discussion, go to the Search Archive link on the WMSN page, www.jiscmail.ac.uk.
3. Scrutiny of what constitutes women's proper work in media narratives is still extremely topical. Diane Negra (2009, 86), e.g., has addressed the 'new archetypes' of female labour as played out in film romances which suggest that if women won't go back to the home, they might at least inhabit the subordinate service roles of table waiting, flight attendant and preschool teaching.
4. See, e.g., the UK gender-equality campaign group Fawcett Society's recent report, *Are Women Bearing the Burden of Recession* (2009), www.fawcettsociety.org.uk/documents/Arewomenbearingtheburdenoftherecession.pdf (retrieved 14 August 2011).
5. Dates given in brackets for programmes or series indicate the year they were first broadcast in Britain.
6. With *The Estate We're In* (2008 and 2010) being a notable exception. This series features Silla Carron, a community activist widely recognized for

her achievements in improving the living conditions of residents in social housing.

7. Diallo appeared on ABC's *Good Morning America* and was interviewed for *Newsweek*, 25 July 2011, 'The Maid's Tale', www.thedailybeast.com/ newsweek/2011/07/24/dsk-maid-tells-of-her-alleged-rape-by-strauss-kahn-exclusive.html (retrieved 9 August 2011).

Bibliography

Adkins, Lisa (1999), 'Community and Economy: A Re-traditionalization of Gender?', *Theory, Culture and Society*, 16 (1), 119–39.

—— (2001), 'Cultural Feminization: "Money, Sex and Power" for women', *Journal of Women in Culture and Society*, 26 (3), 31–57.

—— (2002), *Revisions: Gender and Sexuality in Late Modernity* (Buckingham: Open University Press).

—— (2004), 'Passing on Feminism: From Consciousness to Reflexivity?' *European Journal of Women's Studies*, 11 (4), 427–44.

Ahmed, Sarah (2007), '"You End up Doing the Document Rather Than Doing the Doing": Diversity, Race Equality and the Politics of Documentation', *Ethnic and Racial Studies*, 30 (4), 590–609.

Aikau, Hokulani (2007), 'Between Wind and Water: Thinking about the Third Wave as Metaphor and Materiality', in Aikau, Erikson and Pierce (eds), *Feminist Waves, Feminist Generations* (Minneapolis and London: University of Minnesota Press), 232–49.

Aikau, Hokulani, Erikson, Karla A., and Pierce, Jennifer L. (2007), 'Introduction: Feminist Waves, Feminist Generations', in Aikau, Erikson and Pierce (eds), *Feminist Waves, Feminist Generations* (Minneapolis and London: University of Minnesota Press), 1–45.

Akass, Kim, and McCabe, Janet (2004), 'Introduction: Welcome to the Age of Un-Innocence', in Akass, Kim, and McCabe, Janet (eds), *Reading Sex and the City* (London: I.B.Tauris), 1–15.

Al-Ani, Nora (1990a), 'Don't Ask Her, She's Just the Cleaner', in Scanlon, Joan (ed.) *Surviving the Blues: Growing up in the Thatcher Decade* (London: Virago), 11–15.

—— (1990b), 'No Going Back', in Scanlon, Joan (ed.) *Surviving the Blues: Growing up in the Thatcher Decade* (London: Virago), 16–23.

Alexander, Sally (1994), *Becoming a Woman: And Other Essays in 19th and 20th Century History* (London: Virago).

Allsopp, Richard (1996), *Dictionary of Caribbean Usage* (Oxford: Oxford University Press).

Althusser, Louis (1971), *Lenin and Philosophy and Other Essays*, trans. Ben Brewster (London: NLB).

Anderson, Benedict (1983), *Imagined Communities: Reflections on the Origin and Spread of Nationalism* (London and New York: Verso Books).

Ang, Ien (1985), *Watching Dallas. Soap Opera and The Melodramatic Imagination* (New York: Methuen & Co.).

——(1990), 'Melodramatic Identifications: Television Fiction and Women's Fantasy', in Brown, Mary Ellen (ed.), *Television and Women's Culture: The Politics of the Popular* (London: Sage), 75–88.

——(1991), *Desperately Seeking the Audience* (London, New York: Routledge).

——(1992), 'Living-room Wars: New Technologies, Audience Measurement and the Tactics of Television Consumption', in Silverstone, Roger and Hirsch, Eric (eds), *Consuming Technologies: Media and Information in Domestic Spaces* (London: Routledge), 131–46.

Ang, Ien, and Hermes, Joke (1991), 'Gender and/in Media Consumption' in Curran, James and Gurevitch, Michael (ed.) *Mass Media and Society* (London: Edward Arnold), 109–29.

Anzaldúa, Gloria E. (1987), *Borderlands: The New Mestiza = La Frontera* (San Francisco: Spinsters / Aunt Lute).

Arthurs, Jane (2003), '*Sex and the City* and Consumer Culture: Remediating Postfeminist Drama' *Feminist Media Studies*, 3 (1), 83–98.

——(2004), *Television and Sexuality: Regulation and the Politics of Taste* (Maidenhead: Open University Press).

Ashley, Laura, and Olson, Beth (1998), 'Constructing Reality: Print Media's Framing of the Women's Movement, 1966–1986', *Journal of Mass Communication Quarterly*, 75 (2), 263–77.

Attwood, Feona (2010), 'Representations of Cosmopolitan Sex Work', *Feminist Media Studies*, 10 (1), 109–12.

Awai, Nicole (2007), 'E-mail from "HERE"', *Small Axe: A Caribbean Journal of Criticism*, 11 (3), 109–17.

Baehr, Helen (1980), 'The Liberated Woman in Television Drama', *Women's Studies International Quarterly*, 3, 29–39

Baehr, Helen, and Dyer, Gillian (1987) (eds), *Boxed in: Women and Television* (London and New York: Pandora Press).

Ball, Vicky (2012), 'The 'Feminization' of British Television and the Re-traditionalization of Gender', *Feminist Media Studies*, 12 (2), 248–64.

Banyard, Kat (2010), *The Equality Illusion* (London: Faber & Faber).

BARB (2009), 'Annual % Shares of Viewing (Individuals) 1981–2008' on the *BARB Website*, www.barb.co.uk/facts/annualShareOfViewing?_s=4 [accessed 12 May 2009].

Barbash, Ilisa, and Taylor, Lucien (1997), *Cross-cultural Filmmaking* (Berkeley: University of California Press).

Barthes, Roland (1984), *Camera Lucida: Reflections on Photography* (London: Flamingo).

Bassett, Caroline (2007), *The Arc and the Machine* (Manchester: Manchester University Press).

——(2009), 'With a Little Help from Her Friends', reprint of *Mute* article on cyberfeminism, *Proud to be Flesh: A Mute Magazine Anthology of Cultural Politics after the Net.*, http://metamute.org/ptbf, [accessed 25 August 2011].

Battacharyya, Gargi (2011), 'Will These Emergencies Never End? Some First Thoughts about the Impact of Economic and Security Crises on Everyday Life', in Gill, Rosalind, and Scharff, Christina (eds), *New*

Femininities: Postfeminism, Neoliberalism and Subjectivity (Basingstoke: Palgrave Macmillan), 306–19.

Beck, Ulrich (1992), *Risk Society: Towards a New Modernity* (London: Sage).

Beck, Ulrich, and Beck-Gernsheim, Elisabeth (2001), *Individualization* (London: Sage).

——(1996), 'Individualization and "Precarious Freedoms": Perspectives and Controversies of a Subject-Orientated Sociology', in Heelas, Paul, Lash, Scott, and Morris, Paul (eds), *Detraditionalization* (Oxford: Blackwell), 23–48.

Bell, Melanie (2010), *Femininity in the Frame. Women and 1950s British Popular Cinema* (London: I.B.Tauris).

Benitéz-Rojo, Antonio (1996), *The Repeating Island: The Caribbean and the Postmodern Perspective*, 2nd edn (Durham and London: Duke University Press).

Berlant, Lauren (1997), *The Queen of America Goes to Washington City: Essays on Sex and Citizenship* (London: Duke University Press).

Berry, David M. (2011), 'The Computational Turn: Thinking about the Digital Humanities', *Culture Machine*, 12, 1–19.

Biressi, Anita (2011), '"The Virtuous Circle": Social Entrepreneurship and Welfare Programming in the UK', in Skeggs, Barbara and Wood, Helen (eds), *Reality Television and Class* (London: BFI Publishing), 144–55.

Biressi, Anita, and Nunn, Heather (2008), 'Bad Citizens: The Class Politics of Lifestyle Television', in Palmer, Gareth (ed.), *Exposing Lifestyle Television: The Big Reveal* (Aldershot: Ashgate), 15–24.

——(2010), 'Shameless: Picturing the "Underclass" after Thatcherism', in Hadley, Louisa and Ho, Elizabeth (eds), *Thatcher and After: Margaret Thatcher and her Afterlife in Contemporary Culture* (Basingstoke: Palgrave Macmillan), 137–57.

Bolas, Terry (2009), *Screen Education from Film Appreciation to Media Studies* (Bristol UK/ Chicago USA: Intellect).

Bourke, Joanna (1994), *Working Class Cultures in Britain 1890–1960: Gender, Class and Ethnicity* (London: Routledge).

Bowlby, John (1953), *Childcare and the Growth of Love* (London: Penguin).

Boyce Davies, Carol (1994), *Black Women, Writing and Identity: Migrations of the Subject* (London: Routledge).

Boyle, Karen (2000), 'The Pornography Debates: Beyond Cause and Effects', *Women's Studies International Forum*, 23 (2): 187–95.

——(2005), 'Feminism without Men. Feminist Media Studies in a Post-Feminist Age' in Curran, James and Gurevitch, Michael (eds), *Mass Media and Society*, 4th Edition (London: Arnold), 29–43.

——(2010), 'Selling the Selling of Sex: *The Secret Diary of a Call Girl* on Screen', *Feminist Media Studies* 10 (1), 113–16.

Boyle, Maree, and Parry, Ken W. (2007), 'Telling the Whole Story: The Case for Organizational Autoethnography', *Culture & Organization Journal*, 13 (3), 185–90.

Braidotti, Rosi (1994), *Nomadic Subjects: Embodiment and Sexual Difference in Contemporary Feminist Theory* (New York: Columbia University Press).

——(2002), *Metamorphoses: Towards a Materialist Theory of Becoming* (Cambridge: Polity Press).

Breger, Claudia (2006), 'Gods, German Scholars, and the Gift of Greece: Friedrich Kittler's Philhellenic Fantasies', *Theory, Culture & Society* December 23 (7–8), 111–34.

Briggs, Asa (1979), *The History of Broadcasting in the United Kingdom vol. IV. Sound and Vision* (Oxford: Oxford University Press).

Brown, Maggie (2007), *A Licence to be Different. The Story of Channel 4* (London: BFI).

Brunsdon, Charlotte (1982), 'A Subject for the Seventies', *Screen*, 23 (3–4), 20–9.

——(1995), 'The Role of Soap Opera in the Development of Feminist Television Scholarship' in Allen, Robert (ed.), *To be Continued... Soap Operas Around the World* (Abingdon, New York: Routledge), 49–65.

——(1997), *Screen Tastes: Soap Opera to Satellite Dishes* (London: Routledge).

——(1998), 'Structure of Anxiety: Recent British Television Crime Fiction', *Screen*, 39 (3), 223–43.

——(2000a), *The Feminist, the Housewife, and the Soap Opera* (Oxford: Clarendon Press).

——(2000b), 'Not Having it All: Women and Film in the 1990s', in Murphy, Robert (ed.), *British Film of the 90s* (London: BFI), 167–77.

——(2003), 'Lifestyling Britain: The 8–9 Slot on British Television' *International Journal of Cultural Studies*, 6 (1), 5–23.

——(2006), 'The Feminist in the Kitchen: Martha, Martha and Nigella', in Hollows, Joanne, and Moseley, Rachel (eds), *Feminism in Popular Culture* (Oxford and New York: Berg), 41–56.

Brunsdon, Charlotte, D'Acci, Julie, and Spigel, Lynn (1997) (eds), *Feminist Television Criticism: A Reader* (Berkshire and New York: Open University Press).

Brunsdon, Charlotte, Johnson, Catherine, Moseley, Rachel, and Wheatley, Helen (2001), 'Factual Entertainment on British Television: The Midlands TV Research Group's "8–9 Project"', *European Journal of Cultural Studies*, 4 (1), 29–62.

Brunsdon, Charlotte, and Spigel, Lynn (eds) (2008), *Feminist Television Criticism* (Milton Keynes: Open University Press).

Buckingham, David (2009), 'Creative Visual Methods in Media Research: Possibilities, Problems and Proposals', *Media, Culture & Society*, 31 (4), 633–52.

Burgin, Victor (1982), 'Looking at Photographs', in Burgin, Victor (ed.), *Thinking Photography* (London/New Jersey: Macmillan/Humanities Press International), 142–53.

——(2004), *The Remembered Film* (London: Reaktion Books).

Burton, Antoinette (2006), *Archive Stories: Facts, Fictions, and the Writing of History* (Durham: Duke University Press).

Buss, David M. (1996), 'Sexual Conflict: Evolutionary Insights into Feminism and the "Battle of the Sexes"', in Buss, David M., and Malamuth,

Neill M. (eds), *Sex, Power, Conflict: Evolutionary and Feminist Perspectives*. (New York and Oxford: Oxford University Press).

Butler, Judith (1990), *Gender Trouble. Feminism and the Subversion of Identity* (London: Routledge).

——(1993), *Bodies That Matter* (New York: Routledge).

Carr, Diane, Buckingham, David, Burn, Andrew, and Schott, Gareth (2006), *Computer Games: Text, Narrative and Play* (Cambridge: Polity Press).

Cassell, Justine, and Jenkins, Henry (ed.) (2000/1998), *From Barbie to Mortal Kombat: Gender and Computer Games* (Cambridge, MA: MIT Press).

Cavarero, Adriana (2000), *Relating Narratives: Storytelling and Selfhood* (London: Routledge).

Chun, Wendy, Hui Kyong (2008), 'On "Sourcery," or Code as Fetish', in *Configurations*, 16 (3), 299–324.

C.L. (1978), 'Coronation Street under the Academic Microscope', *Broadcast* (9 January).

Clifford, James, and Marcus, George (eds) (1986), *Writing Culture: The Poetics and Politics of Ethnography* (Berkeley: University of California Press).

Clough, Patricia Ticineto (1992), *The End(s) of Ethnography: From Realism to Social Criticism* (London: Sage).

Clouser, Rebecca (2009), 'Remnants of Terror: Landscapes of Fear in Post-Conflict Guatemala' *Journal of Latin American Geography*, 8 (2), 7–22.

Cockburn, Cynthia (1985), *Machinery of Dominance. Women and Men and Technological Know-How* (London: Pluto).

——(1983), *Brothers: Male Dominance and Technological Change* (London: Pluto).

——(1992), 'The Circuit of Technology: Gender, Identity and Power', in Hirsch, Eric and Silverstone, Roger (eds), *Consuming Technologies, Media and Information in Domestic Spaces* (London: Routledge), 32–48.

Colquhoun, Gary (1995), 'Audience Reaction to Programming around the Watershed', in Hargrave, Andrea Millwood (ed.), *The Scheduling Game: Annual Review 1995* (London, Paris, Rome: John Libbey), 142–47.

Conway, Dennis (2001), *The Complexity of Caribbean Migration*, http://gtuwi.tripod.com/conwaymigr.htm [accessed 23 September 2010].

Cook, Lez (2007), 'Drama on Four 1982–1991'. Conference paper delivered at *Channel 4 – The First 25 Years*. London, BFI Southbank (17–18 November).

Cosslett, Tess, Lury, Celia, and Summerfield, Penny (eds), *Feminism and Autobiography: Texts, Theories, Methods* (London and New York: Routledge, 2000).

Critcher, Chas (1979), 'Sociology, Cultural Studies and the Post-war Working Class' in Clarke, John, Critcher, Chas and Johnson, Richard (eds), *Working-Class Culture: Studies in History and Theory* (London: Hutchinson), 13–40.

Cronin, Anne (2000), *Advertising and Consumer Citizenship* (London and New York: Routledge).

Culley, Margo, and Portuges, Catherine (eds) (1985), *Gendered Subjects: The Dynamics of Feminist Teaching* (Boston: Routledge and Kegan Paul).

Curran, James (2006), 'Media and Cultural Theory in the Age of Market Liberalism', in Curran, James, and Morley, David (2006) (eds), *Media and Cultural Theory* (London: Routledge), 129–48.

D'Acci, Julie (1994), *Defining Women: Television and the Case of* Cagney and Lacey (Chapel Hill: University of North Carolina Press).

Daly, Mary (1979), *Gyn/Ecology: The Metaethics of Radical Feminism* (London: Women's Press).

David, Miriam, and Clegg, Sue (2008), 'Power, Pedagogy and Personalization in Global Higher Education: The Occlusion of Second-wave Feminism?', *Discourse: Studies in the Cultural Politics of Education*, 29 (4), 483–98.

Davis, Jenny (2010), 'Architecture of the Personal Interactive Homepage: Constructing the self through MySpace', *New Media & Society*, 12 (7), 1103–19.

Dayus, Kathleen (1982), *Her People* (London: Virago).

Dean, Jonathan (2010), *Rethinking Contemporary Feminist Politics* (Basingstoke: Palgrave Macmillan).

——(2008), 'Feminist Purism and the Question of "Radicality" in Contemporary Political Theory', *Contemporary Political Theory*, 7 (3), 280–301

Deans, Jason, and Holmwood, Leigh (2009), 'Michael Grade to Step Down as ITV Executive Chairman' at *Media Guardian* (23 April), www.guardian.co.uk/media/2009/apr/23/michael-grade-step-down-itv-chief-executive [accessed 6 May 2009].

De Lauretis, Teresa (1984), *Alice Doesn't: Feminism, Semiotics, Cinema* (Bloomington: Indiana University Press).

——(1987), *Technologies of Gender: Essays on Theory, Film, and Fiction* (Basingstoke and London: Macmillan).

——(1990), 'Upping the Anti (sic) in Feminist Theory', in Hirsch, Marianne, and Fox Keller, Evelyn (eds), *Conflicts in Feminism* (New York and London: Routledge), 255–70.

Derrida, Jacques (1974), *Of Grammatology* (Baltimore: John Hopkins University Press).

Dervin, Brenda (1987), 'The Potential Contribution of Feminist Scholarship to the Field of Communication', *Journal of Communication*, 37 (4), 107–20.

DiCenzo, Maria (2010), 'Pressing the Public: Nineteenth Century Feminist Periodicals and "the Press"', *Nineteenth-Century Gender Studies*, Special Issue: *Nineteenth-Century Feminisms: Press & Platform*, Issue 6 (2), Summer, www.ncgsjournal.com/issue62/issue62.htm [accessed 22 August 2011].

DiCenzo, Maria, Delap, Lucy, and Ryan, Leila (eds) (2011), *Feminist Media History: Suffrage Periodicals and the Public Sphere* (Basingstoke: Palgrave Macmillan).

Doane, Mary Ann (2000), 'Technophilia: Technology, Representation and the Feminine', in Kirkup, Gill, Janes, Linda, Woodward, Kath, and Hovenden, Fiona (ed.), *The Gendered Cyborg: A Reader* (London: Routledge), 110–22.

——(2004), 'Aesthetics and Politics', *Signs*, 30 (1), 1229–35.

Doherty, Thomas (2003), *Cold War. Cold Medium. Television, McCarthyism, and American Culture* (New York: Columbia University Press).

Douglas, Kate (2006), '"Blurbing" Biographical: Authorship and Autobiography', *Biography: An Interdisciplinary Quarterly*, 24 (4), 806–826.

Dow, Bonnie J. (1996), *Prime-time Feminism: Television, Media Culture and the Women's Movement since 1970* (Philadelphia: University of Pennsylvania Press).

——(2004), 'Fixing Feminism: Women's Liberation and the Rhetoric of Television Documentary', *Quarterly Journal of Speech*, 90 (1), 53–80.

Dyer, Richard, Lovell, Terry, and McCrindle, Jean (1977), 'Soap Opera and Women' paper presented by to the Edinburgh International Television Festival, August. In Ann Gray and Jim McGuigan (eds), *Studying Culture*, 35–41. Originally published in the *Edinburgh International Television Festival 1977 – Official Programme*.

Edwards, Steve (1989), 'The Snapshooters of History', *Ten.8* (Birmingham: Ten.8 Ltd).

Ellis, John (2000), 'Scheduling: The Last Creative Act in Television?' in: *Media, Culture & Society*, 22 (1), 25–38.

Ensmenger, Nathan L. (2010), *The Computer Boys Take Over. Computers, Programmers, and the Politics of Technical Expertise* (London: MIT).

Equality and Human Rights Commission (2008), *Sex and Power 2008*, www.equalityhumanrights.com/uploaded_files/sex_and_power_2008_pdf.pdf [accessed 28 August 2011].

Espinet, Ramabai (1993), 'Representation and the Indo-Caribbean Woman in Trinidad and Tobago', in Birbalsingh, Frank (ed.), *Indo-Caribbean Resistance* (Toronto: TSAR Publications), 42–61.

Fanthome, Christine (2003), *Channel 5: The Early Years* (Luton: University of Luton Press).

Feasey, Rebecca (2008), 'Female Students and Feminist Media Criticism: The Pleasures and Frustrations of Teaching Gender Studies', paper presented at the conference *The Point of Feminism*, University of Reading, September.

Fehr, Carla (2008), 'Are Smart Men Smarter than Smart Women? The Epistemology of Ignorance, Women, and the Production of Knowledge', in May, Ann Mari (ed.), *The 'Woman Question' and Higher Education* (Cheltenham and Northampton, MA: Edward Elgar), 102–16.

Felman, Jyl Lynn (2001), *Never a Dull Moment: Teaching and the Art of Performance – Feminism Takes Center Stage* (New York: Routledge).

Felman, Shoshona (1993), *What Does a Woman Want? Reading and Sexual Difference* (Baltimore: Johns Hopkins University Press).

Ferguson, Galit (2010), 'The Family on Reality TV: Who's Shaming Whom?', *Television and New Media*, 11 (2), 87–104.

Fernandez, Maria, and Wilding, Faith (2003), 'Situating Cyberfeminism', in Fernandez, Maria, Wilding, Faith, and Wright, Michelle M. (eds), *Domain Errors! Cyberfeminist Practices* (New York: Automedia), 17–28.

Fine, Michelle (1994), 'Dis-tance and Other Stances: Negotiations of Power inside Feminist Research', in Gitlin, Andrew (ed.), *Power and Method: Political Activism and Educational Research* (London: Routledge), 13–35.

Firestone, Shulamith (1979), *The Dialectic of Sex* (London: Women's Press).

Fiske, John (1987), *Television Culture* (London, New York: Methuen).

Fraser, Nancy (1989), *Unruly Practices: Power, Discourse and Gender in Contemporary Social Theory* (Cambridge: Polity Press).

Freeman, Jo (1973), 'Women on the Move: Roots of Revolt', in Rossi, Alice S. and Calderwood, Ann (eds), *Academic Women on the Move* (New York: Russell Sage Foundation), 1–32.

Freire, Paulo (1970), *Pedagogy of the Oppressed*, trans Myra Bergman Ramos (New York: Seabury Press).

Friedan, Betty (1965/1963), *The Feminine Mystique* (London: Penguin).

Fuller, Matthew (2008) (ed.), *Software Studies. A Lexicon* (Cambridge, MA; London: MIT).

Fuss, Diana (1989), *Essentially Speaking. Feminism, Nature and Difference* (London. Routledge).

Gadamer, Hans Georg (1965), *Wahrheit und Methode: Grundzüge einer Philosophischen Hermeneutik* (Tübingen: Mohr).

Galinsky, Ellen, Salmond, Kimberlee, and Bond, James T. (2003), *Leaders in a Global Economy: A Study of Executive Women and Men* (New York: Families and Work Institute).

Gallagher, Margaret (2001), 'The Push and Pull of Action and Research in Feminist Media Studies', *Feminist Media Studies*, 1 (1), 11–14.

Gallop, Jane (ed.) (1997), *Pedagogy: The Question of Impersonation* (Bloomington: Indiana University Press).

——(2002), *Anecdotal Theory* (Durham: Duke University Press).

Genz, Stéphanie (2006), 'Third Way/ve: The Politics of Postfeminism', *Feminist Theory*, 7 (3): 333–53.

Geraghty, Christine (1991), *Women and Soap Opera. A Study of Prime Time Soaps* (Cambridge: Polity).

Giddens, Anthony (1992), *The Transformation of Intimacy* (Cambridge: Polity Press).

Giles, Judy (2004), *The Parlour and the Suburb. Domestic Identities, Class, Femininity and Modernity* (Oxford: Berg).

Gill, Rosalind (2007a), *Gender and the Media* (Cambridge: Polity Press).

——(2007b), 'Postfeminist Media Culture: Elements of a Sensibility', *European Journal of Cultural Studies*, 10 (2), 147–66.

——(2009), 'Secrets, Silences and Toxic Shame in the Neoliberal University' in Ryan-Flood, Róisín and Gill, Rosalind (eds) *Secrecy and Silence in the Research Process: Feminist Reflections* (London: Routledge), 253–64.

——(2011), 'Sexism Reloaded, or, It's Time to Get Angry Again', *Feminist Media Studies*, 11 (1), 61–71.

Gill, Rosalind, and Scharff, Christina (eds) (2011), *New Femininities: Postfeminism, Neoliberalism and Subjectivity* (Basingstoke: Palgrave Macmillan).

Gillis, Stacy, Gillian Howie and Rebecca Munford (eds) (2007), *Third Wave Feminism: A Critical Exploration* 2nd edn (Basingstoke: Palgrave Macmillan).

Gillis, Stacy, and Rebecca Munford (2007), 'Interview with Elaine Showalter' in Gillis, Stacy, Gillian Howie and Rebecca Munford (eds) (2007), *Third Wave Feminism: A Critical Exploration* 2nd edn (Basingstoke: Palgrave Macmillan), 292–97.

Gilroy, Paul (2007), *Black Britain: A Photographic History* (London: Saqi, in association with Getty Images).

Giroux, Henry (2007), 'When Hope Seems Subversive', *Tikkun*, 19 (6), 38–9.

Gledhill, Christine (2006/1994), 'Pleasurable Negotiations', in John Storey (ed.), *Cultural Theory and Popular Culture: A Reader* (Harlow: Pearson Education), 111–23.

Glissant, Édouard (1989), *Caribbean Discourse: Selected Essays* (Charlottesville: University Press of Virginia).

Goffman, Erving (1959), *The Presentation of Self in Everyday Life* (New York: Anchor Books).

Graff, Agnieszka (2003), 'Lost between the Waves? The Paradoxes of Feminist Chronology and Activism in Contemporary Poland', *Journal of International Women's Studies*, 4 (2), 100–16.

Gray, Ann (1992), *Video Playtime. The Gendering of a Leisure Technology* (London: Routledge).

Gregg, Melissa (2004), 'A Mundane Voice', *Cultural Studies*, 18 (2–3), 363–83.

Grosz, Elizabeth (1994), *Volatile Bodies. Toward a Corporeal Feminism* (Indianapolis: Indiana University Press).

——(2001), *Architecture from the Outside. Essays on Virtual and Real Space* (Cambridge, MA: MIT Press).

Habermas, Jürgen (1987), *The Philosophical Discourse of Modernity* (Cambridge, MA: Massachusetts Institute of Technology).

Hall, Stuart (1992), 'Cultural Studies and Its Theoretical Legacies', in Grossberg, Lawrence, Nelson, Carry, and Treichler, Paul (eds), *Cultural Studies* (New York and London: Routledge), 277–94.

Hall, Stuart, and du Gay, Paul (eds) (1996), *Questions of Cultural Identity* (Thousand Oaks, CA: Sage).

Haraway, Donna (1987), 'Review of Janet Sayers', in McNeil, Maureen (ed.), *Gender and Expertise* (London, Free Association Press), 74–6.

——(1989), *Primate Visions: Gender, Race, and Nature in the World of Modern Science* (London and New York: Routledge).

——(1991), *Simians, Cyborgs, and Women* (London: Free Association Books), 149–81.

——(2002), 'The Persistence of Vision', in Mirzoeff, Nicholas (ed.), *The Visual Culture Reader*, 2nd edn (London: Routledge), 677–84.

Hargrave, Andrea Milwood (1995), *The Scheduling Game: Annual Review 1995* (London, Paris, Rome: John Libbey).

Harris, Anita (2004), *Future Girl: Young Women in the Twenty-First Century* (London: Routledge).

——(2008), 'Introduction: Youth Cultures and Feminist Politics', in Anita Harris (ed.), *Next Wave Cultures: Feminism, Subcultures, Activism* (New York: Taylor & Francis).

Haug, Frigga, et al. (1987), *Female Sexualisation* (London: Verso).

Havens, Timothy (2007), 'The Hybrid Grid: Globalization, Cultural Power and Hungarian Television Schedules' *Media, Culture & Society*, 29 (2), 219–39.

Hayles, N. Katherine (1992), 'The Materiality of Informatics', *Issues in Integrative Studies*, 10, 121–144.

——(1999), *How We Became Posthuman: Virtual Bodies in Cybernetics, Literature, and Informatics* (Chicago: University of Chicago Press).

Hemmings, Clare (2011), *Why Stories Matter: The Political Grammar of Feminist Theory* (Durham, NC: Duke University Press).

Henry, Astrid (2003), 'Feminism's Family Problem: Feminist Generations and the Mother-Daughter Trope' in Dicker, Rory and Piepmeier, Alison (eds), *Catching a Wave: Reclaiming Feminism for the 21st Century* (Boston: Northeastern University Press), 209–31.

——(2004), 'Orgasm and Empowerment: *Sex and the City* and Third Wave Feminism', in Akass, Kim, and McCabe, Janet (eds), *Reading* Sex and the City (London: I.B.Tauris), 65–82.

Herring, Susan C. (2000), 'Gender Differences in CMC: Findings and Implications', *Computer Professionals for Social Responsibility*, 18 (1), http://cpsr.org/issues/womenintech/herring/ [accessed 28 August 2011].

Hill, Annette, and Calcutt, Ian (2001), 'Vampire Hunters: The Scheduling and Reception of *Buffy the Vampire Slayer* and *Angel* in the UK', *Intensities: The Journal of Cult Media*, http://intensities.org/Essays/Hill_Calcutt.pdf [accessed 10 April 2011].

Hilmes, Michelle (2007), 'Front Line Family: 'Women's Culture' Comes to the BBC', *Media Culture & Society*, 29 (1), 5–29.

Hinds, Hilary, and Stacey, Jackie (2001), 'Imaging Feminism, Imaging Femininity: The Bra-Burner, Diana, and the Woman Who Kills', *Feminist Media Studies*, 1 (2), 153–77.

Hirsch, Marianne, and Smith, Valerie. (2002), 'Feminism and Cultural Memory: An Introduction', *Signs*, 28 (1), 1–19.

Hobson, Dorothy (1980), 'Housewives and the Mass Media' in Hall, Stuart, Hobson, Dorothy, Lowe, Andrew, and Willis, Paul (eds), *Culture, Media, Language* (Birmingham: Centre for Contemporary Cultural Studies), pp 105–15.

——(1982), Crossroads: *The Drama of a Soap Opera* (London: Methuen).

——(2003), *Soap Opera* (Cambridge: Polity Press).

Hoggart, Richard (1957), *The Uses of Literacy: Aspects of Working-Class Life, with Special Reference to Publications and Entertainment* (Harmondsworth: Penguin).

Holland, Patricia (2000), '"Sweet It Is to Scan...": Personal Photographs and Popular Photography', in Wells, Liz (ed.), *Photography: A Critical Introduction*, 2nd edn (London and New York: Routledge), 117–64.

Holland, Patricia, and Spence, Jo (eds) (1991), *Family Snaps: The Meaning of Domestic Photography* (London: Virago).

Holloway, Gerry (2005), *Women and Work in Britain since 1840* (London: Routledge).

Hollows, Joanne (2000), *Feminism, Femininity and Popular Culture* (Manchester and New York: Manchester University Press).

Hollows, Joanne, and Moseley, Rachel (eds) (2006), *Feminism in Popular Culture* (Oxford: Berg).

Holmes, Su, and Negra, Diane (eds) (2011), *In the Limelight and under the Microscope: Forms and Functions of Female Celebrity* (London: Continuum).

Huesca, Robert (2002), 'Tracing the History of Participatory Communication Approaches to Development: A Critical Appraisal', in Servaes, Jan (ed.), *Approaches to Development: Studies on Communication for Development* (Paris: UNESCO) 1–36.

Hughes, Christina (2002), 'Pedagogies of, and for, Resistance' in Howie, Gillian and Tauchert, Ashley (eds), *Gender, Teaching and Research in Higher Education: Challenges for the 21st Century* (Aldershot: Ashgate), 99–110.

Hurd, Geoff (1981), 'The Television Presentation of the Police', in Bennett, Tony, Boyd-Bowman, S., Mercer, C and Woollacott, Janet (eds), *Popular Television and Film* (London: BFI and OUP), 53–70.

Husserl, Edmund (1970), *Crisis of European Sciences and Transcendental Phenomenology* (Evanston: Northern University Press).

Irigaray, Luce (1993/1987), *Sexes and Genealogies*, trans. Gilliam C. Gill (New York: Columbia University Press).

——(ed.) (2004), *Key Writings* (New York: Continuum Press).

Johnson, Catherine (2005), *Telefantasy* (London: BFI).

Johnson, Merri Lisa (ed.) (2007), *Third Wave Feminism and Television. Jane Puts it in a Box* (London, New York: Routledge).

Johnson, Richard (1979), 'Culture and the Historians', in Clarke, John, Critcher, Chas, and Johnson, Richard (eds), *Working-Class Culture: Studies in History and Theory* (London: Hutchinson), 41–71.

Juhasz, Alexandra (ed.) (2001), *Women of Vision: Histories in Feminist Film and Video* (Minneapolis: University of Minnesota Press).

Karlyn, Kathleen Rowe (2006), 'Feminism in the Classroom: Teaching towards the Third Wave', in Hollows, Joanne, and Moseley, Rachel (eds), *Feminism in Popular Culture* (Oxford: Berg), 57–76.

Kearney, Mary-Louise (2000), 'Overview: From Rhetoric to Reality', in Kearney, Mary-Louise (ed.), *Women, Power and the Academy: From Rhetoric to Reality* (New York and Oxford: Berghahn Books), 1–17.

Kempadoo, Roshini (2008), 'Amendments: A Fictional Re-imagining of the Trinidad Archive', in *Journal of Media Practice*, 9 (2), 87–99.

Kennedy, Helen (2008), 'Beyond Anonymity, or Future Directions for Internet Identity Research', *New Media and Society*, 8 (6), 859–76.

Kerr, Aphra (2003a), 'Women Just Want to have Fun. A Study of Adult Female Gamers', in Copier, Marinka, and Raessens, Joost (eds), *Level up. Digital Games Research Conference Proceedings* (Utrecht: University of Utrecht Press), 270–85.

——(2003b), *Girls Just Want to Have Fun*. Case Study for the Strategies of Inclusion: Gender and the Information Society (SIGIS) EU funded project, www.rcss.ed.ac.uk/sigis/public/deliverables/D05/1 [accessed 1 April 2007].

Kittler, Friedrich (2008), 'Code (or, How Can You Write Something Differently)', in Fuller, Matthew (ed.), *Software Studies: A Lexicon* (Cambridge, MA; London: MIT Press), 40–7.

Kittler, Friedrich, and Banz, S. (1996), *Platz der Luftbrücke. Ein Gespräch* (Berlin: Oktagon).

Klein, Naomi (2001), *No Logo* (London: Flamingo).

Kuhn, Annette (1984), 'Women's Genres. Melodrama, Soap Opera, and Theory', *Screen*, 25 (1), 18–28.

——(1995), *Family Secrets: Acts of Memory and Imagination* (London: Verso Books).

——(2004), 'The State of Film and Media Feminism', *Signs*, 30 (1), 1221–9.

Kumar, Amitava (2000), *Passport Photos* (Berkeley: University of California Press).

Lakhani, Nina (2008), 'Farewell to "Predictable, Tiresome and Dreary" Women's Studies', *Independent on Sunday* (23 March).

Langhamer, Claire (2005), 'The Meanings of Home in Post-war Britain', *Journal of Contemporary History*, 40 (2), 341–62.

Lanier, Jaron (2010), *You are Not a Gadget* (New York: Knopf).

Lassiter, Luke Eric (2005), *The Chicago Guide to Collaborative Ethnography* (Chicago: University of Chicago Press).

Lawrence, D. H. (1961/1928), *Lady Chatterley's Lover* (London: Penguin).

Lefebvre, Henry (1991), *The Production of Space* (Oxford: Blackwell Publishing).

Letherby, Gayle (2002), 'Claims and Disclaimers: Knowledge, Reflexivity and Representation in Feminist Research', *Sociological Research Online*, 6 (4), www.socresonline.org.uk/6/4/letherby.html [accessed 28 August 2011]

Lewine Jones, Jenny, and Mitra, Barbara (2009), 'Gender Roles in Television Commercials and Primary School Children in the UK', *Journal of Children and Media*, 3(1), 35–50.

Lewis, Jane (1990), 'Myrdal, Klein, Women's Two Roles and Postwar Feminism 1945–1960', in Harold L. Smith (ed.), *British Feminism in the Twentieth Century* (London: Edward Elgar), 78–84.

——(1992), *Women in Britain since 1945: Women, Family, Work and the State in the Post-war Years* (Oxford: Blackwell).

Linn, Pamela (1987), 'Gender Stereotype, Technology Stereotypes' in McNeil, Maureen (ed.) *Gender and Expertise* (London, Free Association Press), 125–51.

Lipsitz, George (1990), *Time Passages: Collective Memory and American Popular Culture* (Minneapolis: University of Minnesota Press).

Liu, Alan (2011), 'Where is Cultural Criticism in the Digital Humanities?' http://liu.english.ucsb.edu/where-is-cultural-criticism-in-the-digital-humanities/Humanities" Original full text of paper presented at the panel on "The History and Future of the Digital Humanities," Modern Language Association convention, Los Angeles, 7 January.

Lockyer, Daphne (2008), 'Kelly Reilly, the new Jane Tennison?' *Timesonline*, http://women.timesonline.co.uk/tol/life_and_style/women/celebrity/article5389311.ece [accessed 18 January 2011].

Looser, Devoney, and Kaplan, E. Ann (eds) (1997), *Generations: Academic Feminists in Dialogue* (Minneapolis: University of Minnesota Press).

López Austin, Alfredo (1990), *Los Mitos del Tlacuache: Caminos de la mitología mesoamericana* (México City: Alianza Editorial Mexicana).

Lotz, Amanda (2001), 'Postfeminist Television Criticism: Rehabilitating Critical Terms and Identifying Postfeminist Attributes', *Feminist Media Studies*, 1 (1), 105–21.

——(2006), *Redesigning Women. Television after the Network Era* (Urbana and Chicago: University of Illinois Press).

Lumby, Catharine (2011), 'Past the Post in Feminist Media Studies', *Feminist Media Studies*, 11 (1), 95–100.

Lundberg, Ferdinand, and Farnham, Marynia (1947), *Modern Woman: The Lost Sex* (New York: Grosset & Dunlap).

Mackenzie, Adrian (2008), 'FCJ-085 Wirelessness as Experience of Transition', *FibreCulture*, 13, http://thirteen.fibreculturejournal.org/ [accessed 28 August 2011].

McCarthy, Anna (2003), '"Must See" Queer TV; History and Serial Form in *Ellen*', in Jancovich, Mark, and Lyons, James (eds), *Quality Popular Television: Cult TV, the Industry and Fans* (London: BFI), 88–102.

——(2007), 'Reality TV: A Neoliberal Theatre of Suffering', *Social Text*, 25 (4 93), 17–41.

McDowell, Linda (1997), *Capital Culture: Gender at Work in the City* (Oxford: Blackwell).

McDowell, Linda, and Court, Gill (1994), 'Performing Work: Bodily Representations in Merchant Banks', in *Environment and Planning D: Society and Space*, 12 (6), 727–50.

McGrath, Roberta (2002), *Seeing Her Sex: Medical Archives and the Female Body* (Manchester and New York: Manchester University Press).

——(2007), 'History Read Backward: Memory Migration and the Photographic Archive', in Grossman, Alan (ed.), *Projecting Migration: Transcultural Documentary Practice* (London: Wallflower Press), 36–52.

McNay, Lois (2000), *Gender and Agency. Reconfiguring the Subject in Feminist and Social Theory* (Cambridge. Polity Press).

McNeil, Maureen (1987), 'Introduction' *Gender and Expertise* (London, Free Association Press), 1–9.

——(ed.) (1987), *Gender and Expertise* (London. Free Association Books).

McRobbie, Angela (1994), *Postmodernism and Popular Culture* (London and New York: Routledge)

——(2004), 'Post Feminism and Popular Culture', *Feminist Media Studies*, 4 (3), 255–64.

——(2005), 'Cutting Girls down to Victoria Beckham's Size', *Times Higher Education Supplement* (14 October), 12.

——(2008), 'Postfeminist Passions', *Guardian*, 25 March, www.guardian. co.uk/commentisfree/2008/mar/25/gender [accessed 28 August 2011].

——(2009a), *The Aftermath of Feminism: Gender, Culture and Social Change* (London and Thousand Oaks, CA: Sage).

——(2009b), 'Inside and Outside the Feminist Academy' *Australian Feminist Studies*, 24 (59), 123–38.

——(2011), 'Preface', in Gill, Rosalind and Scharff, Christina (eds), *New Femininities. Postfeminism, Neoliberalism and Subjectivity* (Basingstoke, New York: Palgrave Macmillan), xi–xv.

Manovich, Lev (2001), *The Language of New Media* (Cambridge, MA: MIT Press).

Marciniak, Katarzyna (2008), 'Foreign Women and Toilets', *Feminist Media Studies*, 8 (4), 337–56.

Marciniak, Katarzyna, Imre, Anikó, and O`Healy, Áine (eds) (2007), *Transnational Feminism in Film and Media* (London: Palgrave Macmillan).

Marie Claire (2007), 'Can we rebrand feminism?' November (UK edition), 156–62.

Mashadi, Ahmad, and Flores, Patrick (2009), 'Foreword', in Tan, Erika, *Persistent Visions* (Singapore: NUS Museum), 7.

Mathurin, Lucille (1995), *The Rebel Woman in the British West Indies during Slavery* (Kingston, Jamaica: Institute of Jamaica Publications).

Media Monkey (2008), 'Gene Hunt is Top Cop Says Poll' *Guardian*, 4 July, www.guardian.co.uk/media/mediamonkeyblog/2008/jul/04/genehuntisto pcopsayspoll?INTCMP=SRCH [accessed 2 May 2011].

Mendelson, Andrew, and Papacharissi, Zizi (2011), 'Look at Us: Collective Narcissism in College Student Facebook Photo Galleries', in Papacharissi, Zizi (ed.), *A Networked Self: Identity, Community and Culture on Social Network Sites* (London: Routledge), 251–74.

Mendes, Kaitlynn (2011), '"The Lady is a Closet Feminist!": Discourses of Backlash and Postfeminism in British and American Newspapers', *International Journal of Cultural Studies*, 14 (6), 1–17.

Mikos, Lothar (1994), *'Es wird dein Leben!' Familienserien im Fernsehen und im Alltag der Zuschauer* (Münster: MAkS Publikationen).

Miller, Nancy (1988), *Subject to Change: Reading Feminist Writing* (New York: Columbia University Press).

Miller, Toby (2007), *Cultural Citizenship: Cosmopolitanism, Consumerism, and Television in a Neoliberal Age* (Philadelphia: Temple University).

——(2009), 'Foreword', in Bolas, Terry (ed.), *Screen Education. From Film Appreciation to Media Studies* (Bristol: Intellect), xi–xii.

Modleski, Tania (1979), 'The Search for Tomorrow in Today's Soap Operas. Notes on a Feminine Narrative Form', *Film Quarterly*, 33 (1), 12–21.

——(1991), *Feminism Without Women: Culture and Criticism in a 'Postfeminist' Age* (London: Routledge).

——(1999), *Old Wives' Tales: Feminist Re-Visions of Film and Other Fictions* (London: I.B.Tauris).

Mohammed, Patricia (1998), 'Towards Indigenous Feminist Theorizing in the Caribbean', *Feminist Review*, 59 (1), 6–33.

Mohanty, Chandra Talpade (1988), 'Under Western Eyes: Feminist Scholarship and Colonial Discourses', *Feminist Review*, 30 (1), 65–88.

Morley, David (1980), *The 'Nationwide' Audience. Structure and Decoding* (London: BFI).

——(2009), 'Mediated Class-ifications: Representations of Class and Culture in Contemporary British Television', *European Journal of Cultural Studies*, 12 (4), 487–508.

Moseley, Rachel (2000), 'Makeover Takeover on British Television' *Screen*, 41 (3), 299–314.

——(2001), '"Real Lads Do Cook...But Some Things Are Still Hard to Talk About". The Gendering of 8–9', *European Journal of Cultural Studies*, 4 (1), 32–9.

Mulvey, Laura (1989/1975), 'Visual Pleasure and Narrative Cinema', in Mulvey, Laura, *Visual and Other Pleasures* (Basingstoke and London: Macmillan), 14–26.

——(2004), 'Looking at the Past from the Present: Rethinking Feminist Film Theory of the 1970s', *Signs*, 30 (1), 1286–92.

Mustafa, Shabbir Hussain (2009), 'Persistent Visions: In Dialogue with Erika Tan', in Tan, Erika, *Persistent Visions* (Singapore: NUS Museum), 12–24.

Myrdal, Alva, and Klein, Viola (1956), *Women's Two Roles* (London: Routledge).

Negra, Diane (2009), *What a Girl Wants? Fantasizing the Reclamation of Self in Postfeminism* (London: Routledge).

Nelson, Robin (1997), *TV Drama in Transition. Forms, Values and Cultural Change* (London: Macmillan; New York: St. Martin's Press).

Newcomb, Horace, and Hirsch, Paul M. (1983), 'Television as a Cultural Forum' *Quarterly Review of Film Studies*, 8 (3), 45–55.

Newman, James (2004), *Videogames* (London: Routledge).

——(2008), *Playing with Videogames* (London: Routledge).

Newton, Julianne H. (2001), *The Burden of Visual Truth: The Role of Photojournalism in Mediating Reality* (Mahwah, NJ: Lawrence Erlbaum).

Nunn, Heather (2011), 'Investing in the "Forever Home": From Property Programming to "Retreat TV"', in Skeggs, Barbara and Wood, Helen (eds), *Reality Television and Class* (London: BFI), 169–82.

Nunn, Heather, and Biressi, Anita (2003), '*Silent Witness*: Detection, Femininity, and the Post-mortem Body', *Feminist Media Studies*, 3 (2), 193–206.

Osborne, John (1957), *Look Back in Anger* (London: Faber and Faber).

Ouellette, Laurie (2010), 'Reality TV Gives Back: On the Civic Functions of Reality Entertainment', *Journal of Popular Film and Television*, 38 (2), 66–71.

Ouellette, Laurie, and Hay, James (2008), *Better Living through Reality TV: Television and Post-welfare Citizenship* (Oxford: Wiley Blackwell).

Paasonen, Susanna (2011), 'Revisiting Cyberfeminism', *Communications*, 36 (3), 335–52.

Palmer, Gareth (2003), *Discipline and Liberty: Television and Governance* (Manchester: Manchester University Press).

Pender, Patricia (2004), 'Whose Revolution Has Been Televised?: *Buffy's* Transnational Sisterhood of Slayers'. Paper presented at Slayage Conference on *Buffy the Vampire Slayer*, Nashville, June.

Penny, Laurie (2011), *Meat Market: Female Flesh under Capitalism* (London: Zero Books).

Pessar, Patricia R. (2001), 'Women's Political Consciousness and Empowerment in Local, National, and Transnational Contexts: Guatemalan Refugees and Returnees', *Identities*, 7 (4), 461–500.

Pinney, Chris (1997), *Camera Indica: The Social Life of Indian Photographs* (London: Reaktion Books).

Poole, Deborah (2005), 'An Excess of Description: Ethnography, Race, and Visual Technologies', *Annual Review of Anthropology*, 34, 159–79.

Probyn, Elspeth (1997), 'New Traditionalism and Post-Feminism: TV Does the Home', in Brunsdon, Charlotte, D'Acci, Julie, and Spigel, Lynn (1997) (eds), *Feminist Television Criticism: A Reader* (Oxford: Oxford University Press), 126–38.

Puri, Shalini (2004), *The Caribbean Postcolonial: Social Equality, Post/Nationalism, and Cultural Hybridity* (Basingstoke: Palgrave Macmillan).

Radner, Hilary (2011), *Neo-feminist Cinema* (London: Routledge).

Radner, Hilary, and Luckett, Moya (1999), *Swinging Single* (Minneapolis: University of Minnesota).

Reddock, Rhoda (1987), 'The Women in Revolt', in Thomas, Roy (ed.), *The Trinidad Labour Riots of 1937: Perspectives 50 Years Later* (Saint Augustine, Trinidad: Extra-Mural Studies Unit, University of the West Indies).

Redfern, Catherine, and Kristin Aune (2010), *Reclaiming the F Word: The New Feminist Movement* (London: Zed Books).

Richards, Michael, Pradip, Thomas N., and Nain, Zaharom (eds) (2001), *Communication and Development: The Freirean Connection* (Cresskill, NJ: Hampton Press).

Riley, Denise (1988), *'Am I that Name?': Feminism and the Category of 'Women' in History* (Basingstoke: Macmillan).

Rivière, Joan (1986/1929), 'Womanliness as a Masquerade', in Burgin, Victor, Donald, James, and Kaplan, Cora (eds), *Formations of Fantasy* (London and New York: Routledge), 35–44.

Rodríguez, Clemencia, and El Gazi, Jeanine (2007), 'The Poetics of Indigenous Radio in Colombia', *Media, Culture & Society*, 29(3), 449–68.

Rohlehr, Gordon (1997), 'The Culture of Williams: Context, Performance, Legacy', *Callaloo: Eric Williams and the Postcolonial Caribbean: A Special Issue* 20 (4), 849–88.

Rose, Gillian (2010), *Doing Family Photography: The Domestic, the Public and the Politics of Sentiment* (Farnham: Ashgate).

Rowbotham, Sheila (1983), *Dreams and Dilemmas* (London: Virago).

——(2010), *Dreamers of a New Day* (London: Verso).

Rowe, Kathleen (1995), *The Unruly Woman: Gender and Genres of Laughter* (Austin: University of Texas Press).

Sanli, Solen (2012), *Women and Cultural Citizenship in Turkey: Mass Media and 'Woman's Voice' Television* (London: I.B.Tauris).

Sarikakis, Katherine, and Shade, Leslie (eds) (2008), *Feminist Interventions in International Communication* (Toronto: Rowman and Littlefield).

Savage, Michael (2008), 'Fury As Paxman Says Middle-Class White Men Have No Chance in TV', in *The Independent* (26 August), www.independent.co.uk/news/media/fury-as-paxman-says-middleclass-white-men-have-no-chance-in-tv-908631.html [accessed 14 May 2009].

Scott, David (2010), 'The Theory of Haiti: The Black Jacobins and the Ethos of Universal History', paper given at London School of Economics.

Seabrook, Jeremy (1982), *Working Class Childhood: an Oral History* (London: Victor Gollancz).

Segal, Lynne (1999), *Why Feminism?* (Cambridge: Polity Press).

Seiter, Ellen (1993), *Sold Separately: Parents and Children in Consumer Culture* (New Brunswick, NJ: Rutgers University Press).

Sevea, Teren (2009), '"Hopping Around" within Time and Space: Transportable Modernity and Escaping the Archive', in Tan, Erika, *Persistent Visions* (Singapore: NUS Museum), 25–7.

Shaw Perry, Barbara (2000), 'Cultural Identity, "Resistance", and Women's Postcolonial Writing from the African-Caribbean/ British Borderlands: Joan Riley's *The Unbelonging*', in Courtman, Sandra (ed.), *The Society for Caribbean Studies Conference Papers*, 1, www.caribbeanstudies.org.uk/papers/2000/olv1p7.pdf [accessed 20 August 2011].

Shepherd, Verene (2002), *Maharani's Misery: Narratives of a Passage from India to the Caribbean* (Kingston: University of the West Indies Press).

——(ed.) (1999), *Women in Caribbean History: The British-Colonised Territories* (Princeton, NJ: Markus Wiener).

Shugart, Helene (2006), 'Ruling Class: Disciplining Class, Race, and Ethnicity in Television Reality Court Shows', *The Howard Journal of Communications*, 17 (79), 100.

Silverstone, Roger, and Hirsch, Eric (eds) (1992), *Consuming Technologies: Media and Information in Domestic Spaces* (London: Routledge).

Silverstone, Roger, Hirsch, Eric, and Morley, David (1992), 'Information and Communication Technologies and the Moral Economy of the Household', in Silverstone, Roger, and Hirsch, Eric (eds), *Consuming Technologies: Media and Information in Domestic Spaces* (London: Routledge), 15–32.

Skeggs, Beverley (1997) *Formations of Class and Gender* (London: Sage).

——(2004), *Class, Self, Culture* (London: Routledge).

——(2010), 'The Moral Economy of Person Production', *Sociologia: Revista do Departamento de Sociologia da FLUP*, XX (2010), 67–84.

Skeggs, Beverley, and Woods, Helen (2008), 'Spectacular Morality: 'Reality' Television, Individualism and The Re-Making of the Working Class', in Hesmondhalgh, David, and Toynbee, Jason (eds), *The Media and Social Theory* (London, New York: Routledge), 177–93.

Smith, Sidonie (1987), *A Poetics of Women's Autobiography: Marginality and the Fiction of Self-Representation* (Bloomington: Indiana University Press).

Sobchack Vivian (1995), 'Beating the Meat/Surviving the Text, or How to Get Out of This Century Alive', in Featherstone, Mike, and Burrows, Roger (ed.) *Cyberspace, Cyberbodies, Cyberpunk: Cultures of Technological Embodiment* (London: Sage), 205–15.

Sollfrank, Cornelia (1999), 'The First Woman Hacker', paper given at NexT: Next Cyberfeminist International, Rotterdam: OBN, 8–12 March.

Spencer, Stephanie (2005), *Gender, Work and Education in Britain in the 1950s* (Basingstoke: Palgrave Macmillan).

Spender, Dale (1996), *Nattering on the Net* (London: Garamond Press).

Spigel, Lynne (1992), *Make Room for TV: Television and the Family Ideal in Postwar America*, 2nd edn (Chicago: University of Chicago Press).

——(2001), *Welcome to the Dreamhouse: Popular Media and Postwar Suburbs* (London: Duke University Press).

——(2004), 'Theorizing the Bachelorette: "Wave" of Feminist Media Studies', *Signs*, 30 (1), 1209–21.

Squires, Judith (2000), 'Fabulous Feminist Futures and the Lure of Cyberculture', in Bell, David, and Kennedy, Barbara M. (eds), *The Cybercultures Reader* (London: Routledge), 360–73.

Steedman, Carolyn (1986), *Landscape for a Good Woman* (London: Virago).

——(1992), *Past Tenses: Essays on Writing, Autobiography and History* (London: Rivers Oram Press).

——(2001), *Dust: The Archive and Cultural History* (Manchester: Manchester University Press).

Stewart, John (1977/78), 'SEFT Potteries Weekend School 'Understanding Popular Television: "Coronation Street"', *Screen Education*, 25 (Winter), 68–71.

Stoler, Ann Laura (2002), *Carnal Knowledge and Imperial Power: Race and the Intimate in Colonial Rule* (Berkeley, Los Angeles, London: University of California Press).

——(2008), *Along the Archival Grain: Epistemic Anxieties and Colonial Common Sense: Epistemic Anxieties and Colonial Commonsense* (Princeton, NJ: Princeton University Press).

Stone, Pamela (2007), *Opting Out?: Why Women Really Quit Careers and Head Home* (Berkeley: University of California Press).

Storey, David (2000/1960), *The Sporting Life* (London, Sydney, Auckland, Houghton: Vintage).

Subedi, Binaya, and Rhee, Jeong-eun (2008), 'Negotiating Collaboration across Differences', *Qualitative Inquiry*, 14(6), 1070–92.

Suchman, Lucy (2006), 'Wajcman Confronts Cyberfeminism', *Social Studies of Science*, 36 (2), 321–7.

Summers, Lawrence H. (2005), 'Remarks at NBER Conference on Diversifying the Science and Engineering Workforce'. Speech presented at Cambridge, MA, 14 January, www.president.harvard.edu/speeches/summers_2005/nber.php [accessed 28 August 2011].

Swindells, Julia (1995), 'Conclusion: Autobiography and the Politics of "The Personal"', in Swindells, Julia (ed.), *The Uses of Autobiography* (London: Taylor & Francis), 205–14.

Tasker, Yvonne (1998), *Working Girls: Gender and Sexuality in Popular Cinema* (London: Routledge).

Tasker, Yvonne, and Negra, Diane (eds) (2007), *Interrogating Postfeminism: Gender and the Politics of Popular Culture* (Durham, NC: Duke University Press).

Taylor, Anne (2008), *Mediating Australian Feminism: Re-reading the First Stone Media Event* (Oxford: Peter Lang).

Thane, Patricia (1994), 'Women since 1945', in Paul Johnson (ed.), *20th Century Britain: Economic, Cultural and Social Change* (London: Longman).

——(2003), 'What Difference did the Vote Make? Women in Public and Private Life in Britain since 1918', *Historical Research*, 76 (192), 268–85.

Thatcher, Margaret (1987), 'Interview with Women's Own ("No Such Thing as Society")', *Margaret Thatcher Foundation*, www.margaretthatcher.org/document/106689 [accessed 29 August 2011].

Thompson, Krista A. (2006), *An Eye for the Tropics: Tourism, Photography, and Framing the Caribbean Picturesque* (Durham, NC: Duke University Press).

Thompson, Robert J. (1996), *Television's Second Golden Age. From* Hill Street Blues *to* ER (New York: Continuum).

Thornham, Helen (2008), '"It's a boy thing": Gaming, Gender and Geeks', *Feminist Media Studies*, 8 (2), 127–42.

——(2009), 'Claiming a Stake in the Videogame: What Grown-ups Say to Rationalize Gaming', *Convergence*, 15 (2), 141–59.

——(2011), *Ethnographies of the Videogame: Gender, Narrative and Practice* (Surrey: Ashgate).

Thornham, Helen, and McFarlane, Angela (2011), 'Discourses of the Digital Native: Use, Non-use and Perceptions of Use in BBC Blast', *Information, Communication and Society*, 14 (2), 258–79.

Thornham, Sue (2000), *Feminist Theory and Cultural Studies Stories of Unsettled Relations* (London: Arnold).

——(2007), *Women, Feminism and Media* (Edinburgh. Edinburgh University Press).

——(2010), 'Media and Feminism', in Curran, James (ed.), *Media and Society* (London: Bloomsbury Academic), 63–82.

Thynne, Lizzie, and Al-Ali, Nadje (eds) (2011), 'Media Transformations', *Feminist Review*, issue 99.

Tooley, James (2002), *The Miseducation of Women* (London: Continuum).

Traub, Valerie (2007), 'The Present Future of Lesbian Historiography', in Haggerty, George E., and McGarry, Molly (eds), *The Companion to Lesbian, Gay, Bisexual, Transgender, and Queer Studies* (Oxford: Blackwell), 124–45.

Turkle, Sherry (1995), *Life on the Screen: Identity in the Age of the Internet* (New York: Simon and Schuster).

Twomey, Breda (2002), 'Women in the Labour Market: Results from the Spring 2001 LSF' in *Labour Market Trends* (March), 109–27.

Tyler, Imogen (2008), '"Chav Mum, Chav Scum": Class Disgust in Contemporary Britain', *Feminist Media Studies*, 8 (1), 17–34.

——(2010), '"Celebrity Chav": Fame, Femininity and Social Class', *European Journal of Cultural Studies*, 13(3), 275–93.

Tyrell, Stacey (2010), *Stacey Tyrell*, http://staceytyrell.com/artwork/1241279_Detail_Postions_As_Desired.html [Accessed: March 5 2011].

Usborne, David (2008), "The Gene Genie gets an LA makeover". *The Independent* (18 May), www.independent.co.uk/news/world/americas/the-gene-genie-gets-an-la-makeover-830371.html [accessed 2 May 2011].

Van der Tuin, Iris (2009), 'Jumping Generations: On Second and Third Wave Feminist Epistemology', *Australian Feminist Studies*, 24 (59), 17–31.

Vergès, Françoise (2003), 'The Island of Wandering Souls: Processes of Creolization, Politics of Emancipation and the Problematic of Absence on Reunion Island', in Edmond, Rod, and Smith, Vanessa (eds), *Islands in History and Representation* (London: Routledge), 162–76.

Vickers, Margaret H. (2007), 'Autoethnography as Sensemaking: A Story of Bullying', *Culture and Organization*, 13 (3), 223–37.

Walby, Sylvia (2002), 'Feminism in a Global Age', *Economy and Society*, 31 (4), 533–57.

——(2005), 'Introduction: Comparative Gender Mainstreaming in a Global Era', *International Feminist Journal of Politics*, 7 (4), 453–70.

——(2011), *The Future of Feminism* (Cambridge: Polity Press).

Walker, Rebecca (ed.) (1995), *To Be Real: Telling the Truth and Changing the Face of Feminism* (New York: Anchor Books).

Walter, Natasha (1998), *The New Feminism* (London: Little, Brown).

——(2010), *Living Dolls: The Return of Sexism* (London: Virago).

Walkerdine, Valerie (1997), *Daddy's Girl. Young Girls and Popular Culture* (London: Macmillan).

——(2006), 'Playing the Game. Young Girls Performing Femininity in Video Game Play', *Feminist Media Studies*, 6 (4), 519–37.

——(2007), *Children, Gender, Videogames. Towards a Relational Approach to Videogames* (Basingstoke: Palgrave Macmillan).

Weber, Brenda (2009), *Makeover TV: Selfhood, Citizenship, and Celebrity* (London: Duke University Press).

——(2010), 'Teaching Popular Culture through Gender Studies: Feminist Pedagogy in a Postfeminist and Neoliberal Academy?', *Feminist Teacher*, 20 (2), 124–38.

Weiner, Gaby (2006), 'Out of the Ruins: Feminist Pedagogy in Recovery', in Skelton, Christine, Francis, Becky, and Smulyan, Lisa (eds), *The Sage Handbook of Gender and Education* (London: Sage), 79–92.

Weissmann, Elke (2009), 'Drama Counts: Uncovering Channel 4's History with Quantitative Research Methods', *New Review of Film and Television Studies*, 7 (2), 189–207.

Welch, Penny (2002), 'Feminist Pedagogy and Power in the Academy', in Howie, Gillian, and Tauchert, Ashley (ed.), *Gender, Teaching and Research in Higher Education: Challenges for the 21st Century* (Aldershot: Ashgate), 113–24.

West, Patrick (2008), 'In an Ugly World, We Need Ugly Newsreaders', *Spiked* (13 June), www.spiked-online.com/index.php?/site/article/5344/ [accessed 14 May 2009].

Whelehan, Imelda (2007), 'Foreword', in Gillis, Stacey, Howie, Gillian, and Munford, Rebecca (eds), *Third Wave Feminism. A Critical Exploration* (Basingstoke, New York: Palgrave Macmillan), xv–xx.

Wilding, Faith (1998), 'Where's the Feminism in Cyberfeminism?', *n. paradoxa: International Feminist Art Journal*, 1 (2), 6–13.

Wilkinson, Helen (1994), *No Turning Back: Generations and the Genderquake* (London: DEMOS).

Williams, Linda (2004), 'Why I Did Not Want to Write This Essay', *Signs*, 30 (1), 1264–72.

Willis, Deborah (ed.) (1994), *Picturing Us: African American Identity in Photography* (New York: New Press).

Wilson, Tony (1993), *Watching Television. Hermeneutics, Reception and Popular Culture* (Cambridge, Oxford: Polity Press).

Winterson, Jeannette (2001/1985), *Oranges Are Not the Only Fruit* (London, Sydney, Auckland, Houghton: Vintage).

Winthrop-Young, Geoffrey, and Gane, Nicholas (2006), 'Friedrich Kittler: An Introduction', *Theory, Culture & Society*, 23 (7–8), 5–16.

Wissler, Holly (2009), 'Grief-singing and the Camera: The Challenges and Ethics of Documentary Production in an Indigenous Andean Community', *Ethnomusicology Forum*, 18 (1), 37–53.

Wolcott, Harry F. (1999), *Ethnography: A Way of Seeing* (Lanham).

Wolf, Naomi (1994), *Fire with Fire* (London: Ballantine Books).

Wollstonecraft, Mary (1992/1792), *A Vindication of the Rights of Women* (London: Penguin).

Woods, Gaby (2009), 'The Interview: Jessica Valenti', *The Observer* (10 May), www.guardian.co.uk/books/2009/may/10/jessica-valenti-feminist-blogger?INTCMP=SRCH [accessed 25 August 2011].

Woodward, Kathleen (1983), *Jipping Street* (1928) (London: Virago).

Woodward, Kath, and Woodward, Sophie (2009), *Why Feminism Matters: Feminism Lost and Found* (Basingstoke: Palgrave Macmillan).

Woolf, Virginia (2002/1929), *A Room of One's Own* (London: Penguin).

Young, Michael, and Willmott, Peter (1967), *Family and Kinship in East London* (London: Routledge and Kegan Paul).

Zweiniger-Bargielowska, Ina (2000), *Austerity in Britain: Rationing, controls, and consumption, 1939–1955* (Oxford: Oxford University Press).

Index

1970s 11–14, 24–6, 29, 53, 57, 68–9, 74, 95, 219–20

Above Suspicion 157, 164, 166, 169
Absence 23, 34, 41, 65, 88–93, 95, 182, 208
Absolutely Fabulous 151
Adkins, Lisa 40–2, 157–8, 160–1
Ahmed, Sara 41–2
Aikau, Hokulani 32–3, 43–4
Ally McBeal 149–55
Amendments 86, 88–91, 100, 101
Angel 143
Anti-feminist backlash 30, 50–1
Archers, The 133–4
Arthurs, Jane 4, 150, 186, 223
Ashes to Ashes 157, 164, 166, 169
Audience measurement 141, 143
Audiences 9, 14, 17, 20, 24, 68, 91, 100, 113, 115, 117–8, 122, 125–6, 134, 141–60, 181, 199, 215
Authorship 2, 7–8, 63–6, 179, 183, 186
Autobiography 63–6, 75–9, 82–3, 86, 219–20
Autoethnography 105, 109, 111, 118

Barthes, Roland 85
Batman 148
BBC 74, 124–40, 145, 151, 158, 161–2, 178, 188
BBC Light Programme 124
Bebo 173
Beck, Ulrich 44–5, 48–9, 157
Bell, Melanie 127–8
Belle de Jour 156, 165, 167–71
Bergstrom, Janet 13–4

Bewitched 147–9
Bikini Beach: Maracus 98–100
Bitch Media 174, 178, 181
Blake's 7 145–6
Blossom 148
Boyle, Karen 4, 121, 169–70
Bra burning 41–3
Braidotti, Rosi 42–3, 197
Bridget Jones 4, 38
Brief Encounter 129
British
    Drama 123, 155–73
    Film Institute (BFI) 11–29
    Sociological Association 2–3, 24
Broadcast 21–2
Brown, Maggie 146–7
Brunsdon, Charlotte 2–3, 14, 34, 42–3, 122, 135, 140–1, 158–64, 167, 217
Buffy: The Vampire Slayer 121, 143, 145–6
Burke, Michael 140

Camera Obscura 13
Capitalism 48, 58
Caribbean 84, 88–90, 94–100
Caroline in the City 148
Cartesian logic 174–5, 177, 197
Channel 4 123, 140–55, 162
Child Care and the Growth of Love 131
Citizen 96, 116, 127, 223–5
Citizenship 128, 216, 223, 225–7
Class 1, 2, 13, 40, 49, 52, 56–8, 63–4, 67–84, 101, 106, 110–1 121, 124–6, 128, 133–6, 148, 151, 160–1, 167, 175, 183, 187–8, 200, 209, 212, 220, 224–5

Class mobility 79–83
Clough, Patricia Ticineto 5, 65–6, 83
Cockburn, Cynthia 199, 201–3, 209–11
Colonialism/post-colonialism 7, 8, 64, 86–9, 91, 93, 96–7, 101–2, 197
Coming Up for Air 128
Consumer
  Capitalism 48
  citizens 159
  culture 158, 159, 161, 163, 168
Contiguity 87, 88, 90–3
Contiguous archives 87–8, 93, 101–2
Coronation Street 16–26, 73
Cosby Show, The 147–8
Counter-memory 85–6
Cronin, Anne 42
Cultural 'feminization' 40, 157–8
Cybill 148, 149, 151

Daily Graphic 129
Dawson, Basil 134
De Lauretis, Teresa 7, 42, 44, 63–5
DeGeneres, Ellen 149
Desperate Housewives 155
Devil Wears Prada, The 43
Dick Barton 125
Dick van Dyke Show, The 147
A Different World 148
Doane, Mary Ann 13–14, 174
Dr Who 145–6
Dyer, Richard 17–18, 21–23, 168–70

Edinburgh International Television Festival 21
Ellen 149
Ellis, John 109, 145
Ethnography 2, 109, 119
Expertise 9, 174, 179–80, 186, 194, 198, 199–215, 222

Facebook 52, 173, 179, 181
Fairy tale 74, 75, 77, 79, 105
Family Secrets 72–4, 78–9, 82–3

Family Ties 147–8
Fawcett Society 50, 52
Fehr, Carla 37
Female Chauvinist Pigs 55
Female-object 63–4
Female subjectivity 49–50
Feminine mobility 156, 158, 161–6, 169
Feminine Mystique, The 38
Femininity 34–5, 39–40, 42, 44, 48, 83, 121, 128, 150, 155, 157, 159, 160–1, 163, 165, 169, 186–7, 192, 194, 196–7, 222–4
  discourses of 161, 186–7, 192
  and feminism 57, 155, 160, 196, 222
  normative 40, 44, 128, 186, 196
  traditional 48, 160, 161, 163, 187
  twentieth-century 157, 159
  youthful 165
Feminism 3–4, 6, 7, 10–12, 24–5, 40–1, 43, 46–62, 63–7, 71, 82, 84–104, 176, 186, 192, 197, 202–5, 208, 217, 223–4, 227
  1970s 12, 24, 25, 71, 192
  in the academy 9, 30, 45, 47–63, 217
  blog 180, 184
  cyber 176, 186, 202–5, 204, 205, 208, 212
  as a discipline 6
  discourses 30
  emergence of 11
  Feminism Without Women 46
  Feminist Waves, Feminist Generations 43, 45–6
  futuristic 7, 173–8
  inter-alia 3–4
  liberal 165, 166
  lived 6, 63–7, 187
  and narrative 63–67, 82, 84–104, 227
  New Media 174, 176, 180–3, 197
  politics of 6, 226
  post- 30, 41, 43, 46, 48–50, 64, 67, 155, 159, 164, 186, 187, 192, 196, 213, 216
  rebranding 30, 32–47
  relaying 29–32

representing 3–4, 10, 30, 33–4, 216
retooling 8, 177, 199–215, 216
second-wave 12, 13, 29, 31, 52, 53,
    59, 123, 132, 136, 155, 160, 179,
    203, 222
success of 49
taken into account 4, 6, 30, 31,
    40, 41, 43, 157, 187, 192
techno 201, 203, 213
and technology 176, 179–185, 186,
    199–215
television 121–4, 223–4
third-wave 32, 43, 47–63
unification of 159–60
Fixing/unfixing 49, 57
Frasier 149
Friedan, Betty 38, 121–22, 132, 222
Friends 149
Front Line Family 125

Gender 2, 3, 6, 30, 42–4, 47–66,
    70–84, 84–104, 122, 145, 185–99,
    208–11, 217, 220
address 153–4
behaviour 37, 130
critique 41, 213
engendering 84–104
fluidity 40
framework 2
gap/divides 30, 185–99
genres 9, 130, 148, 155, 166–7, 217
identities 44, 70–84, 174–5, 199,
    220
ideologies 42, 63–6, 84–104, 122,
    145, 161, 208–11
in/equality 35–6, 41, 45, 55, 83, 160
logic 6
mainstreaming 3, 41, 47–63
mobility 40
performance 40, 101, 161, 199
politics 86, 164, 166–70, 201, 205
reflexivity 42, 44, 159
regulation 38
roles 7, 49, 121–3, 147, 152–4, 164
Studies 3, 47, 49, 54, 222
and technology 185–99, 200–15
transgender 53, 180, 183

Gentle Touch, The 162
Get Smart 147
Ghosting 90–1
Girlzone 43–4
Governor, The 162, 166
Grandmothers 49, 55, 130–1
Guardian 20, 46, 171

Hairy legs 33, 39–41
Haraway, Donna 42, 82, 92–3,
    202, 210
Hero 7, 63, 65–6, 129
heroine 74, 164–6, 168
History 1, 5, 12, 23, 25, 32, 34–5, 39,
    44, 46, 54–5, 58, 63–6, 70, 78–9,
    82, 84–90, 93–4, 97, 101, 105–7,
    110, 112, 119, 123–4, 146, 180,
    215–6, 220, 224
archival 85, 87, 94, 226
British 70
colonialist 7, 64, 89, 93–4, 105
continuities of 14
experience, storytelling 217–220
feminist 82, 84
of film and media studies 11
material 35, 46
metanarratives of 64–6
narrative and 215–6
of PSB 123–4, 146
rewriting 7
her(story) 84–104
Hoggart, Richard 18, 64, 69–70,
    72–3, 77, 80–1
Hollyoaks 148
Housewives 128, 141, 153–4

Identity 42, 105, 111, 168, 184, 212
class 80, 136
cultural 107
ethnic 70, 112, 116
feminist 44, 50, 181
gendered 45, 160, 199
and history 218
management 175
regional 70
and representation 13, 116–9, 173, 174
of the scholar 6

Identity—*Continued*
  self-reflexive 44, 111
  single/plural 50, 111
  sites of identity production 110
  and technology 173
  and transformation 34
  and work 57
I Dream of Jeannie 149
I Love Lucy 147, 148
Images of Women in the Home 222
Images of Women in the
  Media 20, 192
Individualism 32, 160, 165, 167,
  169, 181
Internet 55, 173–5, 179, 181, 203,
  205, 208
Irigaray, Luce 24

Jesse 149–52
Juliet Bravo 162

Kitchen sink drama 68
Kittler, Friedrich 199–200, 205, 207
Klein, Naomi 34
Kuhn, Annette 5, 14, 66, 71–3, 75–6,
  78, 79–82

La Plante, Lynda 157–8, 162–4, 166
Lady Chatterley's Lover 68
*Landscape for a Good Woman: A Story
  of Two Lives* 71–2, 76, 79, 82–3
Lawrence, D. H. 68, 76, 78
Legally Blonde (2001) 43
Lexicon 206–8
Light Entertainment 17
Lived Feminist Identities 6, 63–7
Liver Birds, The 161
Lovell, Terry 14, 21
Lumby, Catharine 215–6, 219

Male-subject 63, 197
Manageress, The 162, 166
Marie Claire 30, 33–5, 37, 39, 41–6
Mary Tyler Moore Show, The 147
Masculinity 40, 44, 57, 121, 157–8,
  199, 203
McCrindle, Jean 21

McHugh, Kathleen 13
McRobbie, Angela 3, 4, 6, 7, 30, 38,
  41–4, 48–51, 150, 156–7, 159–60,
  161, 165, 186–7, 191–2, 216
Midlands Television Research
  Group 140
Miller, Nancy 43
Miseducation of Women 38
Miss Congeniality (2000) 43
Mission Impossible 148–9
Modern Woman: The Lost Sex 39, 130
Modleski, Tania 46, 121
Morley, David 142–3
Mother-daughter relations 29, 32,
  74–5, 82
Motherhood 77, 125, 127–8, 151, 217
Mothers 32, 38, 48–9, 55, 74–5, 77–8,
  80–1, 94–5, 122, 124, 126–8, 130,
  132, 135, 151, 226
Mr Right 141
Mrs Dale's Diary 122, 124–40
Mulvey, Laura 14, 18, 42
Munsters, The 147
My So-Called Life 148
MySpace 173

Negra, Diane 4, 39, 49, 82, 141, 150,
  156, 159, 160, 165, 169–70, 191,
  192, 216–7
Neoliberalism 6, 167, 216
New girl order 123, 158–61, 169–70
News Corp 178
Nunn, Heather 166, 215–27
NYPD Blue 149

Oranges Are Not the Only Fruit 74–5,
  79, 81

Party of Five 148
Patriarchy 7–8, 17, 58, 77, 123, 160–1,
  165, 169–70
Paxman, Jeremy 140
Pedagogy 3, 6, 8, 51–63
'Penis Envy' 33, 36–9
Popular Culture 25, 29–30, 32–47,
  48, 49, 53, 56–61, 64, 73, 125,
  129, 219

Position As Desired 94–5
Positions of exclusion 189–92, 197
Post-feminism 42, 49, 59, 60, 160, 165
  and choice 156, 191, 196–7, 203
  culture and discourse 150, 163–5, 186, 191, 196–7, 203
  femininity 49
  figures of 34, 38, 154, 156, 157, 162–3, 165–6, 190
  gaze 43
  images of 34, 41
  masquerade 44
  politics 32
  popular culture 32–47, 49, 154–5, 157, 159, 160–1, 164, 169–70
  and technology 203, 212
  texts 167, 168–9
  turn 164
Post-war changes and women's lives 127–32, 222
Prime Suspect 162–4, 166
Prime-time television 158–9, 162
Private sphere 7, 10, 37–8, 94, 122, 124, 126–7, 132–5, 150, 152–3, 215, 216, 221–5
Psychoanalysis 25, 73, 76–7
Public sphere 7, 37–8, 45, 126, 132–5, 152–3, 215–6, 218, 220, 221–6

Race Relations Amendment Act 41
Radner, Hilary 158, 160, 163, 167–9
Reflections of the self 104–21
Reflections of others 104–21
Relaying Feminism 29–63, 219
Research Assessment Exercise (RAE) 41
Riley, Denise 45
Rivière, Joan 40, 44
Roseanne 147–9, 151

Scheduling 9, 122, 123, 140–55, 223
Scholarship
  boys 63, 64, 69–70, 72, 82
  girls 70–5, 82
Screen Education 17

Seabrook, Jeremy 69, 70, 72, 81
Second world war 68, 71, 128, 224
Second Wave Feminism see Feminism
Secret Diary of a Call Girl 156–7, 165, 167, 169–70
Serial Drama 24, 124–40
Sex and the City 4, 39, 149–55, 155
Sexuality 54, 68, 71, 74, 76–9, 81, 83, 99, 101, 150, 156, 161, 169–70, 173, 187, 220, 223
Signs 13, 14
Silent Witness 162, 169
Silverstone, Roger 175, 196
Single Girl, the 161–2
Sister/Outsider 55
Skeggs, Beverley 82, 193–4
Sobchack, Vivian 13, 174, 187
Sociology 2, 48, 54, 56–7
Software studies 176, 200, 202, 205–8, 211, 213
Something So Right 148
Spare Rib 178
Spence, Jo 71, 73, 93
Spigel, Lynn 14, 141, 159, 164, 217, 222
Star Trek 145
Star Trek: The Next Generation 145–6
Star Trek: Voyager 14
Steedman, Carolyn 5, 7, 65–6, 71–3, 75 9, 82–3, 86, 92
Stone, Pamela 37, 41
Storytelling 66, 75, 76, 77, 78, 79, 82, 89, 206, 217–21
Suddenly Susan 149–52
Sugar: Maria Magdalena Compos-Pons 96–7
Summers, Lawrence H. 36, 37–39, 45
Sweeney, The 17

Tan, Erika 86–7, 91–2, 102
Techniques of contiguity 88, 90–3
Technological turn 173, 176–7, 187
Textiles 104, 107, 190
Third Wave Feminism *see* Feminism

Thorndike, Edward 37
Tooley, James 38, 39, 45
Tootsie 40
TRAMA Textiles: Weaving the Life of Guatemala 104–121
Trial and Retribution 157, 162, 166, 169
Trinidad 88–90, 98–101
Turkle, Sherry 173

UK Equality and Human Rights Commission 35
Understanding Popular Television 22
Unnatural passions 74
US Women's Liberation Movement 15

Vagina Monologues, The 55
A Vindication of the Rights of Women 39

Walby, Sylvia 3, 49, 215

Walkerdine, Valerie 71, 73, 175, 187, 194, 196–7
Watching Television 141–2
Widows 162, 166
Williams, Linda 14
Williams, Raymond 21, 70, 72
Wilson, Lesley 129, 133–4
Wives 48, 135
Wollstonecraft, Mary 39
Womanliness and Masquerade 40
Women
   centred sitcoms 146–53
   and Film Study Group 11–29, 219
   Media Studies
   Network 216–7
   and Soap Opera 14, 219
   work 151, 156, 166–9
Wonder Years, The 148
Woodward, Kathleen 52, 75
Working-class
   culture 68–70
   lives 67–8, 70–8, 82